Automating Open Source Intelligence

Automating Open Source Intelligence

Algorithms for OSINT

Edited By

Robert Layton

Paul A. Watters

AMSTERDAM • BOSTON • HEIDELBERG • LONDON
NEW YORK • OXFORD • PARIS • SAN DIEGO
SAN FRANCISCO • SINGAPORE • SYDNEY • TOKYO
Syngress is an imprint of Elsevier

Acquiring Editor: Brian Romer
Editorial Project Manager: Anna Valutkevich
Project Manager: Mohana Natarajan
Cover Designer: Matthew Limbert

Syngress is an imprint of Elsevier
225 Wyman Street, Waltham, MA 02451, USA

Notices
Knowledge and best practice in this field are constantly changing. As new research and experience broaden our understanding, changes in research methods, professional practices, or medical treatment may become necessary.

Practitioners and researchers must always rely on their own experience and knowledge in evaluating and using any information, methods, compounds, or experiments described herein. In using such information or methods they should be mindful of their own safety and the safety of others, including parties for whom they have a professional responsibility.

To the fullest extent of the law, neither the Publisher nor the authors, contributors, or editors, assume any liability for any injury and/or damage to persons or property as a matter of products liability, negligence or otherwise, or from any use or operation of any methods, products, instructions, or ideas contained in the material herein.

British Library Cataloguing-in-Publication Data
A catalogue record for this book is available from the British Library

Library of Congress Cataloging-in-Publication Data
A catalog record for this book is available from the Library of Congress

ISBN: 978-0-12-802916-9

For information on all Syngress publications
visit our website at http://store.elsevier.com/Syngress

Working together
to grow libraries in
developing countries

ELSEVIER   Book Aid International

www.elsevier.com • www.bookaid.org

Contents

List of Contributors

Brenda Chawner School of Information Management, Victoria Business School, Victoria University of Wellington, New Zealand

Shadi Esnaashari School of Engineering and Advanced Technology, Massey University, Auckland, New Zealand

Ernest Foo School of Electrical Engineering and Computer Science – Science and Engineering Faculty, Queensland University of Technology, Queensland, Australia

Rony Germon PSB Paris School of Business, Chair Digital Data Design

Iqbal Gondal Internet Commerce Security Laboratory, Federation University, Australia

Hans Guesgen School of Engineering and Advanced Technology, Massey University, New Zealand (Palmerston North campus)

Christian Kopp Internet Commerce Security Laboratory, Federation University, Australia

Robert Layton Internet Commerce Security Laboratory, Federation University, Australia

Seung Jun Lee School of Engineering & Advanced Technology, Massey University, New Zealand

Charles Perez PSB Paris School of Business, Chair Digital Data Design

Agate M. Ponder-Sutton Information Technology & Centre for Information Technology, School of Engineering and Advanced Technology, Massey University, New Zealand

Jim Sillitoe Internet Commerce Security Laboratory, Federation University, Australia

Jason Smith School of Electrical Engineering and Computer Science – Science and Engineering Faculty, Queensland University of Technology, Queensland, Australia

Kristin Stock School of Engineering and Advanced Technology, Massey University, New Zealand (Albany, Auckland campus)

Suriadi Suriadi   School of Engineering and Advanced Technology, College of Sciences, Massey University, New Zealand

Paul A. Watters   School of Engineering & Advanced Technology, Massey University, New Zealand

George R.S. Weir   Department of Computer and Information Sciences, University of Strathclyde, Glasgow, UK

Ian Welch   School of Engineering and Computer Science, Victoria University of Wellington, New Zealand

CHAPTER 1

The Automating of Open Source Intelligence

Agate M. Ponder-Sutton

*Information Technology & Centre for Information Technology, School of Engineering
and Advanced Technology, Massey University, New Zealand*

Open source intelligence (OSINT) is intelligence that is synthesized using publicly available data (Hobbs, Moran, & Salisbury, 2014). It differs significantly from the open source software movement. This kind of surveillance started with the newspaper clipping of the first and second world wars. Now it is ubiquitous within large business and governments and has dedicated study. There have been impassioned, but simplified, arguments for and against the current levels of open source intelligence gathering. In the post-Snowden leaks world one of the questions is how to walk the line between personal privacy and nation state safety. What are the advances? How do we keep up, keep relevant, and keep it fair or at least ethical? Most importantly, how do we continue to "make sense or add value" as Robert David Steele would say, (http://tinyurl. com/EIN-UN-SDG). I will discuss the current state of OSINT and data science. The changes in the analysts and users will be explored. I will cover data analysis, automated data gathering, APIs, and tools; algorithms including supervised and unsupervised learning, geo-locational methods, de-anonymization. How do these interactions take place within OSINT when including ethics and context? How does OSINT answer the challenge laid down by Schneier in his recent article elaborating all the ways in which big data have eaten away at the privacy and stability of private life, "Your cell phone provider tracks your location and knows who is with you. Your online and in-store purchasing patterns are recorded, and reveal if you are unemployed, sick, or pregnant. Your emails and texts expose your intimate and casual friends. Google knows what you are thinking because it saves your private searches. Facebook can determine your sexual orientation without you ever mentioning it." (Schneier, 2015b). These effects can be seen in worries surrounding the recording and tracking done by large companies to follow their customers discussed by Schneier, (2015a, 2015b) and others as the crossing of the uncanny valley from useful into disturbing. These examples include the recordings made by a Samsung TV of consumers in their homes (http://www.theguardian.com/media-network/2015/ feb/13/samsungs-listening-tv-tech-rights); Privacy fears were increased by the cloud storage of the recordings made by the interactive WIFI-capable Barbie (http://www.theguardian.com/technology/2015/mar/13/smart-barbie-that-can-listen-to-your-kids-privacy-fears-mattel); Jay-Z's Album Magna Carta Holy Grail's privacy breaking app (http://www.theguardian.com/music/2013/jul/17/jay-z-magna-carta-app-under-investigation); and the Angry Birds location recording which got targeted by the NSA and GCHQ and likely shared with other Five Eyes Countries (http://www.theguardian.com/world/2014/jan/27/nsa-gchq-smartphone-app-angry-birds-personal-data). The Internet can be viewed as a tracking, listening, money maker for the recorders and new owners of your data. Last but not least there must be a mention of the Target case where predictions of pregnancy were based on buying history.

The Target storey was broken by the *New York Times* (Duhigg, C. "How Companies Learn Your Secrets." February 16, 2012. http://www.nytimes.com/2012/02/19/magazine/shopping-habits.html?_r=0).

The rise of OSINT, data science, business, or commercial has come with the revolution in the variety, volume, and availability public data (Hobbs et al., 2014; Appel, 2014). There has been a profound change in how data are collected, stored, and disseminated driven by the Internet and the advances linked to it. With establishment of Open Source Center and assistant deputy director for open source intelligence in the United States, the shift toward legitimacy of OSINT in the all-source intelligence process was made clear (http://resources.infosecinstitute.com/osint-open-source-intelligence/). The increased importance of OSINT has moved it into the core of intelligence work and allowed a larger number of players to take part, diversifying its uses beyond the original "intelligence community" (Hobbs et al., 2014). Interconnectivity has increased and much of that data can be utilized through open source intelligence methodologies to create actionable insights. OSINT can produce new and useful data and insights; however, it brings technical, political, and ethical challenges and obstacles that must be approached carefully.

Wading through the sheer bulk of the data for the unbiased reality can present difficulties. Automation means the spread of OSINT, out of the government office to businesses, and casual users for helpful or wrong conclusions as in the case of the Boston bomber Redit media gaff (http://www.bbc.com/news/technology-22263020). These problems can also be seen in the human flesh search engine instances in China and the doxing by anonymous and others in positive and negative lights. With more levels of abstraction increasing difficulty is apparent, as tools to look at the tools to look at the output of the data. Due to the sheer volume of data it becomes easier to be more susceptible to cognitive bias. These are issues can be seen in the errors made by the US government in securing their computer networks ("EPIC" fail – how OPM hackers tapped the mother lode of espionage data. Two separate "penetrations" exposed 14 million people's personal information. Ars Technica. June 22, 2015. 2:30pm NZST. http://arstechnica.com/security/2015/06/epic-fail-how-opm-hackers-tapped-the-mother-lode-of-espionage-data/). With the advent of corporate doxying of Ashley Madison and of Sony it can be seen as a private corporation problem as well.

Groups of users and uses include: governments; business intelligence and commercial intelligence; academia; and Hacker Space and Open Data initiatives. Newer users include nongovernmental organizations (NGOs), university, public, and commercial interests. User-generated content, especially social media, has changed the information landscape significantly. These can all have interactions and integrated interests. Collaboration between these groups is common among some, US government contracting IBM and Booz-Allen and also less inflammatory contracted employees; academia writing tools for Business Intelligence or government contracts. These tend to be mutually beneficial. Others where the collaboration is nonvoluntary such as the articles detailing how to break the anonymity of the netflix prize dataset (Narayanan & Shmatikov, 2008); or any of the multiple blog posts detailing similar anonymity breaking methods such as "FOILing NYC's Taxi Trip Data" http://chriswhong.com/open-data/foil_nyc_taxi/ and London bicycle data "I know where you were last summer" http://vartree. blogspot.co.nz/2014_04_01_archive.html) have furthered security and OSINT analysis, sometimes to the ire of the data collectors.

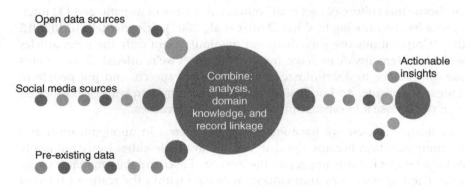

Open source methodology

The extent to which information can be collected is large and the field is broad. The speed, the volume, and variety are enough that OSINT can be considered a "Big Data" problem. Tools to deal with the tools that interface with the data such as Maltego and Recon-ng are becoming more popular and common approaches. These approaches still require setup and a certain amount of knowledge to gain and/or buy access to information. This required setup also includes a certain amount of tuning that cannot be or would be difficult to automate. Fetching the data and to some extent limitation of false positives can be automated. OSINT research continues to push automation further. There is an overall Chelsea Manning, and lean toward the commodification of OSINT; more companies offer more analytical tools and/or software and a service to cash in on what was once a government or very limited field. Many tools are available that require less technical expertise; featuring drag and drop interfaces where the focus is on ease of use and the availability of the data.

Open source intelligence methodology is a synthesis from multiple fields: data science, statistics, machine learning, programming, databases, computer science, and many other fields, but there is no over-arching unifying theory of open source intelligence. The ease of the data creation and acquisition is unprecedented, and OSINT owes this to its rise as well to the complex algorithm, de-anonymization, and fear that has come with them. WikiLeaks, and Snowden, (http://www.theguardian.com/us-news/the-nsa-files), have provided a highly publicised view of the data compiled on the average person with regards to the Five Eyes; we can only assume that similar things are done by other governments (Walsh & Miller, 2015). Commercial organizations have followed suit with worrisome and very public issues surrounding the collection of data. This is a wealth of data as well as a major ethical concern. This is part of the OSINT landscape because (1) people behave differently when they know they are under surveillance (Miller et al., 2005); (2) if this is part of the intelligence landscape this culture of "get it all" others will follow in its path; and (3) intelligence has become big business (Miller et al., 2005). Schneier tells us in 2015 that "Corporations use surveillance to manipulate not only the news articles and advertisements we each see, but also the prices we're offered. Governments use surveillance to discriminate, censor, chill free speech, and put people in danger worldwide. And both sides share this information with each other or, even worse, lose it to cybercriminals in huge data breaches."

And from this view we have an increasing interest in anonymization and de-anonymization because the data that are available either freely publically or for a fee can identify impact on the interested user and the originator of the data. The importance of anonymization of data within the realm of Internet security and its risks are clearly recognized by the U.S. President's Council of Advisors on Science and Technology ("PCAST"):

> Anonymization of a data record might seem easy to implement. Unfortunately, it is increasingly easy to defeat anonymization by the very techniques that are being developed for many legitimate applications of big data. In general, as the size and diversity of available data grows, the likelihood of being able to re-identify individuals (that is, re-associate their records with their names) grows substantially. [...]

Anonymization remains somewhat useful as an added safeguard, but it is not robust against near-term future re-identification methods. PCAST does not see it as being a useful basis for policy (PCAST, 2014).

This 2014 PCAST - Executive Office of the President, 2014, report captures the consensus of computer scientists who have expertise in de- and reidentification: there is no technical backing to say that common deidentification methods will be effective protection against future attempts.

The majority of people have some kind of online presence. There has been an increase not only since its initialization, but in uptake in the last couple of years. Ugander, Karrer, Backstrom, and Marlow (2011) wrote: The median Facebook user has about a hundred friends. Barlett and Miller (2013) said, "Every month, 1.2 billion people now use internet sites, apps, blogs and forums to post, share and view content." (p. 7). In 2015, Schneier tells us, "Google controls two-thirds of the US search market. Almost three-quarters of all internet users have Facebook accounts. Amazon controls about 30% of the US book market, and 70% of the ebook market. Comcast owns about 25% of the US broadband market. These companies have enormous power and control over us simply because of their economic position." (Schneier, 2015a, 2015b). So you can see how the situation could be both exciting and dire as a company, an organization, and an individual. There are a plethora of books on OSINT and its methods, tutorials, and how-to's having been touched by the dust of the "secret world of spies" it is now gathering hype and worry. And because both are warranted treading in this area should be done carefully with an eye toward what you can know and always in mind what privacy should be (Ohm, 2010).

"Loosely grouped as a new, 'social' media, these platforms provide the means for the way in which the internet is increasingly being used: to participate, to create, and to share information about ourselves and our friends, our likes and dislikes, movements, thoughts and transactions. Although social media can be 'closed' (meaning not publically viewable) the underlying infrastructure, philosophy and logic of social media is that it is to varying extents 'open': viewable by certain publics as defined by the user, the user's network of relationships, or anyone. The most well-known are Facebook (the largest, with over a billion users), YouTube and Twitter. However, a much more diverse (linguistically, culturally, and functionally) family of platforms span social bookmarking, micromedia, niche networks, video aggregation and social curation. The specialist business network LinkedIn has 200 million users, the Russian-language VK network 190 million, and the Chinese QQ network 700 million. Platforms such as Reddit (which reported 400 million unique visitors in 2012) and Tumblr, which has just reached 100 million blogs, can support extremely niche communities based on mutual interest.

For example, it is estimated that there are hundreds of English language pro-eating disorder blogs and platforms. Social media accounts for an increasing proportion of time spent online. On an average day, Facebook users spend 9.7 billion minutes on the site; share 4 billion pieces of content a day and upload 250 million photos. Facebook is further integrated with 7 million websites and apps" (Bartlett and Miller, 2013, p. 7).

Schneier tells us that, "Much of this [data gathering] is voluntary: we cooperate with corporate surveillance because it promises us convenience, and we submit to government surveillance because it promises us protection. The result is a mass surveillance society of our own making. But have we given up more than we've gained?" (Schneier, 2015a, 2015b). However, those trying to avoid tracking have found it difficult to inforce. Ethical nontracking (DoNotTrack http://en.wikipedia.org/wiki/ Do_Not_Track) and opt out lists and the incognito settings on various browsers have received some attention and, but several researchers have shown these have little to no effect on the tracking agencies (Schneier; Acar et al., 2014). Ethical marketing and the developers kit for that at DoNotTrack. Persistent tracking within the web is a known factor (Acar et al., 2014) and the first automated study of evercookies suggests that opts outs made little difference. Acar et al. track the cookies tracking a user in three different ways coming to the conclusion that "even sophisticated users face great difficulty in evading tracking techniques." They look at canvas finger printing, evercookies, and use of "cookie syncing. They perform the largest to date automated crawl of the home pages of Top Alexa 100K sites and increased the scale of their work on respawning, evercookies, and cookie syncing. The first study of real-world canvas finger printing. They include in their measurements the flash cookies with the most respawns, the top parties involved in cookies sync, the top IDs in cookies sync from the same home pages and observed the effect of opting out under multiple schemes. A draft preprint by (Englehardt et al., 2014) discusses web measurement as a field and identifies 32 web privacy measurement studies that tend toward *ad hoc* solutions. They then present their own privacy measurement platform, which is scalable and outlines how it avoids the common pitfalls. They also address the case made by most press of the personalization effects of cookies and tracking by crawling 300,000 pages across nine news sites. They measure the extent of personalization based on a user's history and conclude the service is oversold. So based on these the plethora of data could still be useful, gathered less intensely, or in other more privacy-preserving manners.

"We kill people based on metadata" is one of the most quoted or focused-on things that General Michael Hayden, Former NSA head, has said, but other things he said in the same interview were equally important (https://www.youtube.com/watch?v=UdQiz0Vavmc). When General Hayden says the NSA are "…yelling through the transom…"; he means that starting with one phone number the NSA can then expand this by pulling in every number that has called that number and every number that has called those numbers using the interconnections of networks – (see Maltego for similar effects)). Targeted attacks such as these which can expand the available data are covered in depth by Narayanan, Huey, and Felten (2015). The heavy use of statistics and rise of data science allow users to deal less with the data and more with the metadata which can be seen as a lengthening of the weight of the data. Part of this lightening the load is the rise of tools for the less technical.

The advances in open source intelligence automation have been unsurprisingly linked to advances in computing and algorithms; they are focused on the collection of data and the algorithms used to do analysis (Hobbs et al., 2014). There has been a shift toward the public sector not only of the provision of OSINT as a service from private firms but of the use of by marketing and commercial sides of businesses of open source intelligence. The data gathering, insight synthesis, and build of proprietary tools for OSINT are on the rise. Covered here are what algorithms are new, innovative, or still doing well. New sources and ways to find them are covered lightly. Here are presented several common and new algorithms along with breakthroughs in the field. The *ad hoc* quality of the open source intelligence gathering leads to the rise of new original algorithms (Narayanan, 2013 and Acar et al., 2014) and new uses.

THE COMMERCIAL ANGLE

Data science and really the new tend toward tools and hype, "What is hot in analytics" may threaten to distract from the substance of the revolution (Walsh & Miller, 2015). In an October 2012 edition of the Harvard Business Review, the role of a data scientist was called the "sexiest job of the 21st Century." The article discusses the rise of the data expert, with more and more companies turning to people with the ability to manipulate large data sets (http://datasmart.ash.harvard.edu/news/article/the-rise-of-the-data-scientists-611). In 2011, a report by McKinsey predicted that "by 2018 the US would face a shortage of 140,000 to 190,000 workers with deep analytical skills and of 1.5 million managers and analysts with big data skills" (http://www.mckinsey.com/insights/business_technology/big_data_the_next_frontier_for_innovation). "Big Data" has seen a lot of hype and as we sit in what Gartner terms the trough of disillusionment with regard to Big Data; companies are finding additional ways to use data and combine technologies with the concept of recombination to create solutions in the growing trend in the business intelligence space. Business intelligence or business analytics has migrated from IT departments into either its own department or individual departments and often into the marketing department (https://www.gartner.com/doc/2814517/hype-cycle-big-data-). The ability of early adopters in sectors such as risk management, insurance, marketing, and financial services brings together external data and internal data to build new algorithms – to identify risk, reduce loss, and strengthen decision support. Companies want to be seen to be working with world-leading business intelligence companies that can present and synthesize hybrid data.

When the private company Ventana ranked OSINT/BI products in 2015; those that were ranked highly mixed functionality and user experience. Many of the top BI Tools provide user experience and an integrated data management, predictive analytics, visual discovery, and operational intelligence capabilities in a single platform. Modern architecture that is cloud-ready and supports responsive design on mobile devices is a bonus. Combining predictive analytics with visual discovery is popular. Ventana Noted that users preferred all-in-one user technology that addresses the need for identity management and security, especially in a multiple device leaning time (http://www.information-management. com/blogs/Business-Analytics-Intelligence-Hot-Ventana-Research-10026829-1. html?utm_campaign=blogsapr%2022%202015&utm_medium=email&utm_ source=newsletter&ET=informationmgmt%3Ae4238189%3A4131831a%3A&st =email).

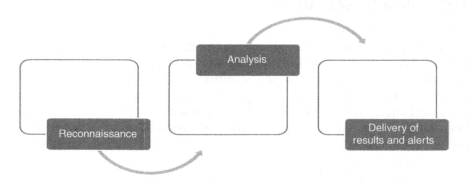

Emphasis is placed on all steps, in order to allow actionable insights to be trusted.

Analysis

Reconnaissance

Delivery of results and alerts

MapReduce and similar algorithms are getting the most use in cloud computing to deal with the quantity and variety of data within OSINT. Originally, a Google proprietary function that has since been genericized, MapReduce is a framework used to process and generate large data sets within a parallel, distributed algorithm on a large number of computers (Dean & Ghemawat, 2010). These computers are nodes in either if they are collocated with the similar hardware a cluster or not a grid. Processing can use unstructured or structured stored data. MapReduce can also process data on or near storage assets in order to reduce loss from transmission distance. Conceptually similar approaches have been in use since 1995 with the Message Passing Interface.

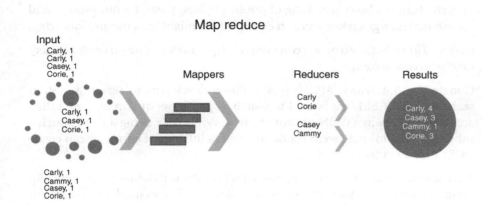

Automation implies tools; the first tool we are going to cover is web crawlers. Because there are many sources the information-gathering process will take time if solely manual techniques are used. A web crawler starts with a list of URLs, the seed list. As the crawler visits these, it identifies all the hyperlinks in the page and adds the new links to the list of URLs. URLs from the list are recursively visited according to a set of policies. If the crawler is performing archiving of websites, it copies and saves the information as it goes. Then, archives are stored in order that they can be viewed, read, and navigated as they were on the live web (Masanès, 2007). One example of this is the Wayback Machine – Internet Archive (http://archive.org/web/).

A crawler can only download a limited number of web pages within a given time, so it prioritizes those downloads. However, because of the numerous possible combinations of HTTP GET (URL-based) that parameters exist, only a small selection of these will return unique content. This is a problem for crawlers, to sort through endless combinations of minor scripted changes to retrieve unique content. For example, an online art gallery offers three options to users; these are specified through HTTP GET parameters in the URL. If users can sort images in four ways, three possibilities for image size, two for file formats, and the option to disable user-provided content, then the same set of content can be accessed with 48 different URLs. Web crawlers can incorporate APIs.

The second set of tools is APIs. Many sites have APIs that return results in a JSON format. APIs require an access_token that free or cost (http://raidersec. blogspot.co.nz/2012/12/automated-open-source-intelligence.html). The JSON output from an API can be imported and handled using Python. This and the ability to make batch requests of API can searching and gathering data easier.

Facebook's Graph API was created to streamline access to information. The "search" feature allows searching of public profiles, posts, events, groups, and more based on a given keyword; an example URL might look like the following:

https://graph.facebook.com/search?q=mark&type=user&access_token=[access_token].

Google Custom Search API: This API allows developers to set up a custom search engine (CSE) that is used to search a specific set of domains, and then access the results in a JSON or Atom format. While only being able to search a subset of domains may seem restricting, with a little bit of effort, we can create a CSE that includes all sites.

After setting up this CSE, we can easily pull results for Twitter users, Linkedin users, documents from companies' websites, etc. For example, Linkedin for Massey University:

site:linkedin.com intitle: "| Linkedin" "at Massey University" -intitle:profiles -inurl:groups -inurl:company -inurl:title

LinkedIn does have its own API; however, this can be expanded to include more sites such as Twitter

site:twitter.com intitle: "on Twitter" "Massey University"

In this way data can be gathered easily and then aggregated. Many new tools include data aggregators this automation is present in greater and lesser degrees depending on the tools. These tools claim to can serve up data and analysis. They promise to be models and sources. These all in one tools for BI/OSINT are on the rise and these are often backed by blogs and information to inform the user. The growing list shows the expansion of the interest in the field and the multiple users and uses, includes: APIs, scrapers, offensive security measures including penetration-testing tools: exiftool data, the harvester, Maltego, Cogito, Cree.py, Metasploit, Scra.py, recon-ng, Panda, R, SAS.

Recon-ng styles itself a web reconnaissance framework; authored by Tim Tomes; sponsored by Black Hills Information Security; and written in Python it can certainly get you some data and store it in its tool database. The tool jigsaw.rb is a ruby script that scrapes the contact website Jigsaw for contact details and generates email addresses on the fly. Maltego has the free community version that is available by itself or in Kali Linux, a Linux distribution available for those investing time in penetration testing and computer security. Kali Linux is one of several Offensive Security projects – funded, developed, and maintained as a free and open-source penetration-testing platform. This tool provides automatic OSINT-gathering techniques using "transforms." The data are then presented and manipulated using an intuitive graphical interface of a force-directed graph. Spokeo is a search engine for social information. By enter a name, email address, username, phone number, etc., one can find information across a variety of social networking platforms and other sources.

There are many other manual and automatic tools that can help us in our OSINT-gathering process, but to talk about what to do with the data now that you have it. NoSQL, big data analytics, cloud, and database as a service (DBaaS), all these have/are new approaches to breaking the code of what is happening and what can be made into actionable insights from that. Tools may not specify which algorithms they use or they make reference which family of algorithms. The tools recon-ng, Maltego, SAS, R, Weka, and Panda all have data-mining utilities. Recon-ng and Maltego are solid and advanced setup and API keys are required, but deep dives may be done on data that the tools acquire. SAS and R have been in use for sometime in research and business and have solid statistical grounding. They are not data-gathering tools abut data mining and data modeling tools as well as languages. Panda PyBrain and SciPy data learning machine learning modlues that are availiable in python. Weka is a java based software for machine learning. These all have in common that they do not gather data, but will take API input and other data formats.

ALGORITHMS

There are overlapping method names within OSINT due to the fusion of disciplines, each with their own vocabularies that deal with the algorithms associated with open source intelligence gathering. Perhaps it is best to say that open source intelligence gathering is open to all the useful algorithms so Statistics, Machine Learning, Pattern Recognition, Computer Science, Applied Mathematics, have claims on the algorithms used for OSINT. Many papers use more than one algorithm or methodology to examine the data and provide a more accurately describe the data and context. Watters (2012); Wibberley and Miller (2014); Jin, Li, & Mehrotra, (2003) are good examples of this multiple method approach. In business and research often many of the algorithms that are gaining ground are unnamed or unspecified in tools. Some standard others are measured by the field they come from: machine learning and natural language processing; event detection; predictive analytics (notably non-machine learning based); network analysis; and manual analysis.

The importance of using algorithms, scientific methods, and isolating the cognitive bias in your open source intelligence can be seen very clearly in the false accusations that appeared on Redit claiming they had discovered the Boston

Bomber, when in fact they had discovered an unfortunate person who had been at the Boston Marathon and then disappeared as he had drowned (http://www.bbc.com/news/technology-22263020).

The algorithms used in OSINT are found for the generalized problems that they solve. The topics describe the problems being solved and how the solver uses them. In the terminology of machine learning, classification is considered an instance of supervised learning, where correctly identified observations are available to be used as a training set. The unsupervised procedure clustering involves grouping data into categories based on measure(s) of similarity or nearness. Semisupervised learning topics such as natural language processing (Noubours, Pritzkau, & Schade, 2013) and adaptive resonance theory (Carroll, 2005) cover a variety of algorithms span learning methods and descriptors. These are well represented in OSINT. Supervised learning includes: structured predictive methods; classification (Watters); decision trees (Watters) and ensemble methods such as bagging, boosting, and random forests, and k means nearest neighbors; neural networks and Naïve Bayes, support vector machine and relevance vector machine, linear and logistic regression (Churn and company attrition models). Neural networks include deep learning. Anomaly detection is a widely discussed set of algorithms which include k - means nearest neighbors and local outlier factors.

Unsupervised learning includes: BIRCH, hierarchical, k-means, expectation maximization, density-based spatial clustering of applications with noise, OPTICS, mean-shift. There are many clustering algorithms differing by what the measure used to cluster the data. Papers using clustering include Herps, Watters, and Pineda-Villavicencio (2013) and Watters.

Cluster analysis or clustering is the task of grouping a set of objects in such a way that objects in the same group are more similar by a decided measure to those in other clusters. It is a common technique for statistical data analysis, used in many fields, including machine learning, pattern recognition, image analysis, information retrieval, and bioinformatics.

Cluster is not one algorithm, but the over arching description of the problems solved. It can be achieved by various algorithms that differ significantly in their notion of what constitutes a cluster and how to efficiently find them. Popular notions of clusters include groups with small distances among the cluster members, dense areas of the data space, intervals, or particular statistical distributions. Clustering can therefore be formulated as a multiobjective optimization problem. The appropriate clustering algorithm and parameter settings (including values such as the distance function to use, a density threshold, or the number of expected clusters) depend on the individual data set and intended use of the results. Cluster analysis as such is not an automatic task, but an iterative process of knowledge discovery or interactive multiobjective optimization that involves trial and failure. It will often be necessary to modify data preprocessing and model parameters until the result achieves the desired properties (Kogan, 2007). The differences between clustering methods and disciplines can be seen in the usage of the results: in data mining, the resulting groups are the matter of interest, in automatic classification the resulting discriminative power is of interest. This can lead to misunderstandings between researchers coming from the fields of data mining and machine learning, since they use the same terms and often the same algorithms, but have different goals.

Herps, Watters, Pineda-Villavicencio only look at the top 50 Alexa sites for Australians making policy suggestions and cluster analysis of site type and overlaps between cookies and relationships between websites (Herps et al., 2013). This analysis culminates in building a directed graph model of the 50 sites; the note that the penetration of Google analytics is 54% of the sample which is closely followed by social media sites. Facebook was storing cookies on 17% of the sites. There is the discussion of the possibility of a privacy feedback loop created by the linking of sites sharing cookies like Facebook and GA. Ending by recommending that Australia adopt laws similar to the European cookie laws due to the pervasiveness of the tracking involved and the amount of data captured.

Reducing the number of independent variables used is an algorithm called dimension reduction. Machine learning and statistics divide this field into feature selection and feature extraction. Feature selection approaches try to find a subset of the original variables. Two strategies are filtering by information gain and wrapper, which is guided by accuracy approaches. These can sometimes be considered combinatorial optimization problems. These algorithms create a reduced space, in which data analysis can sometimes be done more accurately than in the original space. Feature extraction transforms the data in the high-dimensional space to a space of fewer dimensions. The data transformation may be linear, as in principal component analysis but many nonlinear dimensionality reduction techniques also exist. For multidimensional data, tensor representation can be used in dimensionality reduction through multilinear subspace learning.

Random forests are used in Watters et al. to group website output and owners in conjunction with other methods. In machine learning and statistics, classification is the problem of identifying to which of a set of categories a new observation belongs, on the basis of a training set of data containing observations whose category membership is known. Often, the individual observations are analyzed into a set of quantifiable properties. Classifiers work by comparing observations to previous observations by means of a similarity or distance function. The term "classifier" refers to the mathematical function that maps input data to a category.

Re-identification and de-anonymization are booming areas of study covering from record linkage to graph traversal and graph visualization tools: (Narayanan & Shmatikov, 2008) introduce a new simulated annealing-based weighted graph matching algorithm for the seeding step of de-anonymization. They also show how to combine de-anonymization with link prediction – the latter is required to achieve good performance on the portion of the test set not de-anonymized – for example by training the predictor on the de-anonymized portion of the test set, and combining probabilistic predictions from de-anonymization and link prediction. "Even more generally, re-identification algorithms are classification algorithms for the case when the number of classes is very large. Classification algorithms categorize observed data into one of several classes, that is, categories. They are at the core of machine learning, but typical machine-learning applications rarely need to consider more than several hundred classes. Thus, re-identification science is helping develop our knowledge of how best to extend classification algorithms as the number of classes increases." (Narayanan, 2013). The set-theoretic record linkage can be considered within unsupervised learning; by taking the intersections of intersections of multiple openly available databases one can narrow down targets and re-identify people (skydog and security freak at SkydogCon 2012, https://www.youtube.com/watch?v=062pLOoZhk8). Indirect record linkage has been successfully used to group authors of social media (Layton, Perez, Birregah, Watters, & Lemercier, 2013).

While re-identification can cause data leakage, it is mostly used to clarify data. Re-identification is "record linkage" that connects common entities across different databases. Often in real data sets, a useful unique identifier does not exist. In an overview of "record linkage" research of more than a hundred papers, William Winkler of the U.S. Census Bureau discusses the new moves toward automation. Record linkage is used to remove duplicates, or combine records so that relationships in multiple data elements from separate files can be examined. It can be one of the strongest de-anonymization techniques. In the past record linkage was largely a manual process or one that used elementary and *ad hoc* rules. Matching techniques that are based on formal mathematical models subject to testing are now more likely to be in use rather than exceptional (Winkler, 2006). While it can be said that a large amount of re-identification can be done with little more than solid programming and statistics skills (Skydog and security Freak, 2012; Narayanan et al., 2011; Narayanan, 2008, www.youtube.com/watch?v=062pLOoZhk8). "...The history of re-identification has been a succession of surprising new techniques rendering earlier data sets vulnerable" (Narayanan et al., 2015).

In 2000, Sweeney claimed to show 87% of the U.S. population can be uniquely re-identified based on five-digit ZIP code, gender, and date of birth (Sweeney, 2000). The ability to de-anonymize data requires little in the way of advanced analytics and as the tragedy of the data commons and many other ethics publications show there is no way to anonymize data beyond recovery, merely to anonymize beyond current openly available data with no guarantee for the future. This can be seen in the Netflix study (research by Narayanan and Shmatikov revealed that with minimal knowledge about a user's movie preferences, there is an over 80% chance of identifying that user's record in the Netflix Prize data set – a targeted attack (Narayanan & Shmatikov, 2008) and the Target case and the governor case (Sweeney, 2005). Intersecting open data sources is one of the ways to de-anonymize. Leveraging what is known in several data sets to easily find the hiding people within the crowd has become trivial given the right leveraging data.

"Generally the reason a data set can not be de-anonymized is due to the lack of publically published data at this time, like that of the Heritage Health Prize" (El Emam et al., 2012). It has been shown that it is possible to identify Netflix users by cross-referencing the public ratings on IMDb. Even more broad attacks could be possible depending on the quantity and availability of information in possession of the adversary for cross-referencing (Narayanan & Shmatikov, 2008a, 2008b). Data custodians face a choice between roughly three alternatives: sticking with the old habit of de-identification and hoping for the best; turning to emerging technologies like differential privacy that involve some tradeoffs in utility and convenience; and using legal agreements to limit the flow and use of sensitive data (Narayanan, 2011) (Narayanan & Felten, 2014).

Record linkage can include mapping algorithms utilizing multidimensional Euclidean space that preserves domain-specific similarity. A multidimensional similarity join over the chosen attributes is used to determine similar pairs of records (Jin, Li, & Mehrotra, 2003). Likage is very strong in conjunction with geospatial data. This blog is about a publicly available data set of bicycle journey data that contains enough information to track the movements of individual cyclists across London, for a six-month period. "…There are benign insights that can be made by looking at individual profiles – but the question remains whether these kinds of insights justify the risks to privacy that come with releasing journey data that can be associated with individual profiles." (http://vartree.blogspot.co.nz/2014_04_01_archive.html)

Geospatial record linkage and other algorithms can be very powerful. Even Jon Snow's first geospatial analysis in (mapping cholera in 1854) is a case of record linkage and leveraging available data to the common good (Johnson, 2006). Because of the great good gained by geographic data. There is a risk in misunderstanding the anonymization of geospatial data. Narayanan et al. (2015) make the argument that geospatial data cannot or have not yet been able to be anonymized in a way that would ensure the privacy of the data owners or describers. In several examples, geospatial data are leveraged to find patterns and start and ends of journeys lead to knowing places of business and homes ((Narayanan et al., 2015); (Barocas & Nissenbaum, 2014); "FOILing NYC's Taxi Trip Data" http://chriswhong.com/open-data/foil_nyc_taxi/; using British bicycle data "I know where you were last summer" Blog post http://vartree.blogspot.co.nz/2014_04_01_archive.html, "Mapping Where Sex Offenders Can Live" http://automatingosint.com/blog/category/osint/). Spatial analysis is the techniques applied to structures at the human scale, most notably in the analysis of geographic data. Complex issues arise in spatial analysis, many of which are neither clearly defined nor completely resolved, but form the basis for current research. This will be covered in more depth in another chapter. A 2013 study by de Montjoye et al. analysed a mobile phone data set covering 15 months of recorded locations of the connecting antenna each time one of the 1.5 million users called or texted; evaluated the uniqueness of mobility traces (i.e., the recorded data for each user for data points that have antenna location and timestamp). Two random data points uniquely identify over 50% of users. 95% of users are uniquely identifiable using four random data points, which could be revealed through social media then. Geographic data is especially telling using record linkage; that is when multiple data sets are chained together to a non-anonymous data set. These become low hanging fruit easily re-identifying individuals in all of those data sets. In a famous re-identification of the former Governor Weld's medical record used a basic form of this record linkage: Sweeney used gender, date of birth, and ZIP code found through a public data set of registered voters and then used that information to identify him within the de-identified medical database. The geographic data is one of the most telling links in this chain. Hooley and Sweeney's more recent work record linking remains effective on public hospital discharge data from thirty U.S. states in 2013 Hooley and Sweeney, 2013. Other studies like those of Montjoye et al. have cemented that pairs of home and work locations can be used as strong unique identifiers. "…the uniqueness of mobility traces decays approximately as the 1/10 power of their resolution. Hence, even coarse data sets provide little anonymity." (de Montjoye et al., 2013). Geospatial analysis has its own special tools and packages such as: Leaflet.js - web mapping library, GeoEye, Cloudmade - map tiles, Transport For London - data sets of Boris Bike data. There are multiple blogs such as http://spatial.ly/ which has visualizations, analysis, and resources. The API for Wikimapia works like any other API and using this with tools like the geopy Python module https://github.com/geopy/geopy, which handles measurements, can return useful results. An socially responsible example is this map of fracking in the US gives some of the most definitive answers about how much of the US has fracking and where and what kinds of contamination allowing organization of opposition to these occurrences (https://secure3.convio.net/fww/site/SPageServer?pagename=national_parks_public_lands_fracking_2014).

There are exciting things that can be done with the large amounts of collected data. There are very large security risks. Some of the consequences that overt observation brings the negative impact on security and the psychological distrust that results from being watched. These need to be accounted for and coarsening the granulation of the data cannot solve the data privacy issue (de Montjoye et al., 2013). More data sets are becoming publicly available, accessible by data brokers, or by attackers (Schneier, 2015); this means that more targeted attacks can become broad based attacks. New algorithms need to be made and actually measuring the privacy and tracking within the digital world needs to continue and be upgraded. "Even staunch proponents of current de-identification methods admit that they are inadequate for high-dimensional data. These high-dimensional data sets, which contain many data points for each individual's record, have become the norm: social network data has at least a hundred dimensions and genetic data can have millions." (Narayanan et al., 2015) (Erlich et al., 2014). We cannot just let this puzzle slide away as "Arguing that you don't care about the right to privacy because you have nothing to hide is different than saying you don't care about free speech because you have nothing to say." (Edward Snowden, 2015, AMA, http://www.reddit.com/.../just_days_left_to_kill.../crglgh2)

While the focus and users of OSINT have changed and the scope has broadened, much of the backbone remains. Automation has condensed the required time for penetration tests or BI data gathering and report; however the amount of data available has grown exponentially. The investigative structure remains the same, biases must still be accounted for and algorithms remain useful. Knowing the limitations of the algorithms and tools is important. Automation will only get you so far for the moment.

While we may be the bulk of the sources for the new data we are not the totality of it.

There are exciting data sources and helpful analysis to made from them. Sources such as RSOE EDIS – Emergency and Disaster Information Service World OSINT Map (http://hisz.rsoe.hu/alertmap/index2.php), which includes current emergencies; short time events; long time or rolling events; and earthquake and tsunami data with approaching earth objects are still important. The move to contain more is evident even within this fairly old school aggregator of live available data (http://hisz.rsoe.hu/alertmap/index2.php). New data cross correlated with old data or even applied to new techniques can provide useful insights. In the light of the post-Snowden leaks world what are advances in automation and how should they be treated? New data sources are ubiquitous: FitBit and Phone applications, business and tax records, Bing, Google, IRC, IRQ, CDC, Data Monkey, Weiwei. There are solicited/"crowd sourced" insight; public transport through open data requests. An Internet of Things approach can be used; searching it using https://www.shodan.io/. A request can be filed for public data and uses can be very powerful as multiple open community data projects across the world have shown. Anywhere there is a record and an API can be written, data can be gathered.

The data worries and security are ultimately valid; however, use of the gathered data can and has changed how we interact (Bradbury, 2011). We will need to push for positive change just as much as we will need to ensure the data, tools, and algorithms are unbiased. Now that open intelligence has become more open and playing fields are leveling; the need to ensure and encourage positive use is even stronger.

References

Acar, G., Eubank, C., Englehardt, S., Juarez, M., Narayanan, A., & Diaz, C. (2014). The web never forgets: persistent tracking mechanisms in the wild. *ACM conference on computer and communications security*, https://securehomes.esat.kuleuven.be/~gacar/persistent/the_web_never_forgets.pdf.

Appel, E. J. (2014). *Cybervetting: Internet searches for vetting, investigations, and open-source intelligence* (2nd ed.). Boca Raton, FL: CRC Press, ISBN-13: 978-1482238853.

Barocas, S., & Nissenbaum, H. (2014). Big data's end run around anonymity and consent. In J. Lane, V. Stodden, S. Bender, & H. Nissenbaum (Eds.), *Privacy, big data, and the public good: frameworks for engagement* (pp. 52–54). New York: Cambridge University Press.

Bartlett, J., & Miller, C. (2013). The state of the art: a literature review of social media intelligence capabilities for counter-terrorism. *Demos*, 7.

Bartlett, J., & Miller, C. (2013). The state of the art: A literature review of social media intelligence capabilities for counter-terrorism. *Demos*, 4.

Bradbury, D. (2011). In plain view: open source intelligence. *Computer Fraud & Security, 2011*(4), 5–9.

Carroll, J. M. (2005, Feb.). OSINT analysis using adaptive resonance theory for conterterrorism warnings. Paper presented at the *Artificial intelligence and applications* 2005 (pp. 756–760). http://www.scipublish.com/journals/AIA/.

Dean, J., & Ghemawat, S. (2010). Mapreduce: a flexible data processing tool. *Commun. ACM*, 53(1), 72–77.

de Montjoye, Y.-A., Hildalgo, C. A., Verlesysen, M., & Blondel, V. D. Unique in the crowd: The privacy bounds of human mobility, Nature scientific reports 3 (March 2013). doi:10.1038/srep01376. http://www.nature.com/srep/2013/130325/srep01376/full/srep01376.html?ial=1.

El Emam, K., Arbuckle, L., Koru, G., Eze, B., Gaudette, L., Neri, E., Rose, S., Howard, J., & Gluck, J. (2012). De-identification methods for open health data: the case of the heritage health prize claims dataset. *Journal of Medical Internet Research*, 14(1), e33.

Englehardt, S., Eubank, C., Zimmerman, P., Reisman, D., & Narayanan, A. (2014). Web privacy measurement: Scientific principles, engineering platform, and new results. *Manuscript posted at* http://randomwalker. info/publications/WebPrivacyMeasurement.pdf.

Englehardt, S., Reisman, D., Eubank, C., Zimmerman, P., Mayer, J., Narayanan, A., et al. (2015). Cookies that give you away: evaluating the surveillance implications of web tracking. In Proceedings of the 24th International Conference on World Wide Web (WWW '15). International World Wide Web Conferences Steering Committee, Republic and Canton of Geneva, Switzerland, 289–299. WWW 2015. http://randomwalker.info/publications/cookie-surveillance.pdf.

Erlich, Y., Williams, J. B., Glazer, D., Yocum, K., Farahany, N., Olson, M., Narayanan, A., Stein, L. D., Witkowski, J. A., & Kain, R. C. (2014). Redefining genomic privacy: trust and empowerment. PLoS Biol. 2014 Nov 4;12(11):e1001983. doi: 10.1371/journal.pbio.1001983. eCollection 2014. Redefining genomic privacy: trust and empowerment. Erlich Y1, Williams JB2, Glazer D2, Yocum K3, Farahany N4, Olson M5, Narayanan A6, Stein LD7, Witkowski JA8, Kain RC3. *PLoS Biology*.

Herps, A., Watters, P. A., & Pineda-Villavicencio, G. (2013, Nov.). Measuring surveillance in online advertising: a big data approach. In *Fourth cybercrime and trustworthy computing workshop (CTC)* (pp. 30, 35). doi: 10.1109/CTC.;1; 2013.12 URL: http://ieeexplore.ieee.org/stamp/stamp.jsp?tp=&arnumber=6754638&isnumber=6754625.

Hobbs, C., Moran, M., & Salisbury, D. (Eds.) (May 9, 2014). *Open source intelligence in the twenty-first century: new approaches and opportunities (new security challenges)*. Centre for Science and Security Studies, King's College London, UK. Palgrave Macmillan, ISBN-13: 978-1137353313 ISBN-10: 1137353317.

Hooley, S., & Sweeney, L. Survey of publicly available state health databases (white paper 1075-1, Data Privacy Lab, Harvard University, Cambridge, Massachusetts, June 2013), http://dataprivacylab.org/projects/50states/1075-1.pdf.

Jin, L., Li, C., & Mehrotra, S. (2003, Mar.). Efficient record linkage in large data sets. In *Proceedings of the eighth IEEE international conference on database systems for advanced applications (DASFAA 2003)* (pp. 137–146).

Johnson, S. (2006). *The ghost map: The story of London's most terrifying epidemic – and how it changed science, cities and the modern world*. New York. Riverhead Books, ISBN 1-59448-925-4.

Kogan, J. (2007). *Introduction to clustering large and high-dimensional data*. Cambridge: Cambridge University Press, xiii + 222 pp., paperback. ISBN 978-0-521-61793-2.

Layton, R., Perez, C., Birregah, B., Watters, P., & Lemercier, M. (2013). Indirect information linkage for OSINT through authorship analysis of aliases. In *Trends and applications in knowledge discovery and data mining* (pp. 36–46). Berlin, Heidelberg: Springer.

Masanès, J. (2007). *Web archiving*. Berlin: Springer, p. 1.

Miller, D. T., Visser, P. S., & Staub, B. D. (2005). How surveillance begets perceptions of dishonesty: the case of the counterfactual sinner. *Journal of Personality and Social Psychology, 89*(2), 117–128.

Narayanan, A. (2011). An adversarial analysis of the re-identifiability of the heritage health prize dataset, manuscript.

Narayanan, A. (2013). Reidentification as basic science. 33 Bits of entropy blog. Posted May 27, 2013. http://33bits.org/2013/05/27/reidentification-as-basic-science/.

Narayanan, A., & Felten, E. W. (2014). No silver bullet: De-identification still doesn't work. *Manuscript*, http://randomwalker.info/publications/no-silver-bullet-de-identification.pdf.

Narayanan, A., & Shmatikov, V. (2008). Robust de-anonymization of large sparse datasets. In *Proceedings 2008 IEEE symposium on security and privacy*, Oakland, CA, May 18–21, 2008 (pp. 111–125). Los Alamitos, CA: IEEE Computer Society.

Narayanan, A., Huey, J., & Felten, E. W. (2015). A precautionary approach to Big Data Privacy. *Computers Privacy & Data Protection*, http://randomwalker.info/publications/precautionary.pdf.

Noubours, S., Pritzkau, A., & Schade, U. (2013). NLP as an essential ingredient of effective OSINT frameworks. In *Military communications and information systems conference (MCC)* (pp. 1–7). IEEE.

Ohm, P. (2010). Broken promises of privacy: responding to the surprising failure of anonymization. *UCLA Law Review, 57*, 1742–1743.

President's Council of Advisors on Science and Technology (PCAST). Public Meeting Transcript. President's Council of Advisors on Science and Technology (PCAST). (2014). https://www.whitehouse.gov/sites/default/files/microsites/ostp/PCAST/140919_pcast_transcript.pdf.

Schneier, B. (May 17, 2015a). How we sold our souls—and more—to the internet giants. *The Guardian*, https://www.schneier.com/essays/archives/2015/05/how_we_sold_our_soul.html.

Schneier, B. (March 2015b). *Data and goliath: the hidden battles to collect your data and control your world*. New York, NY. US. W. W. Norton & Company, ISBN: 978-0393244816.

Sweeney, L. (2000) Simple demographics often identify people uniquely (data privacy working paper 3, Carnegie Mellon University, Pittsburgh, PA, 2000), http://dataprivacylab.org/projects/identifiability/paper1.pdf.

Sweeney, L. (2005). DHS: Data Privacy and Integrity Advisory Committee FY 2005 Meeting Materials (statement of Latanya Sweeney, Associate Professor of Computer Science, Technology and Policy and Director of the Data Privacy Laboratory, Carnegie Mellon University), http://www.dhs.gov/xlibrary/assets/privacy/privacy_advcom_06-2005_testimony_sweeney.pdf.

Ugander, J., Karrer, B., Backstrom, L., & Marlow, C. (2011). The anatomy of the Facebook social graph, (arXiv Preprint, 2011): 3, http://arxiv.org/pdf/1111.4503v1.pdf.

Walsh, P. F., & Miller, S. (2015). Intelligence and national security. Rethinking 'five eyes' security intelligence collection policies and practice post Snowden.

Watters, P., & University of Canberra. Centre for Internet Safety. (2012). Taming the cookie monster how companies track us online. Centre for Internet Safety, Kambah, A.C.T. http://trove.nla.gov.au/version/189418108.

Wibberley, S., & Miller, C. (2014). *Detecting events from twitter: situational awareness in the age of social media*. In Hobbs, C., Moran, M., & Salisbury, D. (Eds.), *Open source intelligence in the twenty-first century: new approaches and opportunities (new security challenges)*. (pp. 147–167). Centre for Science and Security Studies, King's College London, UK. Palgrave Macmillan, ISBN-13: 978-1137353313 ISBN-10: 1137353317.

Winkler, W. E. (2006). Research report series (statistics #2006-2) overview of record linkage and current research directions. Statistical Research Division. U.S. Census Bureau Washington, DC 20233. https://www.census.gov/srd/papers/pdf/rrs2006-02.pdf.

CHAPTER 2

Named Entity Resolution in Social Media

Paul A. Watters
School of Engineering & Advanced Technology, Massey University, New Zealand

One of the great challenges to automating open source intelligence (OSINT) from sources such as social media is being able to resolve named entities to identify threat actors, and predict their future activities (Watters, McCombie, Layton, & Pieprzyk, 2012). In this context, a named entity refers to a person, place, or thing by its name. For example, my name is "Paul Watters," and I belong to a category called "human," which is a subset of "animal." In more general cases, named entity resolution involves two separate stages: resolving the name, and resolving the category according to an ontology. In the case of OSINT, we assume that the category is known (identifying humans), so the task is somewhat simplified (although it could be the case, through anthropomorphism, that some animals could also be given human names). Sometimes, the same person uses multiple aliases, making actual attribution very difficult (Layton, Perez, Birregah, Watters, & Lemercier, 2013), given that deception is usually involved (Watters, 2013).

Resolving names means associating each named entity with a person on social media (Bontcheva & Rout, 2012). The key problem is obvious: many individuals carry the same name, yet they differ on many key attributes, such as appearance, date of birth, and country of birth. Identifying individuals uniquely and accurately, without human intervention, is a key challenge, since not all of these attributes may be known *a priori*. Thus, an important requirement for named entity resolution is being able to probabilistically determine the true identity of a named individual from a set of possible matches.

Resolving lexical items within a local semantic context is not a new problem (Turney & Pantel, 2010). Yet many of the automated technologies that have been developed over the years have not been very successful in correctly modeling human semantic processing. In this chapter, I will look at one example of this – resolving word senses using automated techniques – and use this as a springboard to suggest some ideas for how named entities could be successfully resolved in the future. Further inspiration for cognitive models could come from further examination of neural system dynamics (Watters, 2000).

The case study I will examine in this chapter involves the wisdom literature of the Bible, including the proverbs of Solomon, which often express themes such as the value of ethical behavior leading to happiness and tangible success, through carefully developed metaphors and similes. The preservation of word and proverb meanings should therefore be a central goal of any attempts at automated machine translations of the kind now commonly available on the Internet. In this chapter, an objective method of assessing the success of machine translations of Biblical proverbs is reviewed, where errors in the translation of meaning are categorized on the basis of dynamical system states (point attractors, limit cycles, and chaotic attractors). Three examples of these system states from Biblical proverbs are then translated from the source language (English) into one of three target languages (French, German, and Italian), using a freely available machine translation system, and their characteristic errors are highlighted. It is concluded that automated machine translation of Biblical proverbs can give rise to serious semantic errors; however, possible strategies for "controling chaos" in these systems are suggested as a basis for future research.

INTRODUCTION

The translation of Biblical literature from the original Greek, Hebrew, and Arameic to modern languages is a task that has long occupied linguists and historians alike, giving rise to often heated debates in the humanities regarding subjectivity of interpretative methods. For example, it has been argued that it is very difficult, if not impossible, to translate a text's meaning outside the cultural environment where it was generated (Sakai, 1997). In Biblical studies, the problem is complicated by the common use of an interlanguage to translate authoritative editions of a Biblical text into other modern languages (for example, translating the English New Revised Standard Version into French). One possible way of resolving issues of subjectivity in translation is to use an automated machine translation system that applies a consistent set of syntactical and grammatical transformations to realize a text in a target language from any source language for which the system has a lexicon and a set of transformational rules. In addition to saving the many years required to translate Biblical texts by using an automated system, the suggestion is also attractive because incremental improvements in linguistic mappings between source and target languages can be updated regularly, with new rules and extra lexical items being added and applied regressively to previous translations.

Although this kind of proposal, at first glance, seems a very attractive proposition for resolving individual differences in the translation of Biblical literature, it rests on the assumption that sets of transformational rules and a source and target lexicon are all that is required for a reasonably accurate translation. These kinds of systems, although varying widely in their implementation, are known as *direct translation* systems, since they do not possess any kind of internal "cognitive" structure, which is found *linguistic knowledge* systems. In this chapter, we will only examine direct translation systems, as they are the most widely adopted systems internationally. The main computational goal of direct translation systems is to balance the processing capacity of a computer and the processing time required to perform a translation, against the accuracy and intelligibility of the target translation. Parsing is very basic, usually involving the replacement of each word in the source language with a lexically retrieved target (i.e., a unidirectional mapping). Although some systems also have the capacity to translate target→source, this is usually achieved by an entirely separate unidirectional mapping. The accuracy of translations generated from translation systems is usually evaluated in terms of the consistency of meaning of the target with respect to the source, and/or vice versa. These translations are acontextual and probabilistic, in the sense that no attempt is made to disambiguate word senses, rather the most frequent word sense is commonly selected (i.e., there is no internal representation of semantics; Layton, Watters & Dazeley, 2012). Knowledge of word order differences forms the basis for simple syntactical transformation rules, which are generally applied after the lexical conversion, for example, the different sequential order of adjectives and nouns in English and French. The morphology of regular verbs is usually handled with dictionary-like lookups, although this often results in the over-regularization of irregular verbs (Palmer, 1990). Direct translation architectures often produce incorrect translations because of the simplified internal representation of linguistic knowledge on which these systems are based. These problems are often exacerbated by the existence of different dictionaries for source→target and target→source translations, which commonly produce noninvertible translations. Despite this, direct translation systems are the most commonly used MT systems, with proponents arguing that they are actually quite useful for "bulk" translations, which are then refined and corrected by a human interpreter.

Of course, not everyone agrees that an enterprise such as machine translation is possible: indeed, given Searle's (1984) distinction between computer information processing (which he claims is purely syntactic) as opposed to human information processing (which is both syntactic and semantic), it might be quite impossible to correctly preserve the meanings of words using an automated translation system. This viewpoint is opposed by the Behaviorist view of human information processing, which posits that once the rules for mapping source and target languages are known, all translations are possible, since Behaviorists do not believe in the "naïve reification of mental structure" (Shannon, 1988). Of course, the success or failure of automated machine translation systems in the processing of "meaning intense" discourse, such as Biblical proverbs, could lend weight to either argument (i.e., successful *direct* translations might support the Behaviorist viewpoint, while semantic processing errors would surely support Searle's position). However, statements about the success or failure of direct translation systems do not necessarily reflect the performance of alternative systems which have linguistic knowledge or which are based on psycholinguistic data or "neural networks."[1]

Evaluating Semantic Processing Performance

One inherent problem in evaluating the success of any machine translation system is that there are very few ways in which the success of translated language can be assessed objectively. In linguistics, an "error" in language production or use is defined by James (1998) as "an unsuccessful bit of language" (p. 1), with the process of error analysis being concerned with describing the conditions under which unsuccessful language arises. Although many researchers make use of judgements and subjective rating scales for evaluation of errors in target language text by a panel of human judges (White & Taylor, 1998), there is always going to be a lot of inter-rating variability between different judges, who no doubt apply different criteria to their judgements of what is an acceptable translation, as opposed to what is unacceptable. Hovy (1998) has suggested that one solution to the problem is to use a "multidimensional" evaluation system, where a translation can be evaluated on many different and presumably correlated scales of fluency, adequacy, comprehensibility, etc. In this sense, covering as many criteria for acceptability as possible might result in a better convergence of judge's ratings (but it also has the potential for greater variation too!).

Watters and Patel (2000) suggested an alternative strategy for the evaluation of machine translation systems known as the iterative semantic processing (ISP) paradigm. The ISP paradigm focusses not only just on translated content, and its subjectively rated acceptability, but also on an objective exploration of the processes which might give rise to consistent semantic processing errors in translation from source to target, but also from target to source. In doing so, the process of machine translation is generalized to be an iterative system in which the source sentence is translated into the target language, which is then reverse translated back to the source language, thus becoming the input for a second source→target translation, and so on. Although this removes the machine translation system from its normal operation in single passes from source to target, it actually facilitates an object evaluation of how much semantic information is lost from iteration to iteration, or alternatively, if no information is lost, for a perfect evaluation to be made (a "10 out of 10"). The act of translation, in either gaining incorrect information, or losing correct information, can

---

[1] Indeed, what is impossible for a direct machine translation system might be entirely possible for an alternative system.

be readily described as one of three possible dynamical system states in terms of desirability. A "point attractor" exists when a parameter converges on a single stable state and remains unchanged in value as time approaches infinity (most desirable state). Alternatively, a limit cycle exists when a changing but regular path in parameter space is achieved with respect to time (undesirable but acceptable state). These two deterministic systems are perfectly capable of describing regular system states where information is neither lost nor gained. Systems that rapidly lose information about their initial states are known as chaotic systems, and were first characterized by Lorenz (1963), and is an unacceptable state. Chaotic behavior is often characterized as divergent paths in parameter space which seem to change randomly, but which actually result from some kind of time-dependent deterministic process. Clearly, system stability arises when point attractors or limit cycles are achieved, and in the context of machine translation, these are the most desirable states. However, chaotic systems are inherently unstable in certain parameter ranges, although a literature now exists on methods for "controling" chaos to achieve stability, and criteria have been developed for assessing interventions which aim to stabilize chaotic orbits.

Characterizing Semantic Processing Errors

Past studies (e.g., Watters & Patel, 1999) have indicated that the most serious errors which affect direct machine translation systems are those that occur in the context of correctly formed sentences in the target language where semantic information is either lost or added from the source sentence, and where this addition or subtraction does not result in a syntactical or grammatical error (i.e., the error is difficult to detect). These kinds of errors are impossible for human interpreters to correct, as the target sentence in each case appears to be grammatically correct. Watters and Patel used a method of source→target inversion of sentences containing metaphor and simile to evaluate how seriously these apparently "invisible" errors could affect the meaning of a sentence. They found that the definitions of many individual words were not linearly invertible, which was largely attributed to the use of dual dictionaries for source→target and target→source translations, and/or the possibility that the dominant (i.e., most frequent) sense of polysemous words was different in both the source and target language (since direct translation systems have no innate capacity to deal with polysemy, as discussed earlier). Another result of the "dual-dictionary" implementation was that the direct translation system examined was unable to inversely translate words that it had actually defined as the target definition of a source word (i.e., information loss). The meaning of source sentences was also skewed by the mis-translation of verbs, such that the depicted action of the sentence was inconsistent with the physical universe, and by the mis-translation of nouns and pronouns. In the latter case, a gender was often "added" to gender-neutral nouns (i.e., information gain), and occasionally, the subject and object of the sentences were reversed.

This study demonstrated, at least for single-step inversions, the utility of checking translations by evaluating the target sentence by reverse translation into the source language. For example, reverse translations provide an objective way for speakers of a source language to evaluate how well the intended meaning of a phrase or sentence is preserved when it is translated into a target language that they do not speak. More generally, the method facilitates the understanding of how compatible the semantic representations in target and source languages really are, since both are described by words in different and possibly semantically incompatible structures. Some theories of language and cognition predict that since all cognition arises from language (Sapir, 1921), or at the very least that language and cognition are inseparable (de Saussure, 1983), speakers of different languages will always have incompatible semantic structures. However, we need not be so pessimistic, since many of the world's languages (or language groups) may have a common origin, perhaps as a result of natural selection (see Pinker (1994) for a discussion). Alternatively, the fact that people can adequately learn languages from different language groups suggests there is at least a capacity for general language learning ability (Romaine, 1995). Indeed, for Indo–European languages, or for Austronesian dialects, one might anticipate a commonality in semantic structure as consistent as other grammatical constructs have proved to be – an optimist might even posit that there is some fundamental relationship between all semantic systems which should facilitate the accurate translation of meaning. This relationship might even be biologically represented in any of the current general language systems which linguists posit to exist in the brain (e.g., the generative assembling device; Corballis, 1991).

Meaning Loss in Biblical Proverbs: A Case Study

The wisdom literature of the Bible, including the proverbs of Solomon, often expresses themes, such as the value of ethical behavior leading to happiness and tangible success, through carefully developed metaphors and similes.

Using the information loss index and cumulative information loss index, we can describe the results of an iterative machine translation in terms of system states. A point attractor will exist when there is an invariant semantic relationship between the source and target sentence. For example, Table 2.1 shows the iterative translations for the proverb "Go to the ant, you lazybones, consider its ways, and be wise." Clearly, there is no information loss after 10 iterations. I_{LOSS} is maintained at zero for each of the ten iterations (i.e., a "perfect" translation). I_{TOTAL} is also zero over all iterations.

The next possible reverse translation system state is a limit cycle, where steady-state variant but predictable interlingual mappings are formed. This means that although one word sense might be incorrectly translated across a translation from source to target, by incorrectly selecting a word sense for example, this

Table 2.1 Point Attractor (English→Italian)

Vanno alla formica, voi i lazybones, considerano i relativi modi e sono saggi.
They go to the ant, you the lazybones, consider the relative ways and they are tests.
Vanno alla formica, voi i lazybones, considerano i modi relativi e sono prove.
They go to the ant, you the lazybones, consider the relative ways and they are tests.
Vanno alla formica, voi i lazybones, considerano i modi relativi e sono prove.
They go to the ant, you the lazybones, consider the relative ways and they are tests.
Vanno alla formica, voi i lazybones, considerano i modi relativi e sono prove.
They go to the ant, you the lazybones, consider the relative ways and they are tests.
Vanno alla formica, voi i lazybones, considerano i modi relativi e sono prove.
They go to the ant, you the lazybones, consider the relative ways and they are tests.

Proverbs 6(6): "Go to the ant, you lazybones, consider its ways, and be wise."

Table 2.2 Limit Cycle (English→German)

Kann Feuer innen getragen werden der Bosom, ohne irgendjemandes Kleidung zu brennen?
Can fire be inside carried the Bosom, without burning somebody clothes?
Kann Feuer innen getragen werden der Bosom, ohne irgendjemandes Kleidung zu brennen?
Can fire be inside carried the Bosom, without burning somebody clothes?
Kann Feuer innen getragen werden der Bosom, ohne irgendjemandes Kleidung zu brennen?
Can fire be inside carried the Bosom, without burning somebody clothes?
Kann Feuer innen getragen werden der Bosom, ohne irgendjemandes Kleidung zu brennen?
Can fire be inside carried the Bosom, without burning somebody clothes?
Kann Feuer innen getragen werden der Bosom, ohne irgendjemandes Kleidung zu brennen?
Can fire be inside carried the Bosom, without burning somebody clothes?

Proverbs 6(27): "Can fire be carried in the bosom without burning one's clothes?"

error is actually corrected in the reverse translation (e.g., by again selecting the incorrect word sense). In this example, "Can fire be carried in the bosom without burning one's clothes?" is shown in Table 2.2. This describes the general situation where a word is incorrectly translated (i.e., $I_{LOSS} = 1$), but which is inversely translated to produce the correct source word (i.e., $I_{LOSS} = -1$). This limit cycle then results in the I_{TOTAL} being zero over all iterations.

The final possible model for an iterative translation system is a chaotic attractor, where variant mappings between source and target occur with rapid short-term information loss after each iteration. This means that although some words remain invariant across all mappings, the information loss of one or two words from source to target (or vice versa) initializes a process of semantic information dissipation which might continue until the sentence is totally unintelligible. It is important to note that both the iterative and cumulative information losses with the chaotic attractor are much higher when compared with the nonchaotic system state. Table 2.3 shows an example of this kind of

Table 2.3 Period Doubling (English→French)

La volonté sage héritent de l'honneur, mais des imbéciles têtus, déshonneur.
The wise will inherit the honor, but the obstinate imbeciles, dishonour.
La volonté sage héritent de l'honneur, mais des imbeciles obstinés, déshonneur.
The wise will inherit the honor, but the imbeciles stubborn persons, dishonour.
La volonté sage héritent de l'honneur, mais des personnes têtues d'imbeciles, déshonneur.
The wise will inherit the honor, but the obstinate people of imbeciles, dishonour.
La volonté sage des héritent l'honneur, mais les personnes obstinées des imbeciles, déshonneur.
The wise will of inherit the honor, but the people stubborn persons of the imbeciles, dishonour.
La volonté sage de héritent de l'honneur, mais des personnes têtues de personnes des imbeciles, déshonneur
The wise will of inherit the honor, but the obstinate people people of the imbeciles, dishonour.

Proverbs 3(35): "The wise will inherit honor, but stubborn fools, disgrace".

process from the English sentence "The wise will inherit honor, but stubborn fools, disgrace," which rapidly loses information about its initial semantic conditions.

It is clear that the iterative process is generating new instances of meanings in several different syntactical forms with the net result of rapid information loss, and an unintelligible translation. In addition, the fact that new term instances are added to every translation is one characteristic of a mathematical model of chaos known as the "period-doubling route," in which the periodicity of a system doubles with each iteration (in the case of a point attractor or limit cycle, this periodicity in minimized). In this case, the extra instance of new terms doubles the period of the occurrence of that particular token (or unique piece of semantic information). Since mathematical methods now exist to control this kind of chaotic activity in systems, it should be possible to evaluate the efficacy of interventions and improvements to machine translation algorithms by determining how they act to control the potential for chaotic semantic instability. In this example, a simple parser for counting the number of unique semantic units in a sentence and for ensuring that this number is preserved across translations would act to reduce the instability of the translation with respect to its initial semantic conditions (i.e., the intended meaning of the source sentence).

Models for Improving Semantic Processing Performance

As seen from the machine translation example, it is possible for algorithms designed to deal with semantic processing to make errors, if they do not process the local context of lexical items. A number of approaches can be taken to ensure that semantic processing is performed correctly, such as representing lexical items in a vector format, and using the surrounding terms to influence term resolution when the input is passed to a classifier. For example, for an application that was attempting to resolve people's identities on a Facebook search, any number of items could be unique to each individual. The key question is, how can one weight the performance of a classifier toward that local context in making lexical decisions (Yarowsky, 1995).

One way to achieve this outcome would be to use a psycholinguistic approach, such as semantic priming, where terms that are colocated with the target term can be used to influence the activation of correct word meanings (Watters, 2002). Previous research used a two-pronged strategy for examining this issue computationally (Yoon, Humphreys, & Riddoch, 2010). First, it was planned to use an easy lexical process task in each priming and no-priming conditions, to show that the supply of context will dramatically improve semantic processing performance. By developing a systematic account of the lexical-semantic processes which may account for traditional performance in semantic processing, there is the potential to predict human performance and generate specific testable hypotheses for named entity resolution (Borthwick, 1999). The competitive model discussed in this chapter forms part of the dual-route cascaded (DRC) model of word and nonword reading (Coltheart, Rastle, Perry, Langdon & Ziegler, 2001); this model has enjoyed wide empirical support over the last three decades. The DRC consists of a nonlexical route consisting of rules that govern how words are properly pronounced based on the idea of letter groupings, and a direct route that accesses the lexicon for each acknowledged regular and irregular words. The semantic processing aspect considers only the activity of the lexical route of the DRC and also the semantic system, though a full account of language process errors in reading (rather than simply lexical processing) can clearly need the combination of each lexical and nonlexical routes to perform phonologic retrieval (Coltheart, Curtis, Atkins, & Haller, 1993). Such a process is not necessary to assist with accurately resolving names within text, however.

The DRC semantic system is realized as a competitive neural network, with a localized system of semantic activation, where every node represents a selected lexical entity. This contrasts with several distributed neural network architectures, wherever there is no specific nodal illustration of words or different lexical units (Li, Farkas, & MacWhinney, 2004). The utilization of distributed representations in developing psychological feature-based models has previously been criticised from the viewpoint of developing testable hypotheses – in scientific theories, there ought to be a detailed likeness between the theoretical entities postulated, and also the empirical observations accounted for. The semantic system presented here expressly uses hypotheses regarding the inner structure (units) of the human semantic processing system, which match

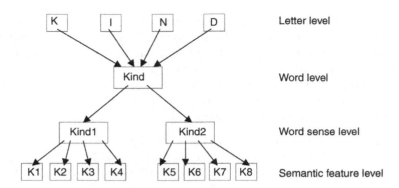

FIGURE 2.1
Semantic processing route of the DRC model for the polysemous term KIND.

knowledge from many years of psychological data and current psychological theories of language processing.

Figure 2.1 shows the schematic structure of the semantic system for the example polysemous term KIND: letter detectors within the sensory activity system offer activation to the "word" level of the system, which then contains separate representations of words that are ready to laterally inhibit one another throughout competition. Every word unit at the "word" level is then connected to a minimum of one unit at the "word sense" level, where different senses of ambiguous words are drawn as different and separate units. Word senses are activated on the idea of a nonlinear operate of relative word meaning frequencies extracted from a large corpus. Alternative word senses are then connected to their associated semantic feature sets, which are extracted from WordNet hypernyms (Scott & Matwin, 1998). The structure of the semantic feature sets is presently nonhierarchical, reflective cognitive psychology knowledge within which the in theory linear relationship between semantic distance and latency expected by early models is found to disappear once term frequency is taken under consideration. Wherever completely different word senses are related to entirely different ideas, it is important that a reductionist approach is most helpful for the type of abstraction that is necessary psychologically, though some researchers have distributed with abstraction as a prerequisite for human information processing (Vaas, 2002).

The models work in an iterative way, with lateral inhibition between words, word senses, and their constituent semantic features playing an important role in generating competitive dynamics. Table 2.4 shows the WordNet hypernyms for the term HAIL. Figure 2.2 gives an illustration of these dynamics at the word level, and Figure 2.3 at the word sense level, for the polysemous term HAIL (which could mean frozen ice, or to hail a taxi). Given that the model

Table 2.4 WordNet Hypernyms for the Two Alternative Senses of the Target Word DEED

Sense 1
⇒ *legal document*, legal instrument, official document, instrument ⇒ *document*, written document, papers – (writing providing information; esp. of an official nature) ⇒ *writing*, writings, written material – (anything expressed in letters; reading matter) ⇒ *written communication*, written language – (communication by means of written symbols) ⇒ *communication* – (something that is communicated between people or groups) ⇒ *social relation* – (a relation between living organisms, especially between people) ⇒ *relation* – (an abstraction belonging to or characteristic of two entities or parts together) ⇒ *abstraction* – (a concept formed by extracting common features from examples)
Sense 2
⇒ *accomplishment*, achievement – (the act of accomplishing something) ⇒ *action* – (something done (usually as opposed to something said); "there were stories of murders and other unnatural actions") ⇒ *act*, human action, human activity – (something that people do or cause to happen)

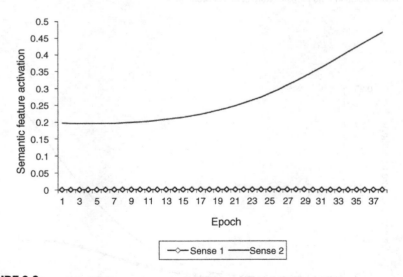

FIGURE 2.2
HAIL lexical resolution – no priming (semantic feature level).

has built-in parameterizations of natural language term frequency (Leacock & Chodorow, 1998), the dominant term is always selected, as long as the difference between the two senses is numerically sufficient. On the other hand, if we prime the model with terms associated with less-dominant senses, representing the local context, then these can influence the dynamics of the network as shown in Figures 2.4 and 2.5.

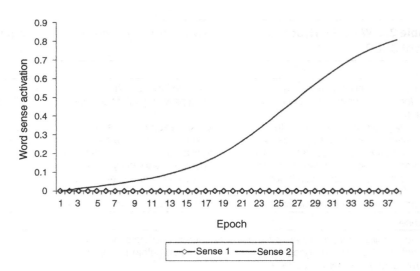

FIGURE 2.3
HAIL lexical resolution – no priming (word sense activation).

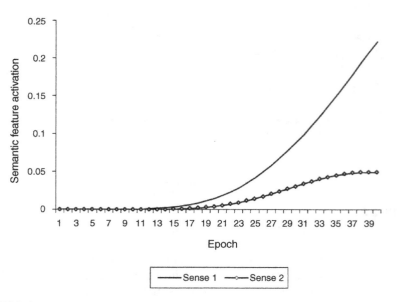

FIGURE 2.4
HAIL lexical resolution – priming (semantic feature activation).

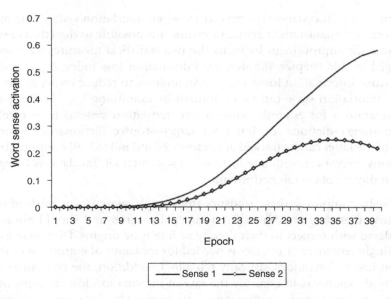

FIGURE 2.5

HAIL lexical resolution – priming (word sense level).

DISCUSSION

In this chapter, I have sketched out two different algorithmic approaches that could be used undertake named entity resolution. The first takes a dynamical systems view of the machine translation process and how it can account for translations that either succeed or fail, and provides a metaphor for how dynamical system states can be related to single-pass translations using the iterative semantic processing paradigm. In the three examples presented in this chapter, I have demonstrated how dynamical system states correspond to the different kinds of translation errors of semantic material in the context of direct translations systems (e.g., word sense disambiguation of polysemous words). In terms of the absolute preservation of meaning across sentences, the aim of the translation system is to form a point attractor in a "translation space," although we have also seen that for practical purposes, limit cycles are also acceptable. Unacceptable translations defined by the iterative method are those that rapidly lose information about their initial semantic conditions, perhaps by a translation system equivalent to the period-doubling route to chaos.

What is important about describing machine translation systems using this methodology is that it is possible to use these states as benchmarks for the performance of translation systems. Thus, when translation systems are modified to correct characteristic semantic errors, it is possible to directly assess the performance improvement by using the two statistical measures we have introduced in this chapter, the iterative information loss index, I_{LOSS}, and the cumulative information losses, I_{TOTAL}. An attempt to reduce errors at any particular translation stage can be monitored by examining I_{LOSS} at that particular iteration – for example, some direct translation systems have excellent source→target dictionaries, but poor target→source dictionaries. Improvement of the latter can be tracked at iteration 2 (and indeed, all even-numbered iterations thereafter), with a reduction in I_{TOTAL} after all translations being the main indicator of overall performance.

Obviously, computing these statistics from single sentences is misleading in the sense that they are drawn from larger discourse, and should always be considered with respect to their literary or linguistic origins. Discourse longer than single sentences or phrases is needed for measures of entropy or of information loss to become statistically reliable. In addition, the computation of numerical exponents to quantify the rate of information loss in terms of the system's entropy (e.g., Lyapunov exponent) needs to be developed and applied to both single sentences and large corpora.

From a neural network perspective, the dynamics of resolving named entities has similarities to resolving the senses of polysemous terms, especially by taking advantage of local context through semantic priming. From the simple examples shown here, it should be obvious how similar contextual information could be used to resolve the identities of individual names on social media. A key question remains as to how such context can be readily gathered using an automated process: for semantic priming of polysemous terms, parameter estimates must be supplied to the model *a priori*, yet fully automated OSINT systems would not necessarily have trusted access (Tran, Watters, & Hitchens, 2005) to this kind of data. Future research is needed to determine the extent to which names can be automatically resolved, versus a set of candidate choices should be presented to a knowledgeable analyst.

References

Bontcheva, K., & Rout, D. (2012). Making sense of social media streams through semantics: a survey. *Semantic Web, 1,* 1–31.

Borthwick, A. (1999). *A maximum entropy approach to named entity recognition.* (Doctoral dissertation, New York University, New York).

Coltheart, M., Curtis, B., Atkins, P., & Haller, M. (1993). Models of reading aloud: dual-route and parallel-distributed-processing approaches. *Psychological Review, 100*(4), 589.

Coltheart, M., Rastle, K., Perry, C., Langdon, R., & Ziegler, J. (2001). DRC: a dual route cascaded model of visual word recognition and reading aloud. *Psychological Review, 108*(1), 204.

Corballis, M. (1991). *The lopsided ape*. New York: Oxford University Press.

Hovy, E. (1998). Evaluation: machine translation. *Newsletter of the European Network in Language and Speech, 7*, 6.

James, C. (1998). *Errors in language learning and use: exploring error analysis*. London: Longman.

Layton, R., Watters, P., & Dazeley, R. (2012). Recentred local profiles for authorship attribution. *Natural Language Engineering, 18*(03), 293–312.

Layton, R., Perez, C., Birregah, B., Watters, P., & Lemercier, M. (2013). Indirect information linkage for OSINT through authorship analysis of aliases. In *Trends and applications in knowledge discovery and data mining* (pp. 36–46). Berlin, Heidelberg: Springer.

Leacock, C., & Chodorow, M. (1998). Combining local context and WordNet similarity for word sense identification. *WordNet: An Electronic Lexical Database, 49*(2), 265–283.

Li, P., Farkas, I., & MacWhinney, B. (2004). Early lexical development in a self-organizing neural network. *Neural Networks, 17*(8), 1345–1362.

Lorenz, E. N. (1963). Deterministic nonperiodic flow. *Journal of the Atmospheric Sciences, 20*(2), 130–141.

Palmer, M. (1990). Customizing verb definitions for specific semantic domains. *Machine Translation Journal, 5*, 5–30.

Pinker, S. (1994). *The language instinct*. Cambridge, MA: MIT Press.

Romaine, S. (1995). *Bilingualism*. Oxford: Blackwell.

Sakai, N. (1997). *Translation and subjectivity*. Minneapolis, MN: University of Minnesota Press.

Sapir, E. (1921). *Language: an introduction to the study of speech*. New York: Harcourt Brace Jovanovich.

Saussure, F. d. (1983). *Course in general linguistics*. London: Duckworth.

Scott, S., & Matwin, S. (1998). Text classification using WordNet hypernyms. In *Use of WordNet in natural language processing systems: Proceedings of the conference* (pp. 38–44).

Searle, J. (1984). *Minds, brains and science*. London: British Broadcasting Corporation.

Shannon, B. (1988). Semantic representations of meaning: a critique. *Psychological Bulletin, 104*, 70–83.

Tran, H., Watters, P., & Hitchens, M. (2005, July). Trust and authorization in the grid: a recommendation model. In *ICPS'05. Proceedings international conference on pervasive services, 2005* (pp. 433–436). New York: IEEE.

Turney, P. D., & Pantel, P. (2010). From frequency to meaning: vector space models of semantics. *Journal of Artificial Intelligence Research, 37*(1), 141–188.

Vaas, R. (2002). Problems of mental causation-whether and how it can exist. *Psyche, 8*, 04.

Watters, P. A. (2000). Time-invariant long-range correlations in electroencephalogram dynamics. *International Journal of Systems Science, 31*(7), 819–825.

Watters, P. A. (2002). Discriminating English word senses using cluster analysis. *Journal of Quantitative Linguistics, 9*(1), 77–86.

Watters, P. A. (2013). Modelling the effect of deception on investigations using open source intelligence (OSINT). *Journal of Money Laundering Control, 16*(3), 238–248.

Watters, P. A., & Patel, M. (1999). Semantic processing performance of Internet machine translation systems. *Internet Research, 9*(2), 153–160.

Watters, P. A., & Patel, M. (2000). Direct machine translation systems as dynamical systems: the iterative semantic processing (ISP) paradigm. *Journal of Quantitative Linguistics, 7*(1), 43–51.

Watters, P. A., McCombie, S., Layton, R., & Pieprzyk, J. (2012). Characterising and predicting cyber attacks using the Cyber Attacker Model Profile (CAMP). *Journal of Money Laundering Control, 15*(4), 430–441.

White, J. S., & Taylor, K. B. (1998). A task-oriented evaluation metric for machine translation. In *Proceedings of the first international conference on language resources and evaluation* (pp. 21–25), Granada, Spain, Vol. 1.

Yarowsky, D. (1995). Unsupervised word sense disambiguation rivaling supervised methods. In *Proceedings of the 33rd annual meeting on Association for Computational Linguistics* (pp. 189–196). Association for Computational Linguistics.

Yoon, E. Y., Humphreys, G. W., & Riddoch, M. J. (2010). The paired-object affordance effect. *Journal of Experimental Psychology: Human Perception and Performance, 36*(4), 812.

CHAPTER 3

Relative Cyberattack Attribution

Robert Layton

Internet Commerce Security Laboratory, Federation University, Australia

INTRODUCTION

Cybercrime and cyberattacks are problems that cause billions of dollars in direct losses per year (Anderson et al., 2013), and even more in indirect losses, such as costs for protection systems such as antivirus programs (Layton & Watters, 2014). While defensive systems have made enormous progress over the last 20 years for these attacks, the escalating battle between attackers and defenders continues (Alazab, Layton, Venkataraman, & Watters, 2010). While it is harder (arguably) to attack systems today than ever before, cyber-based attacks continue to cause damage to online commerce, critical infrastructure, and the population in general.

Defensive systems are unlikely to lead to long-term success in stopping, or at least severely stemming, the flow of cyberattacks. One critical reason for this is that vulnerable software and systems continue to be created, either through the rush of a start-up system attempting to get in to the market first, a graduate programmer (who had not been taught to create prepared queries) introducing an SQL-injection attack (Lee, Jeong, Yeo, & Moon, 2012), or an ambiguity in a design document leading to a vulnerable exchange of information between systems. For these reasons, and many more, it is likely that there will always be ways to attack new systems and programs.

To add to the difficulty in protecting these targets, users who are often unaware of the risks, uninterested in proper security measures, or unable to fulfil those measures (i.e., children) are using these systems leading to more potential exploit opportunity. Cyberattacks targeting users are more prolific than those targeting systems, and this "vulnerability" cannot be patched (Whitten & Tygar, 1999).

One of the most promising means for long-term success in reducing cyberattacks is that of *attribution* (McCombie, Pieprzyk, & Watters, 2009). The risk of prosecution is one of the key ways to reduce crime, as per Situational Crime

37

Prevention (Clarke, 1997). While other avenues, such as a reduction in rewards, are also highly effective, the scope of this chapter is on increasing the risk to the offender, specifically through attribution.

Prosecution, in general, is a difficult concept. It relies on the law-of-the-land (currently ever changing in response to new cyberthreats), the quality of evidence, the society in which the crime is perpetuated, and, quite frequently in the case of online attacks, the requirement of international cooperation on crime. This chapter does not address these issues, but takes a step back to the preceding problem of determining who to prosecute.

One key concept in the issue of *attribution* is that of *absolute attribution*, versus *relative attribution* (Layton & Watters, 2014a, 2014b). In *absolute attribution*, the aim is to determine, with a high degree of confidence, that a particular person performed an attack. This is the role of law enforcement, and a key step to prosecution. In this chapter, we highlight the issues with absolute attribution from a technical point of view, arguing that anonymization tools are quite strong (when used correctly), and that due to this, absolute attribution is unlikely to be reached from pure technical measures, at least when the attacker is informed and motivated to protect their identity.

Sometimes, this is easier than it may otherwise be. For instance, the infamous Mandiant APT1 report attributed the attacks to the developers because they left critical identifying information in their attacks (Mcwhorter, 2013). This information included links to online accounts created by the attackers with their real names, links to the actual locations they were in, and other clues. While the attacks themselves were quite good, there were some mistakes that ultimately led to the attribution of the attack. The clues pointed to the assertion that the attacks were almost certainly state-based attacks against companies in another state.

Attribution itself is a concept that is both easy and hard to define. Due to the organized nature of cybercrime (Galeotti, 2014), attribution could be the answer to any of the following questions, among others:

- "Who performed an attack?"
- "Who wrote the tool to do the attack?"
- "Who designed the attack?"
- "Who organized the attack?"

In this chapter, we explain the concept of pointing, and how the question chosen can dictate the way in which the attribution techniques are pointed, in order to provide the answer. In addition, the techniques themselves that are used are often dictated by the exact question posed.

Relative attribution is the concept of determining that two or more attacks were caused by the same person. We do not attempt to determine who that person is, leaving that to other more investigative techniques. However, there are quite strong reasons for performing relative attribution, including:

1. The linking of attacks provides a better cost benefit for investing more into an investigation (such as in a large organization or law enforcement agency) into the attacks.
2. Relative attribution leads to linking evidence, providing stronger cases for prosecution.
3. Attacks by the same person often follow similar patterns, leading to increased opportunity for cyberdefence.
4. The risk posed by relative attribution can cause attackers to overly generalize their attacks to circumvent attribution. This allows for greater defence.
5. Those that do not overly generalize must frequently, and substantially, alter their attack in order to overcome attribution. This leads to a significant cost for the attack in terms of time, and poses a risk that rushed, untested attacks lead to information leakage.

Relative attribution does have some weaknesses though, which are enumerated later and explained throughout this chapter:

1. The linkage of evidence by relative attribution relies on the quality of the linkage of the attribution itself. This may lead to false positives of evidence linkage, if the attribution is poorly performed.
2. Current relative attribution techniques are susceptible to framing attacks, by which an attacker performs the attack in the style of another person.
3. Current relative attribution is quite weak for complex attacks, for various reasons, such as the lack of available data and research, the difficulty of attribution in large datasets, and a poor understanding of what attribution means.

It should also be mentioned that the use of relative attribution has limits from various laws, etc. For instance, you may not be able to obtain a warrant for more information based on a relative attribution analysis alone. These legal issues are not dealt with in this chapter, with the scope focused on technical means and outcomes.

The rest of the chapter is outlined as follows:

Basic Attack Structure outlines a basic, generic model for how cyberattacks work, across various attack types. The purpose is to outline the specific structures in an attack, not to be a generic model for future analysis. Even with this basic model, however, we can see that there are fundamental problems to attributing cybercrimes that require action outside of the normal viewpoint of cyberattacks.

Anonymization on the Internet outlines ways in which people can be anonymous on the Internet. The purpose is to outline some of the challenges to attribution (both relative and absolute), answering the question of "why don't you just go to arrest the person who owns that computer/IP/network?". The analysis of existing anonymization technologies indicates that while anonymization is hard to achieve, it is easier to achieve this, than it is to achieve effective attribution.

Attribution deals with the question of what attribution is, going further into the definitions of relative and absolute attribution, and how they are performed. We look at absolute attribution, versus relative attribution. This section overviews existing technologies in both spaces, finding that there is significant room for improvement in the techniques.

Limitations and Issues outline the currently known flaws in relative attribution techniques, and how they are characterized. The limitations are currently blocking effective use of attribution technologies in real-world scenarios, but appear to be addressable – that is, in future research.

Research Interest outlines the current research streams that are being performed into relative attribution, and highlights areas that could use interest. Included in this section is an overview of research goals that are not currently being investigated, and how they could be.

Vision and Conclusion summarizes the issues identified in this chapter, highlighting a vision for a long-term future with effective relative attribution techniques, and the advantages of progress in this area. The opportunities that open up with effective attribution, as well as the drawbacks, are considered.

BASIC ATTACK STRUCTURE

We define a cyberattack as any attack that occurs primarily across a computer network, where the entity being attacked is a computer network or system (or both). Brenner (2007) indicated that most cybercrimes are not necessarily new, rather they are "old wine in a new bottle." For example, the cybercrime of a Distributed Denial of Service (DDoS) is simply an extortion performed over the Internet, akin to "protection money" being asked by a local gang. However, we do care about the "cyber-distinction" in this chapter, as we focus primarily on techniques on cyber-based attacks, even if they do have real-world analogies.

We can model a cyberattack through a simple model, composed of an attacking computer or system, a victim computer or system, and an intermediary network that allows a connection between the two (Figure 3.1).

Many types of cyberattacks fit this model (although this is more due to simplicity, rather than generalizability):

- DDoS attacks are composed of many simple messages from an attacking system (or network) to a victim system or network.

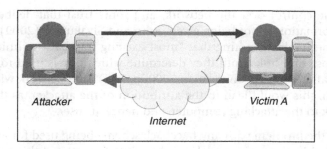

FIGURE 3.1
A simple model of a cyberattack.

- Phishing attacks compose of an attacking message being sent to the victim computer, although the target is primarily the user of the system rather than the system itself.
- Spam is an message, such as an email, being sent to the victim computer
- Malware propagation is performed by an attacking message being sent to the victim's computer, with the intent of exploiting a vulnerability in that system to compromise it.

However, even this over-simplified model shows an immediate problem. The intermediate system between the attacker and the victim is normally not controlled by either the attacker or the victim (who we also later denote as *Victim A*), as most attacks occur through the Internet.

The Internet is composed of computer, routers, network connections, and other systems that relay traffic around the world. These systems are owned by governments and Internet providers mainly, but there are also hobbyists, personal users, system administrators, and many thousands of others that are responsible for components on the chain of getting a message from one computer to another.

While there may be high levels of cooperation between governments and Internet providers (either voluntary or mandatory through legislation), the degree of difficulty in controlling what and how Internet traffic is routed makes it very difficult to perform an action called traceback, by which the victim works out which computer sent the attacking message by tracing the path to the attacker back through the network it came through.

There has been significant research in performing traceback in networks of various sizes. For example, Giani, De Souza, Berk, and Cybenko (2006) investigated using the aggregation of network flows for identifying attacks. Such systems are highly effective in practice, but do not make the assumption, like we do, of an intelligent and motivated attacker. These systems usually rely on having some control over the network, and some trust that deliberate misleading information is not being given. John and Sivakumar (2009) surveyed traceback mechanisms, noting that "most existing traceback techniques start from the upstream links until they determine which one is used to carry the attacker's traffic" (John & Sivakumar, 2009, p. 242). In a network with perfect information, this would lead to the attribution of the attacker, as this would lead us back to the attacking computer, and hence, its user.

Ultimately, the problem with any traceback scheme being used for attribution was identified in the basic model of cybercrime that started this section; the intermediary network between the attacker and the victim is not controlled by the victim, and therefore the victim cannot rely on any information obtained from this network. Despite this, we should not discount network forensic-based methods entirely, as Pilli, Joshi, and Niyogi (2010) noted, as there are still substantial amounts of information in most practical cases, especially where the attacker is human and prone to make mistakes. However, there appears to be a strict upper limit to the utility of such direct attribution techniques.

Clark and Landau (2010) identified this, noting that "The problem isn't attribution, its multi-stage attacks." Suppose that an attacker has the necessary skill-set to compromise a computer. This indicates they (almost definitely) also have the necessary skill-set to compromise a separate computer, from Victim B. Victim B's computer, now controllable by the attacker, can now be used to send messages to Victim A. As Victim B's computer is controlled by the attacker, it can be told to remove any knowledge of the attack message being sent to it, and where it came from.

This is, of course, a gross oversimplification of the way in which anonymization occurs on the Internet. There are also two major attacks against the anonymization that occurs from this concept, which are explained in the next section.

The overall message here is that anonymization is generally easier than attribution, for a number of technical and logical reasons. That said, anonymization is also hard to do properly, and for this reason there are practical attacks that can be used for attribution (including the traceback schemes identified earlier).

As an example of attributing cyberattacks, McRae and Vaughn (2007) employed the concept of catch-release, a method used in fishing research, for phishing research. In a phishing attack, the victim will enter a username and password into a catch, such as a phishing website purporting to be from a trusted bank. By entering a code that loads an image when displayed, the researchers were able to get the attacker to run code that, in some circumstances, gives away the location of the attacker (or at least the IP address of the computer used for viewing the passwords). Such a novel attack relies on the attacker using a web browser to view the websites, but given the way many phishing kits currently work, this assumption was relatively reliable.

Such attribution techniques rely on the attacker making some type of mistake. The scope of this chapter is not to outline such common mistakes and their counter-measures, instead to consider broader concepts and applications of attribution. Therefore, we instead assume that we are targeting a motivated and intelligent attacker, and that we cannot rely on them making a specific mistake.

ANONYMIZATION ON THE INTERNET

The Internet is seemingly paradoxically the world's largest source for massive surveillance, and also one of the safest avenues for sending anonymous messaging that exists today.

The explanation for this paradox is the way in which it is used. Most users of the Internet diligently use the default applications and settings, allowing for almost all of their communications to be tracked, recorded, and analyzed at a later date, as was made painfully clear in the wide-ranging monitoring scandal involving the NSA. Some of this is made mandatory through legislation, others through software developers recording this information for their internal (or, in some cases, external) analysis.

In contrast, other users will instead use programs that aim to hide the user's identity. These technologies are plentiful, although the number that can be trusted is quite small. Further, the list of technologies that can be trusted changes, as exploits or concerns arise.

Perhaps the largest anonymization tool currently in use is The Onion Router (Tor). This system, created by the US Navy in 2004, allowed for anonymous communication by routing messages through a number of other Tor user's computers, in such a way that no-one in the network can intercept messages, who it is intended for, or who it originated from (Dingledine, Mathewson, & Syverson, 2004).

Tor relies on advanced cryptographic concepts, and also safety in numbers. For example, the presence of Tor on a computer may be an indication of wrongdoing on the user's behalf, even if no other evidence exists (although this fact alone could not, and probably should not, lead to a conviction). In order for it to not have this taint, it would need to be used by a large number of people, including those with "nothing to hide" (Solove, 2007).

Another commonly used system for anonymization is the use of VPNs for sending traffic. In a broad generalization, this works the same way Tor does – it sends your traffic through another person's computer (Figure 3.2). The difference is the lack of anonymization between yourself and the VPN provider. In Tor, for example, the "exit node" is the one that actually collects your data, such as the website you are trying to anonymously view, as shown below:

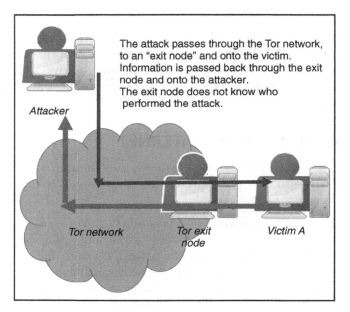

FIGURE 3.2
An attack through Tor.

This exit node does not know who made the request, although it does know the request was made, and the data that were returned (although the data itself can be encrypted).

In contrast, a VPN provider knows exactly who made the request, as there is a direct connection between the client and the VPN provider, as shown in Figure 3.3. VPNs have been used extensively in cybercrimes (de Graaf, Shosha, & Gladyshev, 2013).

This leads to a number of issues, mostly around the trust that can be placed on the VPN to not leak the identity of the client. Conversely, for a law enforcement agency interested in tracking down an offender, a VPN is a better "anonymization" tool for the client/attacker to use, because an LEA can obtain a warrant to get identity information from the VPN provider, whereas such a warrant is nearly pointless to obtain for a Tor-based attack.

The above two examples are legal, legitimate ways to anonymize traffic (at least, they are legal in most jurisdictions, and this assumes that it is legal to access the endpoint's data), even if the messages or attacks it is used for are not legal.

A third example of commonplace anonymization in action is the use (often illicitly obtained) of a compromised computer to send traffic on your behalf.

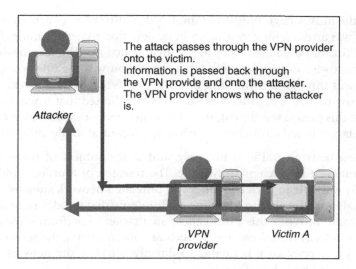

The attack passes through the VPN provider onto the victim.
Information is passed back through the VPN provide and onto the attacker.
The VPN provider knows who the attacker is.

Attacker

VPN provider

Victim A

FIGURE 3.3
An attack through a VPN.

As we described earlier, the attacker will compromise a third system, and tell *it* to both attack the victim, and also to forget who the attacker is. This makes it very difficult to go back through this intermediate platform to the attack.

This method is commonly employed by cybercriminals, and is one of the most troublesome aspects with dealing with botnets. A botnet is a collection of computers controlled by a single (often criminal) botnet master. Botnets, such as Zeus, can be rented out to other users, further hiding the identity of the attacker.

Brennen (2007) identified these "stepping stone" computers as being central to most cyberattacks, and that this is a major point of distinction between a cyber, and noncyberattack, particular for crimes (as opposed to terrorism or war). Consider that for a real-world crime, police may comb the area for clues for the suspect, ask locals for clues, and be on the lookout for that person to perform a crime in that area again. Location, therefore, is a critical component to real-world attacks. In the cyber-relm, however, the attack may be in one country, performing there attack through an intermediary country, to attack a third country as the victim. They may then easily change their attack to another country for the next target.

WEAKNESSES IN ANONYMIZATION

Anonymization technologies have some weaknesses that are difficult to control on behalf of the person aiming to be anonymous.

Perhaps the most straightforward of these is the correlation of activity. In 2013, a person was arrested for accessing child exploitation material online. The person used Tor, and used it correctly as per the instructions. The way in which law enforcement was able to determine that the person was the one accessing the material was through a correlation of activity between website access and the person's use of Tor. A high level of correlation indicated that it was extremely likely that this person was the culprit. While other evidence was used in this trial, this correlation-based attribution is definitely a technical for de-anonymization.

Correlating network traffic is not easy, and is the subject of research for a large number of researchers worldwide. The research of Murdoch and Danezis (2005) was able to correlate otherwise unrelated network streams, and use traffic analysis to be able to identify which intermediate nodes were forwarding information. While this would allow an attacker to perform directed side-channel attacks against these nodes (such as compromising the server hosting the node), the research was unable to directly correlate the network activity with the requester of the information.

As a broader weakness in anonymization is that of specialization versus generalization. An attack that is very generalized is easy to block. Consider for example a spam message. If the message does not use any specialization, the message is easily blocked, for instance by a Bayesian spam filter (Androutsopoulos et al., 2000). In contrast, a spam message that is highly specialized can slip through the filter, as it is composed of more unique components (Lowd & Meek, 2005).

However this uniqueness is difficult to obtain. An attacker would need to perform testing to see if their new spam messages passed through filters, or if it is blocked. This is not trivial to do, so one would imagine a spammer reusing the message, or the concepts that went into developing the message, for more than one spam attack. This specialization allows for a form of attribution we denote as relative attribution, which is similar to the concepts of behavioral crime-patterns.

As the generalization of an attack increases, it becomes easier to block. In contrast, as the attack becomes more specialized, the attack becomes easier to attribute. This is a fundamental concept in attack mitigation through attribution.

ATTRIBUTION AS A CONCEPT

Attribution is the concept of finding the cause for a particular action or object. The concept of attribution is a difficult one, especially when discussing cyberattacks (Figure 3.4). A typical cyberattack today contains people performing the following roles, as a subset of the overall roles:

- Malware writer, who develops the code for a new piece of malware

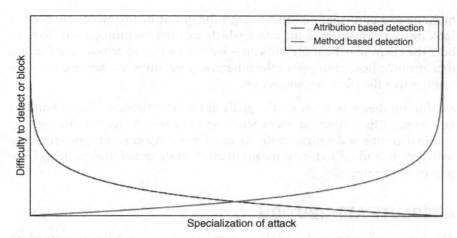

FIGURE 3.4
"While method-based detection becomes more difficult with specialized attacks, attribution-based detection becomes easier." (*Layton and Alazab 2014, p. 2*)

- Phishing/spam writer, who writes the content for a new attack email or website
- Infrastructure owner, such as the botnet operator or "bullet-proof" hosting provider, who controls the infrastructure used for the attack
- Manager, who identifies new attack opportunities and organizes the effort to perform it
- Client, who might pay for someone else to perform an attack

Wheeler and Larsen (2003) defined attribution as "determining the identity or location of an attacker or an attacker's intermediary." They noted that, at least in most public literature, the use of the word was restricted mostly to mean a traceback or source-tracking activity, which we have identified as having severe limitations. Layton and Watters (2014a, 2014b) classified this form of attribution as *direct attribution*, as opposed to *indirect attribution*, which attempts to attribute the attack using techniques that do not rely on directly tracing the attack back to the attacker.

For each of these roles, there may be multiple people, or even multiple teams, performing them. To increase the difficulty, malware is often copied from other sources, combined with new features, and released again. Other malware might only need a configuration change to work for new attackers!

So what does attribution mean in this context? I argue that attributing the crime to any of these people is *possible*; however, it relies on the correct pointing of the attribution technique, and the correct choice of technique itself. To target the malware writer, we need a way to attribute the coding style of the malware to a particular person. To target the infrastructure owner, we need to look instead at features of the attack which are used for propagation. To attribute the client may be more difficult – we need a way to remove the features that attribute instead to one of the other members involved, keeping only the features that the client has impact on.

Attribution therefore relies on the goals of the investigation. This is hardly a new concept, as attribution noncybercrimes has a long history of investigating criminal groups and gangs. As the focus of this chapter is on cybercrime, we will look instead for technical means of attribution, rather than policing techniques and strategies.

ABSOLUTE ATTRIBUTION

Absolute attribution is the goal of determining exactly who performed an action. It relates to the concept of finding the perpetrator of a crime, which is the end-goal of a police investigation. In much the same way, absolute attribution must also come with the necessary evidence to prove such an attribution. This is the part in which many cybercrime investigations fail, as evidence is hard to obtain from a well-performed cyberattack.

Techniques for performing absolute attribution are rare in cyberattacks, due mainly to the previously mentioned issues related to traceback. The issues with using a secondary platform for performing an attack are not as common in noncybercrimes, except perhaps for coercion, in which a third party is forced to perform a crime. However, there are significant differences between these two, namely that using a secondary platform for cybercrime does not always involve the owner of that platform to know about the crime.

In the 2015 cyberattacks on Sony Pictures Entertainment, leaked 100 GB of data from SPE's systems (Bond, 2014), including private details about employees, upcoming movies, details about the network, and so on (Haggard & Lindsay, 2015). The attack was very successful, hitting almost all parts of SPE and causing significant damage to the company. The attack was claimed by a group calling themselves, "Guardians of Peace" (GOP), and wanted the movie *The Interview*, which was highly critical of North Korea's leader, to be banned. The US Government was both quick and confident in attributing the crime to North Korea. However, North Korea denies responsibility for the attack. This indicates the difficulty with performing this type of attribution – the attacker is likely to not admit to the crime, so strong evidence must be presented instead. To date, no such evidence has been made public.

It is also possible that the attack on SPE was performed by another party, using *The Interview* as an excuse and distraction to send blame to North Korea. If so, the technique definitely worked, at least publicly. The difficulty with attribution, particularly in cases where automated methods are employed, is that distraction and disinformation can be particularly harmful, and these framing activities are particularly damaging. This problem is covered more in the section on *Limitations*.

Another high-profile absolute attribution incident occurred when the Stuxnet virus was publicly announced (Fidler, 2011). The virus, which targeted nuclear reactors in Iran, caused damage to the very specific equipment Iran was using to enrich the Uranium. This indicates quite strongly that the attack was (1) state sponsored, and (2) well funded. In turn, this pretty heavily indicated that either the US Government, Israel, or both were being the attacker. However, analysis of the code led at least one high-profile cybercrime expert to indicate that the attack probably was not state sponsored (Parker, 2011). This indicates the problem with code-based analysis for attribution.

Stuxnet was released by the US Government, with cooperation from Israel. We know this primarily because President Obama formally acknowledged the role the US Government had in creating this piece of malware (Edwards, 2014). Without this acknowledgement, we may never have been able to formally attribute this malware – even though (at least with the benefit of hindsight) the perpetrators were fairly obvious once the purpose of the malware was known.

RELATIVE ATTRIBUTION

Relative attribution is akin to the discovery of crime patterns, or even signature crimes, that give investigators clues that the same person performed multiple crimes. This idea of a specific *modus operandi* (Douglas & Munn, 1992) that links a criminal to multiple crimes is pervasive in many forms of investigation, although there has been some significant criticism against criminal profiling (Turvey, 2011), that mostly boil down to the cases of false positive profiles and the overall lack of quality in the results.

Criminal profiling has a long history of analyzing the behaviors of criminals and their attacks (Rogers, 2003). The set of characteristics that go into a crime can be used for profiling, and inform situational crime prevention (Preuß et al., 2007) and possibly to the profiling of the actual criminals, linking multiple crimes performed by the same person. Broadly speaking, this is used quite frequently in many contexts, with varying degrees of success and varying degrees of precision. For example, the characteristics of broken English writing can determine the first language of the writer, such as attributing English text to someone who probably speaks Russian as their first language (McCombie et al., 2008).

Overcoming these limitations is a significant problem, and one that is needed in both cyber and noncyber forms of crime and attribution. Yet despite these issues, relative attribution has a number of significant advantages that suggest its use in criminal investigations is worthwhile. These advantages were identified in the introduction, but are discussed in depth here.

The linking of attacks by perpetrator, even if that perpetrator is not identified, can help investigators perform analysis more quickly. An investigator with a sense of experience in regards to who performed an attack can rely on previous case notes and analyses, using those to focus analysis on key aspects. This is true even in the case where a perpetrator has stolen or bought aspects of their criminal toolkit from others. In the case of a malware distributor, who has purchased malware that was used in a previous attack, relative attribution linking the attacks allows an investigator to guess where some hidden files and system hooks are present, reducing the time for analyzing the attack.

This linking of attacks also provides the means for linking evidence. For example, if relative attribution links two types of cyberattacks, than any evidence obtained from each may be able to be combined to provide a better picture of the perpetrator. As a small and focused (if a little forced) example, if an attack on a user uses a UK English spelling variant, such as *colour*, then we can posit that the author of that attack was English, Canadian, or Australian, with a few other possibilities. If another attack from that same person refers to a hot summer, than we can discount the Northern Hemisphere-based countries and guess that they are Australian.

Defensive measures could also be set up on the guise of per-attacker features, rather than per-attack features. If features that tie a website to a particular hacking group could be identified, this could lead to website blacklists composed of these features, forcing the attacking group to change their method of attack. This would be a significant cost to them and risk a reduced efficacy. This is an important vision for relative attribution and is outlined in detail in the Future Research chapter.

As we identified earlier, increasing the risk of attribution may lead attacks to generalize their attacks, such that attack patterns appear the same across multiple attackers. This would hurt attribution methods, but reduce the effort needed to create defensive systems against those attacks. For those attacks that do not generalize their attack, the other option is a continued (and an expensive) development of new attacks on an ongoing basis, in order to ensure that their attacks are not attributed.

RELATIVE ATTRIBUTION CONCEPTS

Relative attribution is built upon a number of concepts. The first is that of defining what attribution means, and the second is defining how it will be identified. Each of these is critical to the success of the implementation of an effective relative-attribution-based analysis.

We identified earlier what attribution means and that the complexity of the term with regards to cybercrimes. Further, without setting the target for attribution, the analysis may point to all parts of the attack, effectively attributing the attack to the *entire process* for developing and performing an attack, rather than the much more useful target of a specific link in the chain. These issues are also relevant outside of cybercrimes, where digital evidence is also increasingly used (Rogers, 2003).

With regards to identifying the models and features that would be used for relative attribution, the theoretical models that relative attribution is built upon are the concept that behaviors are inherent, hard to hide, and consistent across a person's or group's activity. The validity of these concepts is outlined as follows.

INHERENT VERSUS LEARNT BEHAVIORS

While it is quite obvious that many of our behaviors, such as speaking or writing, are learnt, there is significant debate in whether some of those behaviors are inherent, and to what degree. Further complicating the matter is that some learnt behavior becomes difficult to change, effectively becoming inherent (Bouton, 2014). The concept of changing behavior is otherwise outside the scope of this chapter, but the key concept is that it does appear that some behavior, once learnt, becomes inherent in a person's actions.

HIDING BEHAVIOR

In this chapter, we assumed our attacker is both intelligent and motivated to remain anonymous. Such an attacker could therefore be assumed to be knowledgeable about methods that could be used to attribute their attacks. The problem for the attack, therefore, is how to hide their behavior, so that these attribution methods do not work.

Research by Brennan and Greenstadt (2009) found that when nonexpert writers are simply *asked* to hide their writing style, certain methods of authorship analysis (a form of relative attribution we discuss in Techniques) drop considerably in accuracy. To make this worse, when asked to imitate another author, these same nonexperts were able to cause the attribution method to falsely accuse the framed author, rather than the actual author.

While newer research has been able to improve upon accuracies in this dataset (CITE), the problem still persists, and to date, nobody has formulated an authorship attribution method that is robust against attacks, particularly attacks wherein the attacker is knowledgable about the attribution technique used.

CONSISTENCY OF BEHAVIOR

Research into the consistency of inherent behavior, at least for relative attribution methods, is quite sparse. As examples, Kosba (2014) investigated attributing malicious websites, Bagavandas and Manimannan (2008) investigated the consistency of features in authorship attribution, while Sutanto, Leedham, and Pervouchine (2003) investigated the handwriting features used by document examiners. Findings from these studies suggest that the behaviors used to identify the authors of these documents, from these two different types of attribution, are relatively consistent and useful as markers of authorship.

The evidence appears to be quite strong that, at least where deliberate deception is not used, many behaviors are consistent enough to be used as identifiers for attribution. However, this should not be taken as a free pass – individual features would need to be tested before use.

RELATIVE ATTRIBUTION TECHNIQUES

The specific techniques used to perform relative attribution are generally dependent on the application domain. There are significant differences in the methods used to attribute text, from attributing a business process. In this section, we will overview the techniques used to perform attribution from various means.

Much modern relative attribution is performed either using statistical analysis or extending it via data mining. The benefits are the ability to analyze larger amounts of data, and producing a model that can be tested and verified. The downsides are that the results may not be readable or understandable, which may reduce their ability to influence an investigation or criminal proceedings.

Another important aspect is that the use of automated methods, such as data mining, is reducing the influence the analyst has in directing the outcome. This can be positive, in removing such bias and leading to a more impartial result. This can also be a negative, however, in that these intuitions and background knowledge may lead to faster outcomes if they could be properly used within the attribution process.

Internet security company FireEye released a report outlining sever clues that they use to help identify where attacks come from. The clues included:

1. Keyboard layout, which can help determine the first language of the author
2. Malware metadata, such as compilation information
3. Embedded fonts, which are sometimes different around the world
4. DNS registration, which can be easily faked, but can still lead to linking attacks

5. Language, such as mistakes, which we outline in the next section on authorship analysis
6. Remote administration tool (RAT) configuration, which is often set by the attack based on their personal preferences
7. Behavior of the attack

That last item is quite broad, but represents the nature of relative attribution, linking attacks by behavior. In the next section, we look at how to do such behavioral-based relative attribution using text-based behavior.

AUTHORSHIP ANALYSIS

When the attack consists of documents that have been *written* by an author, the main method for performing attribution is called *authorship analysis*. In authorship analysis, features from within the text are used to model the writing behavior of the author, and lead to a predictive model that can identify the author of a text. If we have a known collection of documents to attribute, the process is called *authorship attribution*, and is performed most often in modern times as a supervised data mining task (Koppel, Schler, & Argamon, 2011) called *classification*.

Authorship attribution studies have been performed on text (Juola, 2006), source code (Burrows, Uitdenbogerd, & Turpin, 2014), malware source code (Layton and Alazab 2014), and even binary programs (Alrabaee, Saleem, Preda, Wang, & Debbabi, 2014). Overall, the effectiveness of the techniques is generally quite high, except for the cases of intelligent adversaries, which is discussed in the next section.

A typical authorship analysis study will begin with a dataset consisting of a set of documents, and the known authors of those documents. This is known as the training set. These documents are processed using a transformer pipeline (Buitinck et al., 2013), which represents these documents as a set of features. A simple example of a feature is the count of the number of words in the document.

The collection of features for each document is represented as a **matrix X**, such that **X[i][j]** is the value of feature **j** (such as the word count) for document **i**. The training dataset also contains the known authors, which can be represented in a **vector y**, such that **y[i]** is the (often codified) author for the document represented in **X[i]**.

Where we want to train a classifier, we might employ cross fold validation. It is beyond the scope of this chapter to discuss methodologies for training classification algorithms, but interested readers are invited to read Layton (2015) for an early introduction, and Bishop (2006) for more experienced analysts.

Once the model has been trained, the model is then used to predict the author of previously unseen documents. We normally assume that the expected author is in the list of authors from the training dataset, with such a problem referred to as a *closed problem*. If this assumption is not valid, that is, the actual author may not be from the training set, then this is an *open problem*. Historically, much of the work in classification has been performed on closed problems, although recent work has investigated the open problem more regularly (Stolerman et al., 2013).

Authorship profiling is the task of attributing other characteristics of the author, based on a study of their writing. For example, certain attributes of broken English may identify whether the author is Chinese or Russian in background (McCombie et al., 2008). Likewise, characteristics of the language from psycholinguistic features to lexical features can identify the age of the author with a good degree of success (Tourney et al., 2012).

The process for attributing these characteristics is known as authorship profiling, and can be performed in a similar way to authorship attribution. For example, rather than having the target vector (**y**) correspond the author, it could be 1 if the author is male, and 0 if they are females. The classification task is then responsible for correlating the features to this expected output. The features that are effective at performing authorship attribution are often also good at performing authorship profiling; however, there are better features for either task (Tourney et al., 2012).

Another method of performing authorship analysis is to use Local n-grams (Kešelj, Peng, Cercone, & Thomas, 2003). This process is based heavily on the above feature-matrix-based methodology, but with several important differences. First, rather than have a global set of features that are extracted for each author (or document), authors are profiled using only features relevant to their writing style. Other features are ignored at this stage. Second, the features that are extracted are exclusively character n-grams, which are overlapping subsequence's of n characters in a row (n is usually a value between 2 and 6, at least for English text). Finally, distances are computed between profiles, rather than using classification algorithms, with profiles with a lower distance more likely to be from the same author.

The following algorithm describes how to extract *LNG-based profiles* for this purpose, which takes two parameters, n: the size of the n-gram, and L: the size of the profile to extract, and computes the profile for a single author.

1. Create an empty profile for the author, where all counts are set to zero
2. For each document known to be from the author:
   a. For each character n-gram in that document, increment the count for the n-gram by one in the author's profile

3. Normalize the counts so that they sum to one.
4. Compute the threshold T, which is the Lth highest count in the author's profile
5. Remove all n-grams from the profile if their normalized count is less than T.

With these profiles computed, there are several distance methods that can be used for prediction. The most straightforward is *SCAP* (Frantzeskou, Stamatatos, Gritzalis, Chaski, & Howald, 2007), which is simply the proportion of overlapping n-grams in each sequence, divided by the overall count.

To perform author prediction using this, we would first profile each of the authors in the training dataset, and then profile the document of unknown authorship. From here, we compute the distance between the author profiles and the document profile. The author profile that has the lowest distance is the predicted author.

LNG-based methods have shown a very high accuracy for many authorship analysis tasks, with comparable performance to other methods (better for some datasets, worse for others).

Where there is now previously known dataset matching authors to writing, the task can be performed as an unsupervised data mining exercise. This process is known as *authorship clustering* (Layton, Watters, & Dazeley, 2012). The aim is to group together documents authored by the same person, even without *a priori* knowledge of shared authorship in a training corpus. This task is considerably harder, but potentially more generalizable to searching for shared authorship, such as in an open source intelligence gathering setting. For instance, we can find social media accounts linked by the same person (Perez, Birregah, Layton, Lemercier, & Watters, 2014).

Authorship analysis has been used for attributing cybercrimes in a large, and growing, number of contexts. For instance, it is the main occupation of the author (Layton et al., 2012), who apply these techniques to cybercrimes such as phishing and spam. Other work, such as Zheng, Huang and Chen (2006), has also applied these techniques to spam.

Attribution techniques have also been applied to source code using techniques similar to authorship analysis above (Layton & Watters, 2014a, 2014b). Work such as this includes supervised authorship analysis, which looks at a known set of programs written by an author, and attempts to see if another program was written by the same author. Other work includes an unsupervised authorship analysis, whereby the leaked source code for the Zeus malware was analyzed to see how many authors are behind it.

LIMITATIONS AND ISSUES

While we covered many of the limitations and issues of current relative attribution techniques preciously in this chapter, it is worth noting these again for the purposes of summarization. In this section, we will highlight the main limitations of work in relative attribution, while the next section will outline possible research directions to resolve it.

Intelligent adversaries are probably the major concern for relative attribution methods to date. An intelligent adversary at present would be quite capable of remaining anonymous under the state-of-the-art methods in relative attribution, by hiding their attacking style and performing analysis before their attack to ensure that these methods do not link their attacks (Brennan & Greenstadt, 2009). While this may seem like a complete failure in the field, there is a significant difference between capability and cost. While the capability is definitely there, the cost for remaining anonymous is increasing as relative attribution methods get better. Just as today's malware authors need to put increasing amounts of work into getting their malware authors through modern antivirus systems, attackers need to consider more complex methods of remaining anonymous against today's attribution techniques.

The problem is perhaps more difficult for remaining anonymous. While a malware author intent only on getting through an antivirus system needs to have it working today, an anonymous attacker needs to consider the future of attribution and how that relates to their attacks – will tomorrow's attribution techniques be able to attribute the attacks to them?

While remaining anonymous is the concern of many attackers, another more insidious problem is that of implicating others in an attack, a framing attack. In this scenario, an attack is performed using the resources and methods considered to belong to another party, in order to implicate them in the attack. As an example, Russian hackers could use Chinese servers and methods, setting their computer's language to Chinese, and leave other clues implicating Chinese attackers in the attack. This would divert attention from the real attackers, and could damage international relations.

Another limitation is that relative attribution does not (by definition) perform absolute attribution. This may limit the ability for some to trust the outcome, or use it in some scenarios. While we have considered the "so what?" question of relative attribution, the message needs to be strictly conveyed about the limitations of a relative attribution, and exactly what the results mean, that is, that two attacks were performed by the same person, but we do not know who that person is. There are possibilities of overcoming this limitation, such as linking an attack to a social media account using relative attribution, and then looking at the social media account for identity information.

RESEARCH STREAMS

Binary attribution for malware is a key area of interest. The concept is that we could use this type of attribution to attribute malware attacks, and this would help with the analysis and blocking of these attacks, and potentially lead to more convictions in this area. Some work has been performed in this area, for instance Rosenblum, Zhu, and Miller (2011) investigated attributing binary programs. This work was quite a successful pioneering study, and has been extended in other research (Alrabaee et al., 2014) but had some important scoping choices that limit its immediate impact, particularly for malware studies:

1. The programs were all single-author, while malware often is multiauthor and often "borrowed" from other sources.
2. The programs were small and single-purpose, while malware is often complexity.
3. The author's were not aware beforehand that they were going to be attributed, and took no efforts to hide their styles.
4. The programs were complete at the time of creation, whereas malware often downloads new parts as it runs.

Addressing these limitations in malware attribution is an important stepping stone for future research.

Improvements also need to be made to text-based authorship analysis methods, particularly to deal with the problems of intelligent adversaries hiding their identity and framing others. These attacks are particularly troublesome to current techniques, and pose a severe limitation on the effectiveness of current techniques, where it can be shown that the attacker is technically adept. Techniques could include intelligent methods for determining when obvious clues of authorship are not quite *right*, indicating that misdirection may be employed by the author.

Unsupervised methods for relative attribution are also a key area of future research and pose a difficult area of research that has a high potential for impact. In unsupervised methods, we do not have any suspects for the author of any document in our dataset, and yet we aim to group those documents by the author. There has been a large body of work on this area (Layton, Watters, & Dazeley, 2013), but the techniques need more robustness. A specific problem for these techniques is scale. While work has been done on scaling supervised authorship analysis techniques, no work (to the author's knowledge) has yet been successful in scaling unsupervised authorship analysis.

CONCLUSIONS

Relative attribution represents a new battlefield of cybersecurity, a generation ahead of the battlefield between malware authors and malware blockers (antivirus). However, the practical usage of attribution techniques is not yet mature, and requires insights into some specific problems. It can be argued that "perfect is the enemy of good," and with that in mind, relative attribution techniques to provide significant advantages *already* for an investigator. For example, relative attribution can help link attacks, and that linkage could be solidified by other investigative work into those attacks.

Relative attribution has significant problems that need to be addressed in research, particularly for the case of an intelligent attacker. These include problems of hiding identities, changing styles, and implicating others in the attack. These problems are significant and need to be carefully considered by investigators. That said, the clues are there that these problems can be addressed, and that relative attribution progress can continue quite strongly.

References

Alazab, M., Layton, R., Venkataraman, S., & Watters, P. (2010). Malware detection based on structural and behavioural features of api calls. In *The 1st International Cyber Resilience Conference* (pp. 1–10). Perth, Western Australia.

Alrabaee, S., Saleem, N., Preda, S., Wang, L., & Debbabi, M. (2014). OBA2: an Onion approach to binary code authorship attribution. *Digital Investigation, 11*, S94–S103.

Anderson, R., Barton, C., Böhme, R., Clayton, R., Van Eeten, M. J., Levi, M., et al. (2013). Measuring the cost of cybercrime. In *The economics of information security and privacy* (pp. 265–300). Berlin, Heidelberg: Springer.

Androutsopoulos, I., et al. (2000). *Learning to filter spam e-mail: A comparison of a naive Bayesian and a memory-based approach.* arXiv preprint cs/0009009.

Bagavandas, M., & Manimannan, G. (2008). Style consistency and authorship attribution: a statistical investigation*. *Journal of Quantitative Linguistics, 15.1*, 100–110.

Bishop, C. M. (2006). *Pattern recognition and machine learning.* Berlin: Springer.

Bond, P. (2014). Sony Hack: Activists to Drop 'Interview'DVDs over North Korea via Balloon. *The Hollywood Reporter, 16.*

Bouton, M. E. (2014). Why behavior change is difficult to sustain. *Preventive Medicine, 68*, 29–36.

Brennan, P., & Greenstadt, R. (2009). *Proceedings of the Twenty-First Conference on Innovative Applications of Artificial Intelligence (IAAI)*, Pasadena, CA, 2009.

Brenner, S. W. (2007). 'At Light Speed' – attribution and response to cybercrime/terrorism/warfare (2007). *Journal of Criminal Law and Criminology, 97*, 379.

Buitinck, L., Louppe, G., Blondel, M., Pedregosa, F., Mueller, A., Grisel, O., et al. (2013). *API design for machine learning software: experiences from the scikit-learn project.* arXiv preprint arXiv:1309.0238.

Burrows, S., Uitdenbogerd, A. L., & Turpin, A. (2014). Comparing techniques for authorship attribution of source code. *Software: Practice and Experience, 44(1)*, 1–32.

Clark, D. D., & Landau, S. (2010). The problem isn't attribution: it's multi-stage attacks. In *Proceedings of the re-architecting the internet workshop* (pp. 11). ACM.

Clarke, R. V. G. (Ed.). (1997). *Situational crime prevention* (pp. 53–70). Monsey, NY: Criminal Justice Press.

de Graaf, D., Shosha, A. F., & Gladyshev, P. (2013). *BREDOLAB: shopping in the cybercrime underworld. In Digital forensics and cyber crime.* Berlin, Heidelberg: Springer, pp. 302–313.

Dingledine, R., Mathewson, N., & Syverson, P. (2004). *Tor: The second-generation onion router*. Washington DC: Naval Research Lab.

Douglas, J. E., & Munn, C. (1992). Violent crime scene analysis: modus operandi, signature, and staging. *FBI Law Enforcement Bulletin, 61.2*, 1–10.

Edwards, C. I. P. M. (2014). An analysis of a cyberattack on a nuclear plant: the stuxnet worm. *Critical Infrastructure Protection, 116*, 59.

Fidler, D. P. (2011). Was stuxnet an act of war? decoding a cyberattack. *IEEE Security Privacy*(4), 56–59.

Frantzeskou, G., Stamatatos, E., Gritzalis, S., Chaski, C. E., & Howald, B. S. (2007). Identifying authorship by byte-level n-grams: the source code author profile (scap) method. *International Journal of Digital Evidence, 6*(1), 1–18.

Galeotti, M. (2014). *Global crime today: the changing face of organised crime*. Routledge. Cambridge, U.K.: Cambridge University Press.

Giani, A., De Souza, I. G., Berk, V., & Cybenko, G. (2006). Attribution and aggregation of network flows for security analysis. In *Proceeding 3rd CERT/CC Annual Workshop Flow Anal.*, 2006.

Haggard, S., & Lindsay, J. R. (2015). *North Korea and the Sony Hack: Exporting Instability Through Cyberspace.*

John, A., & Sivakumar, T. (2009). Ddos: survey of traceback methods. *International Journal of Recent Trends in Engineering, 1*(2), 241–245.

Juola, P. (2006). Authorship attribution. *Foundations and Trends in Information Retrieval, 1*(3), 233–334.

Kešelj, V., Peng, F., Cercone, N., & Thomas, C. (2003). N-gram-based author profiles for authorship attribution. In *Proceedings of the conference pacific association for computational linguistics, PACLING* (Vol. 3, pp. 255–264).

Koppel, M., Schler, J., & Argamon, S. (2011). Authorship attribution in the wild. *Language Resources and Evaluation, 45*(1), 83–94.

Kosba, A. E. (2014). ADAM: automated detection and attribution of malicious webpages. In *Information security applications* (pp. 3–16). Berlin: Springer International Publishing.

Layton, R. (2015). *Learning data mining in python*. Packt Publishing.

Layton, R., & Alazab, A. (2014). Authorship analysis of the Zeus botnet source code. In *Proceedings of the cybercrime and trustworthy computing conference (CTC)*.

Layton, R., & Watters, P. A. (2014a). A methodology for estimating the tangible cost of data breaches. *Journal of Information Security and Applications, 19*(6), 321–330.

Layton, R., & Watters, P. A. (2014b). Indirect attribution in cyberspace. In *Handbook of research on digital crime, cyberspace security, and information assurance*.

Layton, R., Watters, P., & Dazeley, R. (2012). Unsupervised authorship analysis of phishing webpages. In *2012 IEEE International symposium on communications and information technologies (IS-CIT)* (pp. 1104–1109).

Layton, R., Watters, P., & Dazeley, R. (2013). Automated unsupervised authorship analysis using evidence accumulation clustering. *Natural Language Engineering, 19*(01), 95–120.

Lee, I., Jeong, S., Yeo, S., & Moon, J. (2012). A novel method for SQL injection attack detection based on removing SQL query attribute values. *Mathematical and Computer Modelling, 55*(1), 58–68.

Lowd, D., & Meek, C. (2005). *Good word attacks on statistical spam filters*. CEAS. In *Proceedings of the Second Conference on Email and Anti-Spam (CEAS)*, 2005.

McCombie, S., Pieprzyk, J., & Watters, P. (2009). Cybercrime attribution: an Eastern European case study. *The 7th Australian Digital Forensics Conference, secau – Security Research Centre, School of Computer and Security Science* (pp. 41–51). Edith Cowan University, Perth, Western Australia.

McRae, C. M., & Vaughn, R. B. (2007). Phighting the phisher: Using web bugs and honeytokens to investigate the source of phishing attacks. In *Proceedings of the 40th IEEE annual Hawaii international conference on system sciences (HICSS 2007)*.

Mcwhorter, D. (2013). Mandiant Exposes APT1—One of China's Cyber Espionage Units & Releases 3,000 Indicators. Mandiant, February, 18.

Murdoch, S. J., & Danezis, G. (2005). Low-cost traffic analysis of Tor. In *Proceedings of the 2005 IEEE symposium on security and privacy*.

Parker, T. (2011). *Stuxnet Redux: malware attribution lessons learned. Black Hat DC 2011-URL*: www.blackhat.com/html/bh-dc-11/bh-dc-11-archives.html# Parker.

Perez, C., Birregah, B., Layton, R., Lemercier, M., & Watters, P. (2014). REPLOT: *Retrieving Profile Links On Twitter for malicious campagaign discovery. IA Communications.(à paraître)*.

Pilli, E. S., Joshi, R. C., & Niyogi, R. (2010). Network forensic frameworks: survey and research challenges. *Digital Investigation, 7*(1), 14–27.

Preuß, J., Furnell, S. M., & Papadaki, M. (2007). Considering the potential of criminal profiling to combat hacking. *Journal in Computer Virology, 3*(2), 135–141.

Rogers, M. (2003). The role of criminal profiling in the computer forensics process. *Computers Security, 22*(4), 292–298.

Rosenblum, N., Zhu, X., & Miller, B. P. (2011). *Who wrote this code? Identifying the authors of program binaries. In Computer security–ESORICS 2011*. Berlin, Heidelberg: Springer, pp. 172–189.

Solove, D. J. (2007). 'I've got nothing to hide' and other misunderstandings of privacy. *San Diego Law Review, 44*, 745.

Stolerman, A., Overdorf, R., Afroz, S., & Greenstadt, R. (2013). *Classify, but verify: Breaking the closed-world assumption in stylometric authorship attribution*. In IFIP Working Group (Vol. 11).

Sutanto, P. J., Leedham, G., & Pervouchine, V. (2003). Study of the consistency of some discriminatory features used by document examiners in the analysis of handwritten letter a'. In *Proceedings of the Seventh International Conference on Document Analysis and Recognition (ICDAR '03), Vol. 2* (p. 1091). Washington, DC, USA: IEEE Computer Society.

Tourney, R., Yearwood, J., Vamplew, P., & Kelarev, A. V. (2012). Applications of machine learning for linguistic analysis of texts. Machine learning algorithms for problem solving in computational applications: *Intelligent Techniques: Intelligent Techniques, 133*.

Turvey, B. E. (2011). *Criminal profiling: An introduction to behavioral evidence analysis*. New York: Academic Press.

Whitten, A., & Tygar, J. D. (1999). Why Johnny can't encrypt: a usability evaluation of PGP 5.0. In *Usenix Security* (Vol. 1999).

Zheng, R., Li, J., Chen, H., & Huang, Z. (2006). A framework for authorship identification of online messages: writing-style features and classification techniques. *Journal of the American Society for Information Science and Technology, 57*(3), 378–393.

CHAPTER 4

Enhancing Privacy to Defeat Open Source Intelligence

Suriadi Suriadi*, Ernest Foo**, Jason Smith**

**School of Engineering and Advanced Technology, College of Sciences,
Massey University, New Zealand; **School of Electrical Engineering
and Computer Science – Science and Engineering Faculty,
Queensland University of Technology, Queensland, Australia*

INTRODUCTION

To work efficiently, open source intelligence (OSINT) requires access to a substantial amount of users' personally identifiable information (PII). Getting access to such information, unfortunately, proves to be less of a challenge in many circumstances, given the lack of protection applied by organizations in securing users' PII as evidenced by regular reports about data breaches, such as the Sony data breach incident (Lewis, in press) and the Ashley Madison incident (Victor, in press). The revelation by Edward Snowden (Macaskill & Dance, in press) only aggravates the erosion of usres privacy in the digital world.

There are many valid and legitimate reasons why access to users PII is needed. For example, government agencies do need access to users information for the sake, for example, providing appropriate level of health care and protecting national security. Similarly, private businesses also need access to users PII before access to their services can be granted (e.g., an insurance company needs quite detailed information about a user's medical history in deciding health insurance premium). However, problem arises when the custodian of users' information fails to uphold the level of protection to users' PII that is expected of them, leading to various undesirable effects, such as identity thefts.

One way to achieve an acceptable level of balance in this scenario is to use cryptographically enforced methods to exchange users' PII in the form of a privacy-enhancing protocol. This chapter introduces an example of such a protocol that builds upon existing anonymous credential system and extends it into a federated single sign-on setting. This protocol allows for many privacy-respecting principles to be upheld, including the data disclosure minimization principle[1]

---

[1] https://secure.edps.europa.eu/EDPSWEB/edps/site/mySite/pid/74

(critical for preserving users anonymity), while at the same time allowing users' anonymity to be revoked under certain circumstances. Combined with its application in a federated single sign-on environment, this protocol attempts to achieve a balance between privacy, accountability, and practicality.

Scenario

Consider a user u_a who in a single sitting purchases a prescription medicine, posts some comments in two online forums (Forum A and Forum B), and bids for an auctioned item. For privacy reasons, u_a can be anonymous. However, for accountability purposes, some of u_a's PII may have to be revealed when certain conditions are met. Due to the different legislative requirements between different industries, countries, and/or states, the conditions under which u_a's PII can be revealed are likely to be *different* from one service provider to another. For example, the pharmacy may require u_a PII to be revealed if the medicine purchased is found to have serious side-effects, the auction site may need u_a PII if he/she wins the auction, and the online forum may need the PII if u_a posted some illegal material. Assuming that Forum A and Forum B reside in different countries, what constitutes "illegal material" may also be different.

In such a situation, each of these SP needs to have correctly escrowed u_a PII under their respective conditions before providing services. The escrowed PII is only revealed when certain conditions are met. We call this process the CRPI.

Existing ACS (Bangerter, Camenisch, & Lysyanskaya, 2004) provides many privacy-enhancing capabilities. For the purpose of this chapter, we focus on its CRPI capability. This is accomplished through the execution of a PII escrow operation, whereby using a combination of encryption, signature, and zero-knowledge proof techniques, a user's PII is *verifiably encrypted* under a set of *cryptographically binding* conditions. The result of such an operation is a ciphertext that correctly hides some *certified* PII. It can only be decrypted by a trusted ARM when the conditions are satisfied.

Using existing PII escrow operations, if u_a interacts with r-number of SP in a sitting, then r-number of PII-escrow operations have to be performed because each of the PII escrow operations cryptographically binds a user's PII to a set of conditions $Cond_x$ that are *specific* to SP_x for that transaction only. Furthermore, even if u_a only interacts with SP who are all bound by the same legislative requirements, a one-to-one mapping of conditions improves accountability. The conditions used between a user and an SP must contain the identity of the SP involved in that transaction. Consequently, since the conditions are cryptographically bound to the ciphertext, when the conditions are satisfied, the decryption of the PII can be *technically linked* to that particular SP only. As a result, if the revealed PII is abused in the future (such as unauthorized sharing of PII), we could trace the root of such an abuse to only those SP(s) who have received the revealed PII.

Nevertheless, the existing PII escrow operation is inefficient. A PII-escrow operation requires many resource-intensive cryptographic operations (generation of commitments, encryptions, and execution of zero-knowledge proof protocols). Having to perform such operations multiple times in a sitting will result in poor performance, and subsequently, reduced usability. This problem is aggravated for users with limited-power devices. Furthermore, the existing ACS (Bangerter, Camenisch, & Lysyanskaya, 2004) relies on a single trusted ARM for a correct PII escrow operation.

The contribution of this chapter is a protocol called the PIEMCP which allows a user to bind her escrowed PII to multiple sets of conditions (each to be used with different SP), while only having to perform the resources-intensive PII-escrow operation *once*. Furthermore, PIEMCP reduces the trust placed on the ARM and achieves significantly better performance in comparison to the existing approach (Bangerter, Camenisch, & Lysyanskaya, 2004). We achieve this by extending the existing ACS into an FSSO environment (OASIS, 2005) using the TPM (TCG, 2007), secure processor (McCune, Parno, Perrig, Reiter, & Isozaki, 2008), and IBEPRE (Canetti & Hohenberger, 2007), (Green & Ateniese, 2007) technologies. The application of an ACS in an FSSO environment has been previously proposed (Suriadi, Foo, & Jøsang, 2009a); however, the problem of binding PII escrowed under multiple conditions is not addressed. Finally, as the PIEMCP is complex, we have formally verified its security properties using a formal method tool: CPN and the associated state space analysis techniques.

This chapter is organized as follows: Section "requirements and threats" details the security requirements and the threat environment for PIEMCP. Section "preliminaries" describes the notation used and a brief description of the cryptographic schemes and the TPM technologies employed. Section "the PIEMCP" details the PIEMCP. Section "formal security analysis with CPN" provides a formal analysis of the security properties of the PIEMCP. Section "performance analysis of FSSO-PIEMC" analyzes the performance of PIEMCP in comparison to the existing approach. Conclusions and future work are provided in Section "conclusion and future work."

REQUIREMENTS AND THREATS

The main entities involved in the PIEMCP are users (u), IdP, SP, and an ARM. In a FSSO system, an IdP authenticates users and provides authentication information to the SP in a *session*. We define a *session* as a period of time where a user interacts, more or less continuously, with multiple SP after the initial authentication with the IdP and before the user has to re-authenticate with the IdP. As detailed in Section "the PIEMCP," in PIEMCP, such an authentication is performed anonymously using the ACS.

Security requirements: The security requirements for a privacy-preserving system have been previously articulated (Bhargav-Spantzel, Camenisch, Gross, & Sommer, 2006; Suriadi, Foo, & Smith, 2008a; Suriadi, Foo, & Smith, 2008b). In this chapter, we extend existing requirements to satisfy those required by PIEMCP.

Multiple conditions: At the end of every session, the PII escrowed must be able to be bound to multiple sets of conditions, each to be used with a different SP. *Accountable PII disclosure:* In the process of revealing user PII due to the fulfillment of some conditions, the end result should be the revelation of the PII to *only* the SP as stated in the conditions and nobody else. *Authenticated PII:* Prior to conditions fulfillment, IdP, SP, and referees must not learn the value of the user's PII but at the same time be convinced that its encryption is correct; when conditions are fulfilled, the revealed PII must indeed be of correct certified PII. This requirement implies the *confidentiality, conditional release, and revocation* properties detailed in Bhargav-Spantzel, Camenisch, Gross, and Sommer (2006). *Enforceable conditions fulfillment:* A user's PII should never be revealed *before* all designated referees agree that the cryptographically bound conditions are satisfied. This requirement is used in Suriadi, Foo, and Smith (2008a), and it is similar to the *privacy policy, obligations, restrictions, and enforcement* properties detailed in Bhargav-Spantzel, Camenisch, Gross, and Sommer (2006). *Conditions-Abuse resistant:* An SP and an IdP must not be able to fool the user into encrypting their PII under a set of conditions different from those originally agreed. Similarly, an SP or IdP must not be able to successfully revoke the user's PII using conditions different from those originally agreed. This requirement is extended from the more generic *Abuse resistant* property defined in Suriadi, Foo, and Smith (2008a). *Session Unlinkability:* SP and IdP must not be able to link a user from one escrow session to another from the session data gathered.

Threats: We consider threats that arise from malicious users, IdPs, and SPs. A precise explanation of the types of attacks that these entities can perform is provided in Section "formal security analysis with CPN." A malicious user may provide false PII (for escrow) and may attempt to cause unsuccessful revocation of the escrowed PII even when the conditions bound are satisfied. Malicious IdP and SP may attempt (individually or in a collusion) to reveal the escrowed PII in an un-authorized manner (such as when conditions are not fulfilled yet). As is common in an FSSO model, SPs trust IdPs. Collusion between users and IdPs or SPs is unlikely due to conflicting interests: users want to protect their PII, while IdPs and SPs want the exact opposite (the revelation of the PII). We assume the ARM to be opportunistic but risk averse, that is, it is trusted to execute its tasks honestly and not to collude with the IdP and SP; however, it will attempt to learn the value of the PII when the effort required is trivial. By trivial, we mean ability to obtain users PII without having to leave any detectable traces (such as communication logs if it colludes with IdP and/or SP). We argue that this is a realistic assumption of an ARM as its business model relies on its good reputation; however, it does not mean that the ARM will not be opportunistic when its malicious actions cannot be detected or traced.

PRELIMINARIES

$m_a, m_b...m_j$ are plain text data items. $Cipher(Enc_{scheme}, m_i, L, K^i_{pub\text{-}scheme}$ is an encryption of a data item m_i using the Enc_{scheme} encryption scheme under i's public encryption key and under the label L. A label is just a string and it can contain any information. In this chapter, we assume that a label encodes a set of conditions. The plain text m_i can only be recovered by i who has the corresponding private key $K^i_{priv\text{-}scheme})$ as input to decryption algorithm. A signature $S(m_i, K^i_{sign})$ over a message m_i can only be produced using i's private signing key K^i_{sign}. Anybody can verify the signature using the public verification key of i: $VerifySign((S(m_i, K^i_{sign})), K^i_{verify}) = 1$ (valid) or 0 (invalid). A commitment c_{m_i} of a data item m_i is generated using a $Commit$ algorithm, along with a random value r: $c_{m_i} = Commit(m_i, r)$. A commitment is $hiding$: it does not show any computational information on m_i, and $binding$: it is computationally impossible to find another m'_i and r' as inputs to the same $Commit$ algorithm that gives a value $c'_{m_i} = c_{m_i}$. $PK\{(m_a): F(m_a, m_b...m_i) = 1\}$ refers to a zero knowledge proof interactive protocol (PK). PK is executed between a Prover and a Verifier. The data to the left of the colon m_a is the data item that a Prover needs to prove the knowledge of such that the statements on the right side of the colon, $F(m_a, m_b...m_i) = 1$, is correct. A verifier will not learn the data on the left-hand side of the colon, while other parameters are known. The actual protocol involves one or more message exchange(s). At the end of PK, the Verifier will be convinced (or not) that the Prover has the knowledge of m_a without the Verifier learning it.

The ACS (Bangerter, Camenisch, & Lysyanskaya, 2004) is built upon a combination of signature schemes (Camenisch & Lysyanskaya, 2002; Camenisch & Lysyanskaya, 2004), VE scheme (Camenisch & Shoup, 2003a), and commitment schemes. ACS provides many privacy-enhancing services, however, in this chapter, only the CRPI capability is elaborated. In ACS, *unlike* the "usual" certificate (such as X509 certificate), a certificate $Cert_1$ issued to a user u_a is a signature of certificate issuer $CertIssuer_1$ over a collection of PII: $Cert_1 = S(id_a, m_b,...m_i; K^{CertIssuer_1}_{sign})$. A user u_a should keep $Cert_1$ *private*.

We assume that the data item id_a in $Cert_1$ is the explicit identity of u_a, while $m_b,...,m_i$ contain other PII (such as address, date of birth, etc.). The CRPI is accomplished as follows: id_a is *blinded* using a commitment scheme: $c_{id_a} = Commit(id_a, r)$. Then, the value id_a, hidden in c_{id_a}, is encrypted using the

VE scheme (Camenisch & Shoup, 2003a) under the ARM public encryption key, and under a set of

Conditions: $Cipher(Enc_{VE}, id_a, Conditions, K_{public\text{-}VE}^{ARM})$. Then, a *PK* is executed to prove that c_{id_a} is the commitment for id_a contained in $Cert_1$ issued by $CertIssuer_1$. This *PK* also proves that $Cipher_{VE\text{-}id_a}$ is an encryption of id_a hidden in c_{id_a}, under the ARM public key:

$$PK\{(Cert_1, id_a) \quad : \quad c_{id_a} = Commit(id_a, r)$$
$$\wedge \; VerifySign(S(id_a,..., m_i; K_{sign}^{CertIssuer_1}), K_{verify}^{CertIssuer_1}) = 1 \qquad (4.1)$$
$$\wedge \; Cipher(Enc_{VE}, id_a, Conditions, K_{public\text{-}VE}^{ARM})\}$$

In an IBEPRE scheme – such as Chu and Tzeng (2007), Green and Ateniese (2007), a public key is just a label, known as *id*. We denote an IBEPRE of a message m_a under a label id_1 as $Cipher(Enc_{IBEPRE}, m_a, id_1)$. To decrypt, the private key sk_{id_1} has to be extracted from a PKG (who has the master secret key msk). A re-encryption key $rk_{id_1 \rightarrow id_2}$ (which can be generated if one knows sk_{id_1}, id_1, and id_2) is needed to re-encrypt $Cipher(Enc_{IBEPRE}, m_a, id_1)$ into $Cipher(Enc_{IBEPRE}, m_a, id_2)$. The entity performing such a re-encryption does not learn the value of m_a.

To verify that a user is using a genuine TPM in a privacy-preserving manner, a DAA protocol (Brickell, Camenisch, & Chen, 2004) is executed. A successful execution of the DAA protocol convinces a verifier that it is interacting with a genuine TPM platform without learning the "identity" of the platform. Instead, a pair of per-session AIK is generated which can be used by the TPM as its authenticated signing key to sign TPM-generated messages – such as a PCR value – for that session only (a PCR value is the hash value of the modules loaded in a secure execution area of a TPM). Therefore, interactions with the same TPM over multiple sessions are unlinkable – thus privacy preserving.

A TPM platform can be extended to provide the provable isolated execution property as proposed by McCune, Parno, Perrig, Reiter, and Isozaki (2008). This property allows one to prove that a given output is the result of *correct execution* of a set of integrity-protected modules based on some known input. The generation of such proofs only requires a simple signature of the TPM PCR value, input, output, and other supporting parameters. Readers who are interested in the details should consult the referenced chapter (McCune, Parno, Perrig, Reiter, & Isozaki, 2008).

THE PIEMCP

In this section, we detail the PIEMCP that combines the ACS with an IBEPRE scheme, using the *extended TPM* technology that provides the *provable isolated execution* property. Our PIEMCP is designed such that any IBEPRE schemes respecting the definition provided in Green and Ateniese (2007) can be used. We divide PIEMCP into several stages: the setup, PE stage, KE stage, MC stage, and the revocation stage. The setup is performed once. The PE and KE stages have to be performed once per session. The MC stage can be performed multiple times in a session as needed. The revocation stage is executed when an SP believes that some conditions are satisfied, thus needing the PII to be revealed. We assume that the semi-honest ARM also performs the role of a PKG. *Overview:* assume we need to escrow d-number of PII. In PIEMCP, instead of encrypting the PII for the ARM as is currently performed in the ACS, we use a one-time user-generated key for the VE scheme (Camenisch & Shoup, 2003a). The encryptions of the d PII are given to an IdP for escrow. Then, the private portion of the VE one-time key is escrowed as follows: the user's *extended TPM* platform will perform a *provable isolated execution* of `Module1` – given the public key portion of the generated one-time VE keys, performs an IBEPRE of the corresponding VE one-time private key under a set of conditions *Conditions1* (see Table 4.1). Then, the encrypted key is sent to the ARM for escrow, along with the TPM-generated proof to show that the ciphertext is the result of a correct execution of `Module1`. When the escrowed PII needs to be bound to a different set of conditions *Conditions2*, the IdP will request the ARM to re-encrypt the VE private key (generated earlier) under *Conditions2*. When a particular set of conditions, say *Conditions2* are satisfied, the ARM can extract the IBEPRE decryption key to recover the VE private key, which can subsequently be used to recover the PII. The details of PIEMCP are as follows:

Setup: A user u_a obtains a certificate *Cert* containing PII $id_a...m_i$ from a certificate issuer *CertIssuer*. The PII certified by *CertIssuer* is accepted by the IdP and SP in the federation. To verify the issued certificate, the *CertIssuer*'s signature verification key $K_{verify}^{CertIssuer}$ is used.

PII escrow (PE): A FSSO session starts when u_a needs to access services from a service provider *SP*1 who in turn requires the IdP to escrow some of u_a's PII

Table 4.1 `Module1` – IBEPRE Encryption of VE Private Key

Input	$K_{pub\text{-}VE}^u$, *Conditions*, params-IBEPRE
Process	P1.1. Retrieve $K_{priv\text{-}VE}^u$
	P1.2. Verify that $K_{priv\text{-}VE}^u$ is the correct private key for the input value $K_{pub\text{-}VE}^u$
	P1.3. If P1.2 returns true, generate $Cipher(Enc_{IBEPRE}, K_{priv\text{-}VE}^u,$ *Conditions-SP*1) .
	Otherwise, return an error
Output	$Cipher(Enc_{IBEPRE}, K_{priv\text{-}VE}^u,$ *Conditions*) or error

under a set of conditions. *Conditions-SP1* that can be freshly negotiated per session, or preagreed beforehand. A user is responsible to verify that the agreed conditions are formed as follows:

$$\text{Conditions} = K_{enc}^{SP} + \text{one-time random} + \text{list-of-conditions}$$

whereby K_{end}^{SP} refers to the public encryption key of the SP to whom the conditions apply, one-time random refers to a unique *one-time* random value that identifies that particular session between the user and SP, list-of-conditions refer to the set of of conditions that must be satisfied before the associated encrypted message can be recovered.

A start of a session triggers the start of the PE stage (see Figure 4.1). While the existing ACS (Bangerter, Camenisch, & Lysyanskaya, 2004) binds the conditions to the encryptions of those PII directly, in PIEMCP, such binding only occurs during the KE stage. At the PE stage, we use a generic condition string stating that "decryption of these PII should only be performed pending a successful recovery of the associated decryption key that is escrowed in the following key-escrow stage." We denote this condition as *GenCond*. The IdP will not be able to decrypt these escrowed PII because it does not have the decryption key.

1. *SP*1 generates a signed request for PII $m_a...m_c$ to be escrowed to the IdP. This request message includes the *Conditions-SP1*. This request message is redirected through u_a to the IdP.

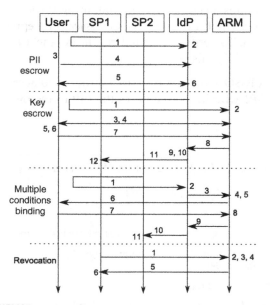

FIGURE 4.1 The PIEMCP message flow.

2. The IdP verifies the request from $SP1$. If valid, it will contact the user to start the PII escrow operation.

3. User u_a generates one-time VE encryption key pair ($K_{\text{pub-VE}}^u$, $K_{\text{priv-VE}}^u$), the commitments $c_a...c_c$ for PII $m_a...m_c$ respectively, and three VE ciphertext of PII $m_a...m_c$ (denoted as $Cipher(Enc_{\text{VE}},(m_a,m_b,m_c),GenCond,$ $K_{\text{pub-VE}}^u)$ for simplicity).

4. u_a sends $K_{\text{pub-VE}}^u$, and $Cipher(Enc_{\text{VE}},(m_a,m_b,m_c),GenCond,K_{\text{pub-VE}}^u)$ to the IdP

5. u_a and IdP engage in a zero proof of knowledge protocol (PK) to prove that the commitments $c_a...c_c$ hide PII $m_a...m_c$ which have been certified in $Cert$ issued by $CertIssuer$. This PK also proves that the VE ciphertexts given correctly encryption $m_a...m_c$ w.r.t. $K_{\text{pub-VE}}^u$. The values of $c_a...c_c$ are given to the IdP as part of the PK procedure.

6. After a successful execution of the above PK, the IdP generates a pseudonym to identify the user for this session and associates it with $K_{\text{pub-VE}}^u$, $Cipher(Enc_{\text{VE}},(m_a,m_b,m_c),GenCond,K_{\text{pub-VE}}^u)$, $K_{\text{pub-VE}}^u$, and $Conditions$-$SP1$.

We cannot simply substitute the execution of the above PK protocol with the *provable isolated execution* capability provided by an *extended TPM* platform. This is because at this stage, the IdP does not have any data that can be used as a source of a *valid input* to a TPM module (garbage-in garbage-out problem). In our protocol, since it is the user who generates and gives $K_{\text{pub-VE}}^u$ to the IdP, the IdP has to verify that the given $K_{\text{pub-VE}}^u$ is correct in relation to the encrypted PII – which can only be achieved by the execution of the PK protocol. Only after a successful PK operation can we use $K_{\text{pub-VE}}^u$ and other publicly known value as valid input to a module to be executed by an *extended TPM* platform.

Key escrow (KE): The public key parameters for the IBEPRE scheme used are known to all participants.

1. The IdP signs $Conditions$-$SP1$ and sends $S(Conditions$-$SP1, K_{\text{sign}}^{IdP})$ + $Conditions$-$SP1$ in a redirection message through the user to the ARM.

2. The ARM verifies the signature. If valid, it stores $Conditions$-$SP1$ and continues. Otherwise, halt.

3. u_a and ARM engage in a DAA protocol to verify the use of valid TPM platform and to generate a pair of AIK keys, denoted as $K_{\text{verify-AIK}}^{\text{TPM-}u_a}$, $K_{\text{sign-AIK}}^{\text{TPM-}u_a}$.

4. As AIK should only be used to sign messages generated internally by a TPM, u_a's TPM should also generate a one-time signing key to sign messages from u_a (but not TPM-internally generated messages): $K_{\text{verify}}^{u_a}$, $K_{\text{sign}}^{u_a}$. The user's TPM can send $K_{\text{verify}}^{u_a} + S(K_{\text{verify}}^{u_a}, K_{\text{sign-AIK}}^{\text{TPM-}u_a})$ to the ARM for verification.

5. u_a runs `Module1` on the *extended TPM* platform to perform an IBEPRE encryption of $K^u_{\text{priv-VE}}$ under *Conditions-SP1* (see Table 4.1). This module will generate an output:

$$Cipher(Enc_{\text{IBEPRE}}, K^u_{\text{priv-VE}}, Conditions\text{-}SP1)$$

6. The platform should generate the proof of correct execution of `Module1`. This proof would contain information on the *extended TPM*'s PCR values (before and after execution) calculated from the value of `Module1`, the inputs, output, and other necessary information. This proof is signed using $K^{\text{TPM-}u_a}_{\text{sign-AIK}}$. See McCune, Parno, Perrig, Reiter, and Isozaki (2008) for details of how such proof is generated.

7. The TPM proof + $Cipher(Enc_{\text{IBEPRE}}, K^u_{\text{priv-VE}}, Conditions\text{-}SP1)$ are sent to the ARM.

8. The ARM verifies the TPM proof. If valid, the ARM stores *Conditions-SP1* + $Cipher(Enc_{\text{IBEPRE}}, K^u_{\text{priv-VE}}, Conditions\text{-}SP1)$, and sends a signed $Cipher^{Conditions\text{-}SP1}_{\text{IBEPRE-}K^u_{\text{priv-VE}}}$ to the IdP.

9. The IdP verifies the received message from the ARM. If valid, it generates a one-time pseudonym *pseudo_a* to identify the user for that particular session only.

10. The IdP stores *pseudo_a*, and links it with $Cipher(Enc_{\text{IBEPRE}}, K^u_{\text{priv-VE}}, Conditions\text{-}SP1)$, $K^u_{\text{pub-VE}}$, *Conditions-SP1*, and $Cipher(Enc_{\text{VE}}, (m_a, m_b, m_c), GenCond, K^u_{\text{pub-VE}})$.

11. The IdP then sends a signed response message back to *SP1*. Included in the response are *pseudo_a*, $Cipher(Enc_{\text{IBEPRE}}, K^u_{\text{priv-VE}}, Conditions\text{-}SP1)$, *Conditions-SP1*, and $Cipher(Enc_{\text{VE}}, (m_a, m_b, m_c), GenCond, K^u_{\text{pub-VE}})$.

12. *SP1* verifies the response message from the IdP. If valid, *SP1* now has the necessary data such that when *Conditions-SP1* are satisfied, $m_a...m_c$ can be recovered with the help of the ARM.

Multiple Conditions Binding (MC): This stage is started when u_a goes to another *SP2* who also needs the escrowed PII but this time bound to a different set of conditions *Conditions*.

1. *SP2* generates a signed request for u_a's escrowed PII $m_a...m_c$ to be bound to *Conditions-SP2*.

2. The IdP verifies the request from *SP2*. From this request, the IdP will also detect that it has an open authenticated session with a user known as *pseudo_a*.[2]

---

[2] The IdP can detect such an open authenticated session with *pseudo_a* because in the existing FSSO protocols, the request message that *SP2* generated earlier is actually sent through a redirection from the user to the IdP, thus some authenticated session information (such as cookies) can be passed along to the IdP from the user machine.

3. The IdP retrieves *Conditions-SP1* associated with *pseudo$_a$*, and sends a signed re-encryption request to the ARM by sending *Conditions-SP1* and *Conditions-SP2′*.

4. The ARM verifies the request, and checks if it has the same *Conditions-SP1*. If not, stops.

5. To verify that the IdP has not given an invalid *Conditions-SP2′* to the ARM, the ARM prepares a message *multiple-bind = Conditions-SP1 + Conditions-SP2′*, and generates a signature over *multiple-bind*.

6. The ARM sends $S(multiple-bind, K_{sign}^{ARM})$ to u_a.

7. u_a, who knows *Conditions-SP1* and *Conditions-SP2* verifies the *multiple-bind* message and its signature. If valid, u_a sends a signed 'OK' message using $K_{verify}^{u_a}$ to the ARM.

8. The ARM verifies the response from the user. If it is valid, it then retrieves $Cipher(Enc_{IBEPRE}, K_{priv-VE}^u, Conditions\text{-}SP1)$, and re-encrypts it under *Conditions-SP2* to generate $Cipher(Enc_{IBEPRE}, K_{priv-VE}^u, Conditions\text{-}SP2)$ (the ARM can do the re-encryption as it knows $Cipher(Enc_{IBEPRE}, K_{priv-VE}^u, Conditions\text{-}SP1)$, msk, *Conditions-SP1*, and *Conditions-SP2*).

9. The ARM stores *Conditions-SP2* and $Cipher(Enc_{IBEPRE}, K_{priv-VE}^u, Conditions\text{-}SP2)$, and sends a signed re-encrypted ciphertext to the IdP.

10. The IdP verifies the ARM reply. If valid, it then sends a signed response message back to *SP2*. Included in the response are *pseudo$_a$*, $Cipher(Enc_{IBEPRE}, K_{priv-VE}^u, Conditions\text{-}SP2)$, *Conditions-SP2*, and $Cipher(Enc_{VE}, (m_a, m_b, m_c), GenCond, K_{pub-VE}^u)$.

11. *SP2* verifies the response returned from the IdP. If valid, then *SP2* knows that $m_a \ldots m_c$ can be recovered with the help of the ARM when *Conditions-SP2* are satisfied.

Revocation: When an SP, say *SP1*, believes that *Conditions-SP1* are satisfied, it will start the revocation stage:

1. *SP1* sends a revocation request containing *Conditions-SP1* to *n*-referees.

2. Each referees verifies if *Conditions-SP1* is fulfilled, the request message and checks if it has the same *Conditions-SP1′* stored. If so, it checks if the SP it is talking to is the same as the identity of *SP1′* as stated in *Conditions-SP1′*.

3. The ARM verifies if *Conditions-SP1′* are satisfied. If not, stops.

4. If satisfied, then the ARM extracts $sk_{Conditions\text{-}SP1}$ which is the private key for *Conditions-SP1*.

5. ARM generates a message $rev = sk_{Conditions\text{-}SP1} + Conditions\text{-}SP1$. It then signs *rev* and encrypts it using the public encryption key as stated in *Conditions-SP1* string for *SP1* (any secure encryption algorithm can be used here).

6. $SP1$ decrypts and verifies the ARM response, obtains $sk_{Conditions\text{-}SP1}'$ and then decrypts $Cipher(Enc_{IBEPRE}, K^u_{priv\text{-}VE}, Conditions\text{-}SP1)$ to recover $K^u_{priv\text{-}VE}$. Next, it uses $K^u_{priv\text{-}VE}$ to decrypt $Cipher(Enc_{VE}, (m_a, m_b, m_c), GenCond, K^u_{pub\text{-}VE})$ to reveal m_a, m_b, m_c.

FORMAL SECURITY ANALYSIS WITH CPN

The PIEMCP involves large multiparty communication, employs complex cryptographic primitives, and uses the extended TPM functionalities. These factors, combined with the numerous message exchanges between users, IdP, SP, and ARM in a multi-stage execution, make the PIEMCP a complex system. In order to verify, with high assurance, the achievement of the security properties of a complex system such as PIEMCP, a formal approach is required.

We use the CPN and state space analysis as the formal method techniques to model PIEMCP and to verify its security properties as detailed in Section "requirements and threats." The use of CPN as the formal method technique to model and verify large complex systems is well known (Billington & Han, 2007; Gordon, Kristensen, & Billington, in press; Smith, Tritilanunt, Boyd, Nieto, & Foo, 2007; Kristensen, Christensen, & Jensen, 1998).

We have formally modeled the PIEMCP using the CPN technique. From the CPN model, a state space is generated. A state space contains the information of all the possible states of the protocol. We can query this information to verify the security properties of PIEMCP. Specifically, we translate the security properties into a series of queries that can be verified against the information contained in the space space.

Attack Scenarios

In verifying the security properties of the PIEMCP, we have incorporated the following malicious behaviours into the CPN model in accordance with the threat model detailed in Section "requirements and threats."

1. A malicious user can perform the following actions:
   a. provide incorrect PII and incorrect one-time VE public key to the IdP during the PE stage,
   b. provide incorrect `Module1` result during the KE stage,
   c. use hard to fulfill $ConditionsX'$ (which are different from the originally agreed conditions with the SP_x) as input to `Module1` (the IBEPRE of the VE private key).
2. Both malicious IdP and SP can perform the following actions:
   a. give easy-to-fulfill conditions $ConditionsX'$ to the ARM (which are different from those originally agreed between a user and an SP_x) during the KE stage and MC stage,

b. attempt to start the revocation stage using conditions which are not yet fulfilled,

c. attempt to start the revocation stage using incorrect (non-existent) easy-to-fulfill conditions,

d. attempt to fool users into using the same condition string with two or more SP,

e. attempt to learn PII which has been revealed to another SP.

3. An opportunistic but risk-averse ARM may attempt to recover PII when it is trivial to do so. Specifically, if an ARM manages to obtain enough data to decrypt $Cipher(Enc_{VE}, (m_a, m_b, m_c), GenCond, K_{pub-VE}^u)$ without having to deliberately collude with other entities, it will do so.

Verification Results

A detailed description of the model is provided in Suriadi, Ouyang, Smith, and Foo (2009b) and Suriadi, Ouyang, and Foo (2012). Our model implicitly assumes that the cryptographic primitives and the TPM provable execution technology behave as they are expected to.

We verify the achievement of the PIEMCP security properties with *and* without the existence of the attack scenarios described earlier. This two-stage approach allows us to be confident that the protocol does provide the security properties in a normal environment and in an environment under attack. Again, due to space limitations, an exhaustive explanation of the state space analysis that we have conducted is not possible. Readers who are interested in the detail of our analysis should refer to Suriadi, Foo, and Smith (2009c).

In summary, our state space analysis confirms that in the absence *and* presence of the attack scenarios detailed earlier, the PIEMCP achieves the multiple conditions, accountable PII disclosure, authenticated PII, enforceable conditions fulfillment, conditions-abuse resistant, and session unlinkability properties as long as the implicit assumptions encoded into the model holds (the TPM provable execution technology and the cryptographic primitives employed behave as expected).

Removing Trusted ARM

The need to place a certain amount of trust on a PKG is inherent in most identity-based encryption schemes (Baek, Newmarch, Safavi-Naini, & Susilo, 2004). In PIEMCP, although the ARM plays the role of a PKG, we do not assume that it is a fully trusted entity either. Instead, we assume a stronger threat model whereby an ARM can be opportunistic but risk-averse (see Section "requirements and threats" for details). Nevertheless, there may be situations when the existence of such an ARM is not possible. In this case, an alternate solution to PIEMCP is required. We can extend the PIEMCP to cope with this situation in a fairly straightforward manner. An outline of how we can remove the need for a trusted ARM is given as follows. The PE stage remains the same. However, during the KE stage, instead of using an IBEPRE scheme, we require the user to encrypt the generated one-time VE private key using the custodian-hiding group encryption scheme (Liu, Tsang, Wong, & Zhu, 2005) under a set of conditions *Conditions*1. Essentially, this encryption scheme allows users to distribute the trust from a single ARM to a set of *n* referees. The MC stage in this scenario is similar to the KE stage: the user has to perform another group encryption of the one-time VE private key, but this time under a different set of conditions *Conditions*2. During revocation, at least k ($k \leq n$) referees have to agree on the conditions fulfillment before the VE private key can be recovered. Obviously, to reap the benefits of a group encryption, we require that at least $k > 1$.

Performing the custodian-hiding group encryption requires significant amount of computational resources. Having to perform such encryption multiple times with each of the SP within a session will severely reduce the performance of the system, especially for the users. Nevertheless, such a reduction in performance may be acceptable in exchange for a stronger privacy protection.

PERFORMANCE ANALYSIS OF FSSO-PIEMC

We measure the performance of PIEMCP using the number of cryptographic operations that have to be performed by users, IdP, SP, and ARM. We show that our protocol provides a significantly better efficiency as compared with the existing approach (Bangerter, Camenisch, & Lysyanskaya, 2004).

We base the calculation on the number of signature creation (`Sign`), signature verification (`Verify`), generic encryption and decryption (`Enc` and `Dec`), commitments generations (`comm`), encryption and decryption of VE (`Enc(VE)` and `Dec(VE)`), *PK* operations for proving correct commitments (`PK-comm`), *PK* operations for proving correct VE encryptions (`PK-VE`), execution of the DAA protocol (`DAA`), the encryptions and decryptions operations for the IBEPRE scheme (`Enc(IBEPRE)`) and (`Dec(IBEPRE)`), IBEPRE re-encryption (`Renc(IBEPRE)`), and IBEPRE private key extraction (`Ext(IBEPRE)`).

Of these operations, the `PK-VE`, `PK-comm`, and `DAA`, consume the most computational resources as they require numerous computationally-intensive modular exponentiations (modex). As an example, based on a rough estimate, the `PK-VE` operation requires a prover (e.g. a user) to perform roughly 10 modex, while a verifier (e.g., an IdP) needs to perform approximately 13 modex – see Camenisch and Shoup (2003b) for details. Table 4.2 summarizes the total online cryptographic operations for PIEMCP. As explained in Section "the PIEMCP," the first round of interaction between a user and an SP triggers

Table 4.2 Online Performance Summary for PIEMCP

Players		User	IdP	SP	ARM
PII + Key Escrow (1st SP)	Max	d(comm + Enc(VE) + PK-comm + PK-VE) + 1 DAA + 1 Sign + + 1 Enc(IBEPRE)	d(PK-comm + PK-VE) + 2 Sign + 2 Verify	1 Sign + 1 Verify	1 DAA + 1 Sign + 2 Verify
	Opt	1 DAA + 1 Enc(IBEPRE) + 1 Sign	2 Sign + 2 Verify	1 Sign + 1 Verify	1 DAA + 1 Sign 1 + Verify
Each of the next r SPs (MC)		1 Sign + 1 Verify	2 Sign + 2 Verify	1 Sign + 1 Verify	2 Sign + 2 Verify + 1 Renc(IBEPRE)
Revocation				1 Sign + 1 Dec(IBEPRE) + d(Dec(VE) 1 Verify + 1 Dec	1 Verify + 1 Extract 1 Sign 1 Enc

the PE and KE stages. Subsequent interactions with other SP only trigger the execution of the MC stage. Therefore, Table 4.2 breaks the required cryptographic operation between the PE + KE stages (combined), the MC stage, and the revocation stage.

The proposed PIEMCP suffers from inefficient first-round operation (PE and KE stages) for the user, IdP, and ARM due to the required PK-comm, PK-VE, and DAA operations. However, the efficiency of the subsequent rounds is massively improved, especially for the users who only need to do one signature generation and one signature verification – a very useful property for users with low-powered devices. Of course, the majority of operations are now transfered to the ARM who has to perform a re-encryption (which may include a private key extraction and a re-encryption key generation) for each of the r SP. However, even so, they are all based on efficient elliptic curve cryptography operations. Besides, it is very likely that an ARM would operate using a system with a considerable amount of computational powers.

Comparison to Existing Approach

Assume we need to escrow d-number of PII. In the existing approach, every single interaction with a different SP requires the execution of the PII escrow operation: for d PII to escrow, a user has to generate d commitments and d VE encryptions. In addition, the user and the SP have to perform

Table 4.3 Performance Comparison Between PIEMCP and the Existing Approach (Bangerter, Camenisch, & Lysyanskaya, 2004) for Interactions With r-Number of SP in a Session

Players	User	IdP	SP	ARM
PIEMCP	d(PK-comm + PK-VE + Enc(VE) + comm) + 1 DAA	d(PK-comm + PK-VE)		1 DAA + r Renc(IBEPRE)
Existing Approach (Bangerter, Camenisch, & Lysyanskaya, 2004)	$r \times d$ (PK-comm+ + PK-VE)		$r \times d$ (PK-comm + PK-VE)	

d (PK-comm + PK-VE). So, if a user in a session interacts with r number of SPs, a user has to perform $r \times d$ (commitments + VE + PK-comm + PK-VE) operations, while each SP has to perform $r \times d$ (PK-comm + PK-VE).

To simplify the comparison, let us just consider the main cryptographic operations: Enc(VE), comm, PK-comm, PK-VE, DAA, and Renc(IBEPRE). See Table 4.3 for a summary of the performance comparison. In comparison with the existing approach, the PIEMCP improves the performance by roughly a factor of r: regardless of the number of SP a user interacts with in a session, the PIEMCP only has to perform the resources-intensive cryptographic operations (PK-comm, PK-VE, DAA) *once*. While the ARM still has to perform roughly r Renc(IBEPRE), such operations require a much less computational resources as compared with performing $r \times d$ (comm + Enc(VE) + PK-comm + PK-VE).

The recent advancement in the ACS (Camenisch & Groß, 2008) improves the performance of the system by significantly reducing the computational complexity required to *prove the knowledge and properties* of users PII contained in an anonymous certificate in a zero-knowledge manner. Nevertheless, it is unclear whether such a performance improvement also applies to the CRPI capability as well. Besides, in terms of performance, our initial investigation shows that the improved ACS still requires at least one *PK* operation to be executed with each of the r SP that the user interacts with in a session – our proposal does not have to endure such a computational inefficiency.

CONCLUSION AND FUTURE WORK

We have proposed a protocol that allows the escrow of users' PII bound to multiple conditions. The PIEMCP proposed requires less trust to be placed on the ARM, while achieving significantly better performance in comparison to the existing approach (Bangerter, Camenisch, & Lysyanskaya, 2004). The security properties of the newly proposed protocol have been formally verified using CPN and state space analysis techniques. Furthermore, this protocol can be used to counter the privacy-eroding tendency facilitated by indiscriminate surveillance of OSINT technologies.

References

Baek, J., Newmarch, J., Safavi-Naini, R. , & Susilo, W. (2004). A survey of identity-based cryptography. In: *AUUG 2004*.

Bangerter, E., Camenisch, J., & Lysyanskaya, A. (2004). A cryptographic framework for the controlled release of certified data. In B. Christianson, B. Crispo, J. A. Malcolm, & M. Roe (Eds.), *Security protocols workshop, Vol. 3957 of LNCS* (pp. 20–42). Springer.

Bhargav-Spantzel, A., Camenisch, J., Gross, T., & Sommer, D. (2006). User centricity: a taxonomy and open issues. In A. Juels, M. Winslett, & A. Goto (Eds.), *DIM* (pp. 1–10). ACM.

Billington, J., & Han, B. (2007). Modelling and analysing the functional behaviour of tcp's connection management procedures. *STTT, 9*(3–4), 269–304.

Brickell, E. F., Camenisch, J., & Chen, L. (2004). Direct anonymous attestation. In V. Atluri, B. Pfitzmann, & P. D. McDaniel (Eds.), *ACM conference on computer and communications security* (pp. 132–145). ACM.

Camenisch, J., & Groß, T. (2008). Efficient attributes for anonymous credentials. In P. Ning, P. F. Syverson, & S. Jha (Eds.), *ACM conference on computer and communications security* (pp. 345–356). ACM.

Camenisch, J., & Lysyanskaya, A. (2002). A signature scheme with efficient protocols. In S. Cimato, C. Galdi, & G. Persiano (Eds.), *SCN, Vol. 2576 of LNCS* (pp. 268–289). Springer.

Camenisch, J., & Lysyanskaya, A. (2004). Signature schemes and anonymous credentials from bilinear maps. In M. K. Franklin (Ed.), *CRYPTO, Vol. 3152 of LNCS* (pp. 56–72). Springer.

Camenisch, J., & Shoup, V. (2003a). Practical verifiable encryption and decryption of discrete logarithms. In D. Boneh (Ed.), *CRYPTO, Vol. 2729 of LNCS* (pp. 126–144). Springer.

Camenisch, J., & Shoup, V. (2003). Practical verifiable encryption and decryption of discrete logarithms (slides). In: *The 7th workshop on elliptic curve cryptography (ECC 2003)*, University of Waterloo, Waterloo, ON, Canada.

Canetti, R., & Hohenberger, S. (2007). Chosen-ciphertext secure proxy re-encryption. In P. Ning, S. D. C. di Vimercati, & P. F. Syverson (Eds.), *ACM conference on computer and communications security* (pp. 185–194). ACM.

Chu, C. -K., & Tzeng, W. -G. (2007). Identity-based proxy re-encryption without random oracles. In J. A. Garay, A. K. Lenstra, M. Mambo, & R. Peralta (Eds.), *ISC, Vol. 4779 of LNCS* (pp. 189–202). Springer.

Gordon, S. Kristensen, L. M., & Billington, J. (2007). Verification of a revised wap wireless transaction protocol. In: ICATPN (Billington and Han, pp. 182–202).

Green, M., & Ateniese, G. (2007). Identity-based proxy re-encryption. In J. Katz, & M. Yung (Eds.), *ACNS, Vol. 4521 of Lecture notes in computer science* (pp. 288–306). Springer.

Kristensen, L. M., Christensen, S., & Jensen, K. (1998). The practitioner's guide to coloured petri nets. *STTT, 2*(2), 98–132.

Lewis, D. Sony pictures: The data breach and how the criminals won, Forbes.

Liu, J. K., Tsang, P. P., Wong, D. S., & Zhu, R. W. (2005). Universal custodian-hiding verifiable encryption for discrete logarithms. In D. Won, & S. Kim (Eds.), *ICISC, Vol. 3935 of LNCS* (pp. 389–409). Springer.

Macaskill, E. Dance, G. Nsa files: Decoded, The Guardian.

McCune, J. M., Parno, B., Perrig, A., Reiter, M. K., & Isozaki, H. (2008). Flicker: an execution infrastructure for TCB minimization. In J. S. Sventek, & S. Hand (Eds.), *EuroSys* (pp. 315–328). ACM.

OASIS. Assertions and Protocols for the OASIS Security Assertion Markup Language (SAML) V2.0, OASIS, oASIS Standard (March 2005).

Smith, J., Tritilanunt, S., Boyd, C., Nieto, J. M. G., & Foo, E. (2007). Denial-of-service resistance in key establishment. *IJWMC, 2*(1), 59–71.

Suriadi, S., Foo, E., & Smith, J. (2008a). A user-centric protocol for conditional anonymity revocation. In S. Furnell, S. K. Katsikas, & A. Lioy (Eds.), *TrustBus, Vol. 5185 of Lecture notes in computer science* (pp. 185–194). Berlin: Springer.

Suriadi, S. Foo, E., & Smith, J. (2008). Conditional privacy using re-encryption. In: J. Cao, M. Li, C. Weng, Y. Xiang, X. Wang, H. Tang, F. Hong, H. Liu, Y. Wang (Eds.), *IFIP international conference on network and parallel computing workshops 2008* (pp. 18–25). Shanghai, China: IEEE Computer Society.

Suriadi, S., Foo, E., & Jøsang, A. (2009a). A user-centric federated single sign-on system. *Journal of Network and Computer Applications, 32*(2), 388–401.

Suriadi, S., Ouyang, C., Smith, J., & Foo, E. (2009b). Modeling and verification of privacy enhancing protocols. In K. Breitman, & A. Cavalcanti (Eds.), *International conference on formal engineering methods, Vol. 5885 of Lecture notes in computer science* (pp. 127–146). Berlin, Germany: Springer.

Suriadi, S. Foo. E. & Smith, J. (2009). Private information escrow bound to multiple conditions using re-encryption (full version), Tech. rep., Information Security Institute – Queensland University of Technology, http://eprints.qut.edu.au/20847/1/MultipleConditions.pdf.

Suriadi, S., Ouyang, C., & Foo, E. (2012). Privacy compliance verification in cryptographic protocols. In K. Jensen, W. van der Aalst, M. Ajmone Marsan, G. Franceschinis, J. Kleijn, & L. Kristensen (Eds.), *Transactions on Petri Nets and Other Models of Concurrency VI, Vol. 7400 of Lecture Notes in Computer Science* (pp. 251–276). Berlin, Heidelberg: Springer.

TCG, Trusted Platform Module Specification - Part 1 Design Principles Version 1.2 Revision 103, TCG (July 2007).

Victor, D. The ashley madison data dump, explained, The New York Times.

CHAPTER 5

Preventing Data Exfiltration: Corporate Patterns and Practices

Shadi Esnaashari*, Ian Welch**, Brenda Chawner†

*School of Engineering and Advanced Technology, Massey University, Auckland, New Zealand; **School of Engineering and Computer Science, Victoria University of Wellington, New Zealand; †School of Information Management, Victoria Business School, Victoria University of Wellington, New Zealand

Open source intelligence (OSINT) relies on adversaries being able to gain access to corporate data. One way that companies can defeat OSINT is to implement policies that prevent intrusion and data exfiltration. Yet, time and time again, companies routinely fail to set and implement realistic data exfiltration and access policies.

In this chapter, we will give an overview of what we have done in our research into the area of data exfiltration by companies, and to what extent they control data access (both logical and physical). We also propose that because censorship[1] is a fast growing area, researchers should investigate it more profoundly. We believe that there are issues with implementing censorship, especially with how the system is working now. Some of these issues we identified from our research include blindly purchasing a blocked list by authorities and implementing censorship based on that, filtering many benign contents as objectionable materials, not treating many similar websites in the same way, not being transparent to the users at the time of blocking, and not being responsible for wrongly implementing censorship.

Our findings show that the system of implementing censorship which is widely used had many problems. Thus, it is our duty to address this problem and ask for support in this area. If we do not address this practice and fight against it, blocking will be implemented more and more and consequently will affect more people accessing their desired material.

In what follows, we summarize our discussion into three sections, namely what is happening around the world, what is happening in New Zealand, and what we can do about it.

---

[1] We uses censorship in a number of senses in this chapter, but primarily, we mean restricting access to certain types of data on the basis of a security *policy*.

WHAT IS HAPPENING AROUND THE WORLD?

Web censorship is a phenomenon across the globe. Governments monitor and censor the Internet. The policy for implementing censorship is similar to a black box for the users. Users do not know about the traffic that has been monitored and classified as censored. Everyday more and more users find the Internet has been under surveillance, controlled, and fragmented.

Users believe that Internet access means accessing whatever Internet offers and not having access to the approved application and content. Saltzer who is one of the key players in the development of the Internet in 1981 mentioned about principles of the End-to-End: "Application specific functions ought to reside in the end hosts of a network" (Saltzer, Reed, & Clark, 1984). This principle is not being considered nowadays when the data is captured through control of either side of the connection. These activities make the open Internet under threat. By implementing censorship, also known as filtering, users are prevented from accessing the desired content considered unsuitable for them by governments.

Motivation of governments to implement censorship and take control of the Internet has increased due to huge use of the Internet. Governments easily shape the Internet based on the norms and culture of the society. Therefore, censorship has become political, social, religious, and child pornographic lookalikes in different countries.

Different countries have different scenarios and degrees of censorship for their citizens. For example, China has the strongest censorship in the world by blocking social websites such as Facebook, Twitter, Tumblr, and political websites related to political leadership, etc. Some countries, such as Saudi Arabia, consider religious morals in implementing censorship.

Iran, as another example, talks about fragmenting the Internet and is going to have "Iranian Internet." It allows the flow of information within the country but not beyond the country.

Filtering the Internet has profit for authorities. Considering the economy, making limitation on Internet is more profitable. Considering social and political aspects, authorities are capable of taking control of the society and preventing it from harmful activities that are against the law and not suitable for the government. To put everything in a nutshell when governments close the Internet, it is much easier to control it.

While some people believe that censorship is not self-regulated and the governments are responsible for implementing the censorship, there are others who believe that censorship is not a great idea and it affects the users' needs and trust. People who oppose censorship believe that there are different issues with the practice of blocking. For example, people will not be able to access their desired material which has an effect on trust in the society, its knowledge, and democracy.

Censorship regarding films, books, and games is clear and transparent for the users but not for the websites and services. This lack of transparency will leave people confused as to whether the website is blocked or offline. The other impact of lack of transparency in implementing censorship is that benign content is sometimes blocked and classified as offensive content by authorities. If censorship is transparent the benign websites that are considered offensive will be clarified and the beneficial content will not be restricted for people. Moreover, secretly implementing the censorship would make citizens lose trust in governments.

The idea of filtering comforts parents and authorities that their children or staffs are prevented from accessing the unwanted content. This may give a false sense of security to parents which is not appealing. The government, Internet Service Providers, and families are responsible to teach parents how to prevent their children from accessing inappropriate content. It is also beneficial if parents can teach their children to be responsible for their safety instead of waiting for their parents to provide safety for them. Most of the people in general and children in particular access the Internet through their phones which increases the concern of their families.

Censorship or filtering is an offense to democracy. It is similar to the government holding the users' hands to prevent them from doing things that, it thinks, can offend them. The problem is that government thinks that by censoring websites they could prevent users from accessing the inappropriate content. This is true for just a portion of the society, as there are many ways for the motivated people to bypass censorship.

WHAT IS HAPPENING IN NEW ZEALAND?

New Zealand is a digital country since Internet is used in four out of five New Zealand homes (Household access to the Internet, 2013). In terms of Internet access, New Zealand is one of the countries with the highest Internet access rate. There are different reasons that have led the number of Internet users to increase such as a decrease in the price of broadband, mobile access, ADSL, and motivation for applying for jobs online, etc. More than 93% of the Internet in New Zealand is provided by Internet Service Providers (ISPs) such as TelestraClear, Telecom, and Vodafone. These Internet Service Providers have implemented filtering in conjunction with Department of Internal Affairs (DIA).

DIA states that the URLs that are mostly related to child abuse materials are restricted and no one knows exactly what they have blocked. Once the government starts blocking, they can start to filter websites that are not convenient for them. All requests will be routed to the government servers. The user's request will be compared to the blocked list. If it is matched with their black list, the request will be denied. This blocked list is revised by staff each month to have an updated blocked list every time (Wikileaks, 2013).

In Wikileaks (2013), it is published that Child Exploitation Filtering System costs $150,000 which is given freely to the ISPs to block around 7000 objectionable sites. It is also published that the number of blocked websites is five times more than the ones in the UK list and twice as much as those in Australia. It is in contrast to what is heard from the public and published by OpenNet Initiative (ONI) that censorship in Australia is more than it is in New Zealand. Techliberty (2013) announced, "The Government has no Mandate to Filter the Internet." They mentioned that censorship was not covered by law and still no laws were passed in the Parliament. They believe that implementing censorship to mass websites is against the Bill of Rights.

Even if censorship is legitimate, implementing it secretly does not give good sense to people. As a response to this, DIA claims that publishing list of websites is a pointer to the crime and DIA uses its power not to publish it. Starting to implement censorship gives power to governments to implement more censorship whenever and whatever they like.

A survey commissioned by InternetNZ (2013) about public thoughts about the government's Internet filter has shown interesting results about this study. Only 9% of the people knew whether or not their ISP used government filter. The ISPs that provide more than 90% of the NZ Internet market use government's censorship program. Only 23% of the people wanted the government to filter their Internet connection. It is also worth mentioning that authorities know that even implementing censorship is not effective and motivated people will access the desired content. Given that, what is the reason for breaching the privacy and freedom of the citizens? Prior to this action, the citizens cannot trust the government.

DIA has clarified that censorship has been applied to child pornography sites. The question remains why they do not consider other ways such as requesting the servers hosting these sorts of websites to delete them. Child pornography is illegal in almost all countries. Thus, it is a better idea to fight against this issue globally by removing it from Internet and not implementing censorship on what brings dishonesty for governments. Even if the government believes that child pornography is blocked, it is still there. There are lots of websites with the same content.

SPECIFYING THE PROBLEM

There are problems with the level of filtering such as:

1. In New Zealand censorship is applied secretly and is not transparent for people. One of the effects of implementing censorship secretly is that some of the websites are incorrectly blocked. For example, German couples could not access a political site in Germany through Te Papa Museum free WiFi because it was categorized as Japan's porn websites (Te Papa Museum, 2013).
2. It is mentioned that only child abuse websites are blocked which is not true and there are more websites and services that are blocked. Based on the work we have done, depending on the organizations, there are other categories of websites and services that are blocked as well.
3. If filtering is applied for children in order to keep them safe on the Internet, it is hard for adults to bypass it. At the same time, those who were the target of censorship could bypass it.
4. If organizations are against child pornography, they should fight against this issue globally not breaching privacy of people.
5. Censorship or filtering operates as an offense to democracy. It is similar to the government holding the users' hands to prevent them from doing things that, it thinks, can offend them. The problem is that government thinks by censoring websites, they could prevent users from accessing the inappropriate content. This is true for just a portion of the society, as there are many ways for the motivated people to bypass censorship.
6. Authorities who implement censorship are not responsive. Even the authorities mention that users should inform in case things are wrongly blocked, they are not easy to convince.

PROBLEMS ARISING BY IMPLEMENTING CENSORSHIP

There are different problems that arise in the society by implementing censorship.

First, implementing censorship affects the economy of the businesses because customers cannot get the direction or information from the website. Second, implementing censorship will give good sense of safety to parents that their children are safe on the Internet but actually the content is still there. Third, filtering will affect the knowledge of the society. For example, filtering sexual material will prevent young people from accessing the healthy information, making young people blind in terms of their future safety. The other effect is the performance of the Internet. Since all the traffic needs to go through DIA, it may cause a performance issue and will make a single point of failure. Fifth, distrust will come to the society, and citizens of the country will not trust the government as they know they are censoring more than child pornography websites.

SO, WHAT SHOULD BE DONE?

We were motivated to conduct this study to find out about the scale of the problem to find the blocked websites and services in order to make transparency for people. It is clear that blocking has been applied to websites other than child abuse, but finding all the blocked content has not been easy. Although the list of blocked websites is not published by DIA, the users of the Internet know about the probability of censoring some websites. Child abuse websites are blocked by government but different sites and services are blocked at different times by ISPs and organizations. All the filtering affects principles of human rights organizations. But because Internet filtering is so widespread and supported by strong opposition, it is so hard to debate.

Finding a unique and reliable way of finding censorship was not easy. We had limitation in terms of using different ports as most of the desired ports for us were blocked in different organizations. Therefore, we had to make lots of changes in our implemented tool for each organization. Also due to the importance of censorship subject, we had to use manual analyses as well as automatic ones.

Our experience in places such as organization 1, organization 2, organization 3, organization 4, organization 5, organization 6, organization 7, and organization 8 showed how these places treated their WiFi users differently and how they restricted the use of Internet to specific traffic and websites through specific ports.

We tried to access a variety of URLs from different categorizations using our implemented tool to find out about the prevalence of censorship in different organizations. It was thought that there might not be much content blocking in organizations in New Zealand, but there were of course ports and services that were blocked. Our results showed that not only lots of ports and services had been blocked but also there were lots of URLs from each category which had been blocked.

For example, in a short distance from organization 5, organization 1 offers free Internet to their customers but with more restrictions in accessing the websites and using ports. Organization 1 restricts access to most services by blocking ports such as FTP, SSH, SMTP, DNS, POP3, RPC, NetBIOS, IMAP, SNMP, SMB, and MTP/SSL. In organization 1 we also tested the free WiFi with our first round of URLs. Out of 180 URLs, 114 URLs were censored. These include categories from proxy, gambling, malicious sources, adults, file sharing, anonymizer websites, racism, drug, religions, and games. If they were eager not to allow access to objectionable material, it was possible for users to access it through their mobile phones or other free WiFis close to them.

In contrast, organization 5 provides open access to all the services. Almost all the tested URLs were also open access, except four URLs.

In organization 4 most of the ports we tested were open to use, except for DNS (port 53), RPC (port 135), NetBIOS (port 139), and SNMP (port 161). These ports were expected to be blocked as they were not used generally in local networks. But it was interesting how organization 4 used different ways of implementing censorship for different contents. For example, for some of the websites from jokes and adult entertainment category they were clear by providing transparent blocked messages. For some of the websites from Peer-to-Peer (P2P) or adult entertainments category, they sent an error message.

The problem was that a consistent pattern had not been used for all blockings. Organization 4 was one of the organizations with high number of content blocking. At organization 3 access to ports SMB (port 445), SMTP (port 25), DNS (port 53), RPC (port 135), and NetBIOS (port 139) was blocked. We expected to have these port blockings because of security purposes. But it is interesting how organization 3 did over-blocking by implementing benign websites as offensive ones and how they categorized these blocked websites wrongly. For example, organization 3 blocked access to some online shops selling children's toys and they categorized it under "Pornography; Extreme." Our experiment in organization 3 identified that the URLs had been blocked from different categories such as proxy, gambling, malicious sources, adults, file sharing, anonymizer, racism, and drug.

In organization 6, all the services we test were open, except Transmission control protocol (TCP) access to remote SMTP server's port 25 that was prohibited. With this blocking it was not possible to send email via SMTP. This sort of blocking was very common because this port could be used by hackers for generating spam.

In terms of content blocking, organization 6 blocked some of the content from adult entertainment by redirecting them to administrator's desired content.

Organization 2 provided access to all services. They had a couple of blockings that were not transparent for users. In their strategy, they redirected the request for objectionable content from adult entertainment to administrator's desired content.

Organization 8 provided access to all services. In terms of content blocking they redirected the request to desired content of authorities. In some cases, a transparent error message was shown to the users.

Organization 7 was extreme in terms of service blocking. Ports 25, 53, 80, 110, 143, 443, and 993 were open and all others were closed. In terms of content blocking they blocked content from pornography and P2P websites.

Our interview with organization 1 and organization 3 showed that, for example, organization 1 applied blocking due to two important reasons: security and network efficiency. Organization 1 also mentioned that this was all about the policy and history of the organization and its loyalty to the organizations it was registered with.

Organization 3 mentioned that their organization was a great brand and they wanted to keep the great brand of their organization and its family environment. But they had less information regarding their blocking system. For example, they did know that they had blocking from alcohol, drug, and gambling websites.

We also obtained interesting feedback from organization 2. The IT professionals from this organization pointed out that they were not responsible for their free WiFi. It is interesting that they offered free WiFi but they were not responsible for that. It shows how blindly they implemented the system based on what they purchased.

The variety of the results of what was blocked showed that ISPs and blocking software did not have a set of agreed approaches for implementing blockings. More open discussion about what it is appropriate to block and what should be available is needed.

We would like to argue that implementing censorship at a national level is not a good idea and implementing censorship by individuals is a better decision. There is another solution to identify adults from young children. Then, we can ask adults whether or not they want censorship and give them all the information about censorship, how they implement it, and what the categorization is. We also need to teach them how to report if the censorship is incorrectly applied.

It is also possible that parents who need to implement the blocking for their children get information through their ISPs when they subscribe for the services. This solution will be helpful for children who need safety on the Internet.

It has to be mentioned to the authorities and parents who like to prevent users and children from watching these objectionable materials in their sites that at the same time there are different sources of getting Internet for people. Therefore, if one of these free WiFis blocks some websites, the users still have access to 3G. So free Internet Service Providers cannot worry about downloading banned materials. And, it is not their responsibility to control their Internet usage. Therefore, blocking content could not be effective when people access different sources to get information. It is, then, better to implement blocking on individual computers and cellphone devices through parents.

Educating people is very important. Government could educate parents how to keep their children safe on the Internet. At the same time government and parents can teach children how to keep themselves safe and not wait for their parents and government to keep them safe in the Internet.

Thus, we believe we could consider other solutions as suggested here:

1. We should not apply blocking at national level, and let individuals implement blocking.
2. We should educate children about how to be safe on the Internet.

3. We should fight against the issue of child pornography globally.
4. We should be transparent for the users by providing the list of blockings in terms of content and services.
5. We should be helpful with providing reasons for blockings.
6. We should be more cautious in choosing the software for implementing blocking.
7. We should not rely on the available blocked lists and being more cautious on categorizing blocked content.

SUMMARY

This chapter discussed the prevalence of Internet blocking around the world and particularly in New Zealand. We presented the problems of implementing central censorship and the issues raised by these problems. We emphasized that nobody knew what was happening on the Internet and what would happen to the Internet in the future. There was a need for a system to collect, analyze, provide visibility to manage the Internet better. We mentioned that censoring free movies and music prevented illegal downloading of files which were against the copyright agreement. Censoring child pornography kept children safe. But when it came to censoring adults' jokes, and political websites, it was annoying for people. We also discussed that there was a regulation in adults and circumvention tools. It was not ethical to restrict adult, entertainment and social networks for people.

References

Euthanasia activist wants New Zealand website blacklist released—wikileaks. (2013). https://wikileaks.org/wiki/Euthanasia_activist_wants_New_Zealand_website_blacklist_released Accessed 01.07.13.

Household access to the Internet—statistics New Zealand. http://www.stats.govt.nz/browse_for_stats/people_and_communities/households/household-access-to-the-internet.aspx Accessed 01.07.13.

Saltzer, J. H., Reed, D. P., & Clark, D. D. (1984). End-to-end arguments in system design. *ACM Transactions on Computer Systems*, 2(4), 277–288.

Survey on internet filtering, internetnz. https://internetnz.net.nz/news/blog/2012/Survey-Internet-Filtering Accessed 08.08.13.

Te papa does not know why it is censoring the Internet, tech liberty nz. http://techliberty.org.nz/te-papa-internet-censorship/ Accessed 02.06.13.

Why we oppose internet filtering, tech liberty nz. http://techliberty.org.nz/why-we-oppose-internet-filtering/ Accessed 08.07.13.

CHAPTER 6

Gathering Intelligence on High-Risk Advertising and Film Piracy: A Study of the Digital Underground

Seung Jun Lee, Paul A. Watters

School of Engineering & Advanced Technology, Massey University, New Zealand

INTRODUCTION

In recent years, cyber security threats have increase exponentially, putting corporate information technology (IT) budgets under severe strain, as managers try and work out the best way to organize and fund defences against potential cyberattacks. These are often centered around web and cloud services (Tran, Watters, & Hitchens, 2005).

The research literature suggests that the problem will endure: Shane and Hunker (2013) implied from wide perspective that the overall size and elaboration of cybercrime will continue to increase constantly. Furthermore, Shane and Hunker (2013) indicated the fact that every few months or even every couple of weeks appears to continually produce up-to-date news of the worst-ever cybercrimes or cyber theft activities that may be still occurring as huge concerns around the globe. As a typical example of such serious cyber theft incidents from Arthur (2011) (as cited in Shane and Hunker (2013)) also implied that the seriousness of the cyber theft or cybercrime activity can certainly be realized through the consecutive cyber thefts incident of more than 100,000,000 PlayStation user confidential accounts from Sony which has significantly occurred in April 2011. Therefore, this particular incident provides a meaningful implication to both the public and industries that it is important for them to consistently maintain the robust cybersecurity infrastructure and ensure the effective protection countermeasures for sustaining particularly their intellectual properties and copyright contents against various types of potential cybercrime activities or threats such as illegal film and music contents piracy, high-risk online advertising and links to piracy and banking malware, etc.

However, it is a current fact that the sustainability of ensuring or protecting their valuable intellectual properties/contents against potential cyber threats or privacy is primarily associated with the effective establishment of the

89

optimized security countermeasures or solutions that may often lead the relevant organizations or rightsholders into generating a large amount of budgets for constructing the optimized security countermeasures efficiently.

Furthermore, people often ask, why is going to the cinema so expensive? Or why do bank charge such expensive bank fees for their accounts? The answer, partly, is that the security measures that are put in place are very expensive.

As illustrated in Figure 6.1, this particular numerical data shows that Google in July 2015 alone received very surprisingly 54,810,885 notifications to remove or eliminate items from the search index that infringe copyright. Assuming that the cost of sending a single notification in regard to copyright-violated contents is approximately between $10 and $100, this means that many hundreds of millions or even billions of dollars are immensely spent on security measures. Imagine if this money could be spent elsewhere in the industry. For instance, these kinds of possible scenarios can be appeared by giving monetary grants to young film makers or funding emerging artists to record their first CD, etc.

As illustrated in Figure 6.2, this particular trend graph from the recent Google Transparency Report (2015) shows about the total number of URLs requested to be removed from search per week. According to Google Transparency Report (2015), this trend graph indicated that the following six enormous measurements of URLs requested by copyright owners and reporting organizations were observed as follows based on the several timeframes:

1. On week of July 18 in 2011, it was measured as 129,822 URLs in total.
2. On week of July 23 in 2012, it was measured as 1,669,841 URLs in total.
3. On week of July 29 in 2013, it was measured as 4,536,644 URLs in total.
4. On week of August 04 in 2014, it was measured as 6,957,143 URLs in total.
5. On week of July 27 in 2015, it was measured as 12,773,487 URLs in total.
6. On week of August 03 in 2015, it was measured as 12,241,970 URLs in total.

Copyright removal requests received for search in the past month

54,810,885 URLs requested to be removed

81,161 Specified domains

5,987 Copyright owners

2,671 Reporting organizations

FIGURE 6.1

A numerical information about the most recent copyright removal requests received for search in the past month as of August 15, 2015. *(Source from: Google Transparency Report (2015))*

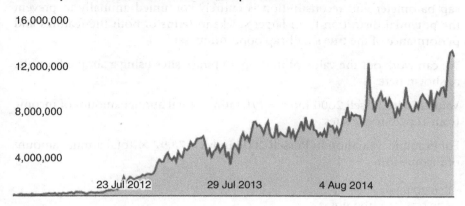

FIGURE 6.2
A trend graph showing URLs requested to be removed from search per week as of August 15, 2015.
(Source from: Google Transparency Report (2015))

As illustrated in Figure 6.2, one of the most significant findings from this trend graph clearly implied that there is an enormously increasing trend in regard to URLs requested by both copyright owners and reporting organizations to be removed from the week of July 18, 2011 to week of August 03, 2015. Furthermore, Figure 6.2 shows that the highest value of URLs requested to be removed was measured particularly on week of July 27, 2015 and very surprisingly 12,773,487 URLs in total were appeared to be removed during this particular timeframe (i.e., week of July 27, 2015). Most recently, Figure 6.2 shows that 12,241,970 URLs in total were measured during the week of August 03, 2015.

The question of whether security budgets are being effective is therefore critical to the future success of creative industries, as is the case for justifying expenditure on countermeasures in any security environment. To make budgets effective, security managers need to assess the risk posed by different threats. In the case of film piracy, this can be done by looking at the value of the sites that are responsible for enabling piracy. We can use a standard business valuation methodology—such as the price/earnings (P/E) ratio—to do this.

According to Russell Indexes (2015), it is primarily defined that "The Russell 2000 Index is designed to calculate the performance of the selected small-cap stock market index or segment in accordance with the U.S. equity universe. The Russell 2000 Index can be described as a subset of the Russell 3000 Index, which accounts for about 10% of the market capitalization of the index. It is primarily consisted of about 2000 shares of the small securities on the basis of a mixture of both present index membership and their stock market cap.

The Russell 2000 is established to offer a broad, unbiased and impartial small-cap barometer and reconstitution is entirely continued annually to prevent the potential distortion from larger stocks in terms of both the features and performance of the true small-cap opportunity set."

We can work out the value of the Top 20 piracy sites using a simple formula, as shown here:

Valuation in Russell 2000 Index = P/E ratio × Total annual amount of income from Top 20 rogue sites

For example, valuation in Russell 2000 Index = 78.97 × Total annual amount of income from

Top 20 rogue sites
$$= 78.97 \times \$63,409,908.24$$
$$= \$5,007,480,453.71$$

Thus, the size of the threat is significant—film piracy is more than a $5 billion enormous industry!

In this chapter, the question of whether countermeasures against piracy are effective, is essentially addressed. In particular, the assumption that the risk posed by piracy or rogue websites is uniform, is questioned. Indeed, while the evidence suggests that the number of piracy websites is continually growing, and that rightsholders continue to issue numerous complaints, no-one has examined before whether these websites in fact attract any users at all. If a profile can be developed by identifying the key attributes of commercially successful piracy or rogue websites, this could be used in the future to classify new piracy websites into the categories of successful versus unsuccessful sites, and informed decisions about budget expenditure could be made on a rational basis.

ADVERTISING AND RISK

This particular section introduces about the following five related contents comprehensively in regard to this chapter:

1. The Digital Millennium Copyright Act (DMCA)
2. Chilling Effects Database
3. Google Transparency Report (i.e., Copyright removal requests from Google index)
4. Mainstream advertising will be basically discussed and how piracy is funded or supported.
5. High-risk advertising will be basically discussed and their links to piracy websites will also be introduced briefly in this particular chapter.

THE DIGITAL MILLENNIUM COPYRIGHT ACT (DMCA)

This particular section describes briefly about the DMCA as follows.

Google Transparency Report (2015) highlighted that the DMCA is a copyright law from the United States that is primarily designed to deviate from monetary liability for copyright infringement or violation in the online service or business provider such as Google. According to Wikipedia (2015a, 2015b), the beginning of the DMCA has been officially enacted since on October 28, 1998 in the United States. In the DMCA, Google Transparency Report (2015) also indicated that relevant online operators or service providers have the responsibilities to remove material that is allegedly a copyright infringing claims or violated contents immediately. Therefore, Google Transparency Report (2015) emphasized that one of the core requirements in the DMCA is that online service providers such as Google should respond immediately by removing these copyright violated materials or claims (i.e., or by disabling access to these copyright-violated contents) in relation to safe harbor provisions if certain requests are received or reported that essentially satisfies the requirements of the DMCA. Furthermore, Google Transparency Report (2015) confirmed that Google complies faithfully with respect to the requirements of the DMCA in regard to responding to the removal requests of copyright for the purpose of providing more assurance and transparency particularly for supporting their users.

CHILLING EFFECTS DATABASE

This particular section describes briefly about chilling effects database as follows.

Chilling Effects (2015) indicated that Chilling Effects is a distinct collaboration from the Electronic Frontier Foundation and the following various law school clinics based in the United States such as George Washington School of Law, Berkeley, Stanford, and Harvard. According to Chilling Effects (2015), it is primarily a research-based project from the foundation of the Berkman Center for Internet and Society in regard to stopping and desisting about online contents. Chilling Effects (2015) also indicated that the main feature of Chilling Effects is to collect complaints and also analyze about various types of online activities such as removing or deleting content online. According to Chilling Effects (2015), the aim of this particular effect is largely classified into the following three goals: (1) to educate the communities or public, (2) to promote effective research about various types of complaints received particularly on the deletion request from service providers or online publishers, and (3) to provide the highest transparency as possible.

Furthermore, Google Transparency Report (2015) highlighted that in place of removed content or material, Google appeared to connect their distinct search results with the requests suggested and posted by Chilling Effects when Google is able to implement it within legitimate scope.

GOOGLE TRANSPARENCY REPORT

This particular section describes about Google transparency report as follows.

Google Transparency Report (2015) suggested that Google currently provides the following seven extensive transparency reports in terms of these main aspects as follows:

1. Google provides a detailed transparency report about various requests for removing content from government.
2. Google provides detailed transparency report about government various requests to hand over some information such as user data and account information about Google users.
3. Google also provides detailed transparency information on either demands or requests by copyright holders upon their request to remove search results.
4. Google provides detailed transparency report about overall information about Google product traffic such as traffic patterns since 2008 and the availability regarding Google products around the globe in the real-time based, etc.
5. Google provides detailed transparency report about comprehensive statistics based on weekly detection from the number of malware websites including phishing websites. Detailed Google transparency report about which networks basically host or contain malware websites is also provided in terms of overall safe browsing aspects from Google.
6. Detailed Google transparency report on the overall content/traffic volume of email exchange between other service providers and Gmail is provided by Google to ensure the protection against snooping over the Internet. According to Google Transparency Report (2015), this particular Google transparency report also provides detailed information through the optimized encryption method of email in transit.
7. Google also provides a detailed transparency report about statistics on European privacy requests for removing content from search results through the implementation of Google's distinct data protection removal process in Europe.

Furthermore, Google Transparency Report (2015) showed that the following main significant contents can be described as follows in regard to requests to remove content perspectives:

- Copyright owners and their representative organizations regularly send requests to Google to remove content from search results that may contain a high possibility of connecting particular link to material or contents that is allegedly violated copyrights. Furthermore, Google Transparency Report (2015) indicated that each request basically names particular URLs to be deleted and then Google provides a list of the domain parts of the requested URLs for processing content removal under a specifically designated domain.

- Google Transparency Report (2015) also indicated that around the globe, there are currently a large number of requests received from various government agencies to Google in regard to requesting content or information removal from various Google-related products. This particular transparency report from Google Transparency Report (2015) indicated that the basic reviews from these various government agencies to remove content is first determined by Google carefully to decide and ensure whether the corresponding contents should be deserved to remove because of the violation of a law/copyrights or relevant policies from Google before any action is undertaken.

As illustrated in Figure 6.3, one of the most significant findings from this trend graph clearly implied that there is an enormously increasing trend between December 2011 and December 2012 in relation to the requests from government agencies around the world to remove content. During the timeframe between December 2012 and June 2013, Figure 6.3 also shows that an immensely

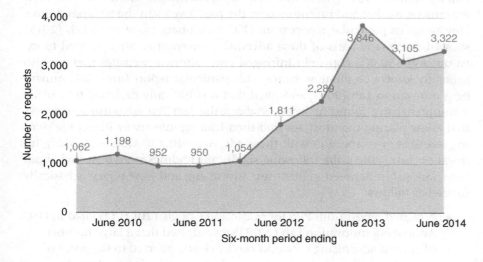

FIGURE 6.3

A trend graph showing the total removal requests received from Google in regard to government requests around the world to remove content since 2009. *(Source from: Google Transparency Report (2015))*

increasing trend was observed in regard to government requests around the globe to remove content due to the violation of a relevant copyright law or product policies as determined by Google.

The significant research process of this chapter is particularly focused on the essential data collection from Top 20 Specified Domains within the following main section – due to copyright, Requests to remove content in Google Transparency Report (2015). Based on data from this Top 20 Specified Domains, the research methodology has been examined and implemented to generate the significant results by utilizing k-means cluster analysis, to develop approach to grouping together which presents the highest revenue risk to rightsholders or copyright owners based on Top 20 most complained rogue websites (i.e., Specified Domains from Google Transparency Report (2015)). For more detailed information, this particular process to obtain the significant findings generated in the research will be discussed in Chapter 3 – Research Methodology section.

MAINSTREAM ADVERTISING AND HOW PIRACY IS FUNDED

This particular section describes about mainstream advertising and how piracy is funded.

An advertising transparency report from University of Southern California (USC) Annenberg Innovation Lab (2013) in January 2013 indicated the fact that the new advertising networks currently seem to show enormous growth of advertising market and inventory over the past 5 years in the wideband time. However, this particular report from USC Annenberg Innovation Lab (2013) showed that many parts of these advertising inventories are appeared to exist on over 150,000 copyright infringed entertainment websites that are also generally known as pirate websites. This particular report from USC Annenberg Innovation Lab (2013) indicated that it is basically designed to provide a comprehensive monthly overview about the Top Ten advertising networks that allow placing the most ads and then leading into many illegal file sharing websites in connection with these ads. According to USC Annenberg Innovation Lab (2013), the following significant findings were observed about the relationship between mainstream advertising and how piracy is basically funded as follows:

- A related report from PRS for Music and Google (2012) (as cited in USC Annenberg Innovation Lab (2013)) investigated that a large number of current advertising networks can be clearly affected to support the various activities of pirate websites which are mainly based on the category of movie and music. This report from PRS for Music and Google (2012) indicated that 86% of the peer-to-peer (P2P) search sites with illicit file sharing content or distributed material are appeared to be funded financially by advertising method. PRS for Music and Google (2012) implied from this significant finding that a variety of main brands are not really realized about the fact that advertising is primarily an important source of funding to support the key activities of piracy-based illicit industries such piracy movie or music sites.

- A related information from Google Transparency Report (2013) (as cited in USC Annenberg Innovation Lab (2013)) indicated that over 2,300,000 particular URLs have been observed particularly from Filestube.com in terms of copyright violation. Hence, this enormous result from Google Transparency Report (2013) implied that these serious activities from illegal file sharing or piracy websites are affected very negatively indeed to the creative industries or community around the globe by maintaining to steal the important intellectual properties or assets such as copyrighted material or unique trademark.

- Furthermore, USC Annenberg Innovation Lab (2013) in February 2013 suggested that it can be clearly seen from the corresponding list based on the discovered infringing websites that particularly many young adults appeared to be seen as having a strong attraction to the following categories such as mobile phone, car, car insurance, and credit rating agencies on the piracy sites. Hence, USC Annenberg Innovation Lab (2013) implied a possible reason behind this meaningful finding that the frequency of advertising occurred in the case of American Express can be seen often on rogue or piracy sites as an example.

HIGH-RISK ADVERTISING AND THEIR LINKS TO PIRACY WEBSITES

This particular section describes about high-risk advertising and their links to piracy websites as follows. This is more important that just looking at whether companies are being wayward, because high-risk advertising exposures to children such as online gambling, scams, pornography, banking malware, etc., in the real life can be very harmful through a number of various real studies or cases that have already been widely examined and implemented in Australia, New Zealand, and Canada as follows.

HIGH-RISK ADVERTISING: CASE STUDIES IN CANADA

This particular chapter from Watters (2015) indicated the fact that although most nations around the globe are currently appeared to maintain an imperfect regulation in terms of censorship, at the same time, the sovereign rights to defend themselves should be recognized. This chapter also suggests that

Table 6.1 Frequency by Ad Category – High-Risk Ads

	Sex Industry	Malware	Download	Gambling	Scams
N	805	1172	106	113	489
Percentage	30.0%	43.6%	3.9%	4.2%	18.2%

Source from: Watters (2015).

Watters (2015) examined and implemented an effective approach about how the unregulated Internet regulation can be seriously influenced to produce significant harms to the users. This chapter showed that in the sample based on Canadian users, the overall 5000 pages of rogue websites have been considered and analyzed on the basis of particularly the most complained TV shows and movies. In this chapter, Watters (2015) also identified that 12,190 advertising items in total were found and 3025 ads in overall were appeared as visible ads category. As a result, this chapter from Watters (2015) highlighted that the following significant findings were found: (1) 89% of these ads above delivered to Canadian users were appeared as high-risk ads and (2) 11% of these ads above delivered to Canadian users were appeared as mainstream ads. As illustrated in Table 6.1, this particular table from Watters (2015) shows the overall frequency distribution for the case of high-risk ads only in terms of ads category such as malware, gambling, scams, download, etc. Table 6.1 shows that the highest risk category from advertising was appeared as malware (i.e., 43.6%) which allows the banner ads to prevalently lead into the other potential high-risk links including malwares. In Table 6.1, the next highest risk ads were appeared from ads based on sex industry (i.e., 30.0%) and also from ads based on scams (i.e., 18.2%) respectively.

HIGH-RISK ADVERTISING: CASE STUDIES IN AUSTRALIA

This particular section describes about high-risk advertising and their links to piracy websites in Australia. As an objective of this particular chapter from Watters (2014), a systematic approach has been evolved to analyze and investigate about online advertising to target on Australians. Watters (2014) suggested that this chapter is particularly concentrated on sites for the Top 500 DMCA complaints in regard to mainly TV and movie content which were supported by Google. As a result, this systematic approach from Watters (2014) highlighted that the following significant findings were found: (1) 99% of these ads were appeared as high-risk ads and only 1% of these ads were appeared as mainstream ads. (2) This chapter showed that in the sample, only one website was found in regard to displaying mainstream ad only; this chapter also showed that the other remaining sites appeared to contain no ads or only ads were

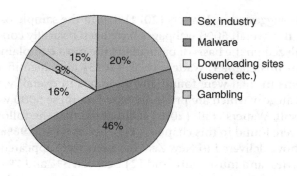

FIGURE 6.4
A pie-chart distribution of high-risk advertisings. *(Source from: Watters (2014))*

displayed by sources generated from high-risk, or mainstream ads were observed as a small number.

As illustrated in Figure 6.4, this particular table from Watters (2014) shows the overall distribution for the case of high-risk ads only in terms of ads category such as malware, gambling, sex industry, and downloading sites. Figure 6.4 shows that the highest risk category from advertising was appeared as malware (i.e., 46.49%) which allows the banner ads to prevalently lead into the other high-risk links including malwares. In Figure 6.4, Watters (2014) indicated that the second highest risk ad was appeared from ads based on sex industry (i.e., 20.18%). Furthermore, Watters (2014) showed that 14.91% category was appeared on the basis of scams that consist of various types (e.g., investment scams). In Figure 6.4, this particular category for scams (i.e., 14.91%) is basically referred to the corresponding light blue allocation where it displays a distribution: 15% from the pie-chart distribution. Moreover, Figure 6.4 shows that in comparison, the prevalence of high-risk advertising from both malware (i.e., 46.49%) and downloading sites (i.e., approximately 16%) in Australia is higher than the prevalence of high-risk ad from both malware (i.e., 43.6%) and downloading (i.e., 3.9%) in Canada, as shown in Table 6.1. On the other hand, Table 6.1 shows that in comparison, the prevalence of high-risk advertising from both sex industry (i.e., 30.00%) and scams (i.e., 18.2%) in Canada is higher than the prevalence of high-risk advertising from both sex industry (i.e., 20.18%) and scams (i.e., 14.91%) in Australia, as shown in Figure 6.4.

HIGH-RISK ADVERTISING: CASE STUDIES IN NEW ZEALAND

This particular section describes about high-risk advertising and their links to piracy websites in New Zealand. According to the previous related chapter from Watters (2014) (as cited in Watters, Watters, & Ziegler (2015)) this chapter used an approach as suggested by Watters (2014) that in the sample based on New Zealand users, the overall 5000 webpages have been basically considered, captured, and analyzed on the basis of particularly the most complained TV shows and movies. In this chapter, Watters et al. (2015) also identified that 5547 advertising items in total were found and 2268 ads in overall were appeared as visible ads category which are primarily based on these 5000 webpages collected. As a result, Watters et al. (2015) highlighted that the following significant findings were found in this chapter: (1) between 93 and 96% of these ads as indicated above delivered to New Zealand users were appeared as high-risk ads for TV, movies, and music only, and (2) between 3% and 7% of these ads delivered to New Zealand users were appeared as mainstream ads.

As illustrated in Table 6.2, this particular table from Watters et al. (2015) shows the overall frequency distribution for the case of high-risk ads only in terms of overall ads category such as malware, gambling, scams, sex industry, and download. Table 6.2 shows that the highest risk category from advertising was appeared as malware (i.e., 57.71%) which allows the banner ads to prevalently lead into the other potential high-risk links including malwares or malicious code. In Table 6.2, Watters et al. (2015) also showed that the next highest risk ads were appeared from ads based on sex industry (i.e., 14.55%) and also from ads based on download (i.e., 11.80%) and followed by ads on scams (i.e., 9.50%) respectively. Furthermore, Table 6.2 shows that in comparison, the prevalence of high-risk advertising from both malware (i.e., 57.71%) and gambling (i.e., 6.43%) in New Zealand is higher than the prevalence of high-risk ads from both malware (i.e., 46.49%) and gambling (i.e., 3.00%) in Australia, as suggested by Watters (2014) and Figure 6.4. On the other hand, Watters (2014) showed that in comparison, the prevalence of high-risk advertising from sex industry (i.e., 20.18%), download (i.e., approximately 16%), and scams (i.e., 14.91%) in Australia is higher than the prevalence of high-risk advertising from sex industry (i.e., 14.55%), download (i.e., 11.80%), and scams (i.e., 9.50%), respectively, in New Zealand as shown in Table 6.2.

According to Watters et al. (2015), this particular chapter already showed that between 93 and 96% of these ads delivered to New Zealand users were appeared or classified as high-risk ads for TV, movies, and music only. Between 3% and 7% of these ads were appeared as mainstream ads in the case of New

Table 6.2 Frequency by Ad Category – High-Risk Ads

	Sex Industry	Malware	Download	Gambling	Scams
N	317	1,257	257	140	207
Percentage	14.55%	57.71%	11.80%	6.43%	9.50%

Source from: Watters et al. (2015).

Zealand. Therefore, this result implies that the allocation of high-risk ads (i.e., between 93 and 96%) delivered to New Zealand users certainly have less high-risk ads compared with the allocation of high-risk ads (i.e., 99%) delivered to Australians as identified by Watters (2014). A recent chapter from Watters (2015) also confirmed that 89% ads primarily delivered to Canadian users were appeared as high-risk ads for the most complained TV shows and movies. This particular chapter from Watters (2015) showed that 11% ads delivered to Canadian users were appeared as mainstream ads. Hence, this result clearly implies that the allocation of high-risk ads (i.e., between 93 and 96%) delivered to New Zealand users as identified by Watters et al. (2015) certainly have more high-risk ads compared with the allocation of high-risk ads (i.e., 89%) delivered to Canadians as identified by Watters (2015).

Watters et al. (2015) also provided an important implication that high-risk ads on malware were appeared as 57.71% across TV and movie sites only. However, Watters et al. (2015) provided a significant finding in this chapter that enormously 96.34% ads for music category only were classified as malware.

RESEARCH CHALLENGES

The challenge is to develop a robust approach to grouping together which present the highest revenue risk to rightsholders or copyright owners. Techniques like cluster analysis can be used effectively to group together sites based on a wide range of attributes, such as income earned per day and estimated worth. The attributes of high earning and low earning websites could also give some useful insights into policy options which might be effective in reducing earnings by pirate websites. For example, are all low-value sites based in a country with effective Internet controls (Watters, McCombie, Layton, & Pieprzyk, 2012)? One of the practical data-mining techniques such as a decision tree or classification tree could help rightsholders to interpret these attributes (Layton, Watters, & Dazeley, 2012).

This chapter demonstrates that we can use a standard business valuation methodology such as the price/earnings (P/E) ratio to enhance the effectiveness of security budgets by assessing the risk posed by different threats or potential cyberattacks from the perspective of security management. This chapter also demonstrates that online advertising is a critical source of supporting the various illicit activities of piracy music or piracy movie sites. In addition, this chapter implies that high-risk advertising exposures to people especially children such as online gambling, scams, sex industry, and banking malware can be very harmful through a number of various real cases in countries such as Canada, Australia, and New Zealand. This chapter also demonstrates that their links to piracy websites may lead into the associated links containing various types of malwares that can be further threats or social issues to both the users and many nations around the globe. Furthermore, this chapter describes about mainstream advertising and also demonstrates regarding how piracy is funded or supported in regard to mainstream advertising environment.

References

Arthur, C. (2011). Sony suffers second data breach with theft of 25m more user details. Guardian UK, May 3, 2011. Retrieved July 27, 2015 from the WorldWideWeb: http://www.guardian.co.uk/technology/blog/2011/may/03/sony-data-breach-online-entertainment

Chilling Effects. (2015). About chilling effects. Chilling Effects Electronic Frontier Foundation. Retrieved July 27, 2015 from the WorldWideWeb: https://chillingeffects.org/pages/aboutGoogle Transparency Report. (2015). Transparency Report (Access to information). Google Inc. Retrieved July 27, 2015 from the WorldWideWeb: https://www.google.com/transparencyreport/?hl=en

Layton, R., Watters, P., & Dazeley, R. (2012). Recentred local profiles for authorship attribution. *Natural Language Engineering, 18*(03), 293–312.

Russell Indexes. (2015). Russell 2000 Index. Russell Investments. Retrieved July 27, 2015 from the WorldWideWeb: http://www.russell.com/indexes/americas/indexes/fact-sheet.page?ic=US2000

Shane, P. M., & Hunker, J. A. (2013). *Cybersecurity: Shared risks, shared responsibilities.* Durham, NC: Carolina Academic Press.

Tran, H., Watters, P., & Hitchens, M. (2005, July). Trust and authorization in the grid: a recommendation model. In *Proceedings IEEE international conference on pervasive services (ICPS'05)* (pp. 433–436).

USC Annenberg Innovation Lab. (2013). USC Annenberg Lab Ad Transparency Report (January 2013). USC Annenberg Innovation Lab. Retrieved July 27, 2015 from the WorldWideWeb: http://www.annenberglab.com/sites/default/files/uploads/USCAnnenbergLab_AdReport_Jan2013.pdf

Watters, P. (2015). Censorship is futile possible but difficult: a chapter in algorithmic ethnography. *First Monday, 20*(1), .

Watters, P., Watters, M. F., & Ziegler, J. (2015, January). Maximising eyeballs but facilitating cybercrime? Ethical challenges for online advertising in New Zealand. In *IEEE 2015 48th Hawaii international conference on system sciences (HICSS)* (pp. 1742–1749).

Watters, P. A. (2014). A systematic approach to measuring advertising transparency online: An Australian case chapter. In *Proceedings of the second Australasian web conference*, Vol. 155 (pp. 59–67). Australian Computer Society, Inc.

Watters, P. A., McCombie, S., Layton, R., & Pieprzyk, J. (2012). Characterising and predicting cyber attacks using the Cyber Attacker Model Profile (CAMP). *Journal of Money Laundering Control, 15*(4), 430–441.

Wikipedia. (2015). Chilling Effects. Wikimedia Foundation, Inc. Retrieved July 27, 2015 from the WorldWideWeb: https://en.wikipedia.org/wiki/Chilling_Effects

Wikipedia. (2015). Digital Millennium Copyright Act. Wikimedia Foundation, Inc. Retrieved July 27, 2015 from the WorldWideWeb: https://en.wikipedia.org/wiki/Digital_Millennium_Copyright_Act

CHAPTER 7

Graph Creation and Analysis for Linking Actors: Application to Social Data

Charles Perez, Rony Germon
PSB Paris School of Business, Chair Digital Data Design

I read somewhere that everybody on this planet is separated by only six other people. Six degrees of separation. Between us and everybody else on this planet. The president of the United States. A gondolier in Venice. Fill in the names. I find that A) tremendously comforting that we're so close and B) like Chinese water torture that we're so close. Because you have to find the right six people to make the connection. It's not just big names. It's anyone. A native in a rain forest. A Tierra del Fuegan. An Eskimo. I am bound to everyone on this planet by a trail of six people. It's a profound thought.

John Guare, Six Degrees of Separation, 1990

INTRODUCTION

The world is evolving and increasingly getting more and more complex. From a technological perspective, this is expressed by the amount of generated data, for example with personalized services provided to Internet users. The challenge of modeling such complexity for gathering information requires appropriate models and algorithms to work with. One of the most natural ways to represent our world is to consider objects and their interactions and communication/exchange. Internet, humans, enterprises, proteins are all related to this paradigm of interactions. An enterprise, a society or a social network takes roots in relationships between employees, individuals (Easley, 2010). Genes, proteins are getting efficient in the way they interact together through chemical exchanges. The secrets of our brain may be related to the challenge of modeling the interactions between neural cells.

The graph theory provides a model for analyzing entities and the relationships between them. In this chapter, we introduce key concepts of graph theory and more precisely of social network analysis. From graph creation through entity disambiguation, relationships identification, and weighting to the graph analysis, we present here a set of metrics and tools that can contribute to the information gathering. In particular, a case study of this chapter presents how to use social media to gather intelligence. We highlight the graph creation and analysis using a Twitter dataset of approximately 100,000 tweets related to open source intelligence from the January 26, 2015 to the April 26, 2015.

THE SOCIAL NETWORK MODEL

A Brief History of Graphs and Social Networks

Social network analysis is at the intersection of multiple fields. Historically, it is tightly related to sociology, psychology, mathematics, anthropology, and network science.

The mathematician Leonard Euler introduced the concept of graphs in 1741. He modeled the city of Konigsberg (currently Kaliningrad, Russia) as a graph (whose bridges were edges and nodes were areas of land) and proved that there was no possible path to cross all of the seven bridges of the city without crossing one at least twice (Euler, 1741). Figure 7.1 illustrates the model proposed by L. Euler: red lines represent bridges and gray areas represent lands. The problem was solved by observing the parity of the number of links connected to each node. For a path crossing all bridges to exist, L. Euler observed that nodes with an odd number of links must be either starting or ending point of the path. Thus, number of nodes with an odd number of links must not exceed two. The graph presented in Figure 7.1 does not match this condition proving that there was no possible path. This problem, which remained unsolved for many years, appears to be easy when applying the graph model. With this work, L. Euler introduced the mathematical foundations of network science.

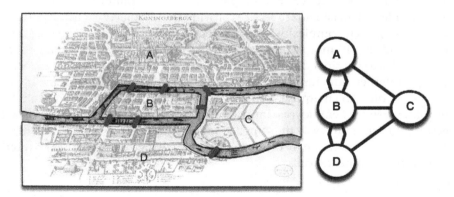

FIGURE 7.1

The old city map of Konigsberg and the graph proposed by Euler to model the city. We observe the seven bridges (red on the left and represented by links on the right) and four pieces of land (gray areas on the left represented by nodes on the right).

Jacob Levi Moreno, the founder of *sociometry* in the 1930s, proposed to model social relationships as a *sociogram*. Moreno (1934) defined the sociogram as a process to visualize the position of each individual within a given group, as well as the interrelation of all other individuals. He applied such a technique for many different groups such as baby groups, public school and high school students. The process of building a sociogram for a group of students was based on questionnaires. It was often asked to the students to mention the classmates they would prefer for "sitting next to" or "staying in the same class." A possible way to build the sociogram from the questionnaire would be based on the mutual mentions. Such work allowed identifying students who were unchosen, mutual pairs, triangles, or even very often mentioned such as stars. These observations lead J. L. Moreno to focus a part of his work on phenomena such as leadership, isolation, rejection, reciprocity, and popularity.

Georg Simmel is known as the first sociologist to refer to structural approach for social interactions. His famous citation "Society arises from the individuals and the individual arises out of association" clearly highlights this perspective (Simmel, 1955). G. Simmel supported the idea that the nature of relationships may be more important than the group itself when analyzing many human behaviors that is the core of social network analysis.

John Barnes, a famous anthropologist, is often identified as the first author to refer to the concept of social network in the famous article "Class and Committees in a Norwegian Island Parish" (Barnes, 1954). In this article, J. Barnes studied the social relations between members of Bremnes (a Parish in Western Norway) and used the following words for describing the situation he observed: "Each person is, as it were, in touch with a number of other people, some of whom are directly in touch with each other and some of whom are not. Similarly each person has a number of friends, and these friends have their own friends; some of any one person's friends know each other, others do not. I find it convenient to talk of a social field of this kind as a network. The image I have is of a set of points some of which are joined by lines. The points of the image are people, or sometimes groups, and the lines indicate which people interact with each other." These last words are often referred to as the first definition of social networks.

The psychologist Stanley Milgram has made a very famous and controversial contribution to social network analysis with an article on small-worlds (Milgram, 1967). S. Milgram conducted an experiment to capture the number of intermediates between any people in the United States. For this purpose, he randomly picked couples of American citizens (one being a source and one being a target). In the experiment, the source must transmit a letter to the target under certain conditions. If the source knows the target, then it can send the mail directly to the target and the chain is over. If the source does not know personally the target, he must send the letter to one of his friends who might be the most likely to know the target personally. If the source has no idea of such an individual, then it could use a geographical criterion for sending the letter to the right person. S. Milgram measured the average number of hops that were required (on a set of 64 letters that reached their destination) to finally obtain the famous *six degrees of separations*.

Harrison White (White, 1976) has made an important improvement in the analysis of social networks applying matrix algebra and clustering techniques. This contribution allowed bypassing the limitations of manual investigations using a more sophisticated and automatic approach of analysis.

In 1973, Mark Granovetter in "The strength of weak ties" makes a first conceptual bridge between micro and macrolevels of sociological theory. M. Granovetter shows how small-scale interactions (strength of interpersonal ties) influence and impact on large-scale patterns such as diffusion, social mobility, social cohesion, etc. (Granovetter, 1973).

Although relationships have always existed between humans and entities in general, the revolution of information technology in the early 1990s has permitted keeping tracks of many of those relationships. The storage of users' everyday online activities by social networks, smartphones, laptops, sensors, and, more globally, through the Internet made available many open sources of open data that provide a large field of application for analysis: the digital. For this reason, the field of network science and social network analysis have known a growing interest and an increasing number of contributions during the last decade (Scott, 2000). In 2014, the first *Encyclopedia of Social Network Analysis and Mining* (ESNAM) has been published giving an overview of the domain (Alhajj & Rokne, 2014).

Conceptual Framework

A graph is commonly defined by the two following core elements: nodes (or entities, items) and edges (or relationships, ties, connections). A graph is formally denoted $G(N, E)$, where N represents the set of nodes, and E the set of edges. The set of nodes may represent web pages, user profiles, humans; the set of edges illustrates relationships between these entities, such as hyperlinks, friendship, similarity, acquaintance. For example, a friendship-based social network is represented as a graph whose nodes are profiles and edges exist if two profiles are friends.

Two types of networks can represent Twitter: the friendship (Wang, 2010) (Figure 7.2, left) and the mention networks (Figure 7.2, right) (Huberman, Romero, & Wu, 2008). The friendship network represents the followers/ followees' relationships while the mention network is built based on user

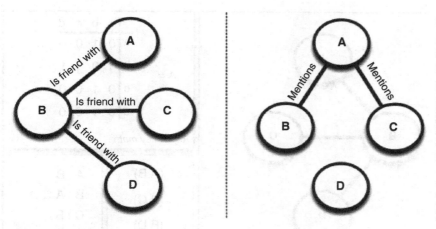

FIGURE 7.2

Two examples of undirected social graphs. The friendship graph (on the left side) illustrates profiles connected to each other by friendships. The mention graph (on the right side) illustrates profiles that have mentioned each other on a given social network such as Twitter.

mentions in tweets (in the form @screename). Researchers showed that the mention network could help better understand the communication and importance of actors on Twitter than a friendship network: static friends/followers structures do not highlight actual interactions between profiles that are revealed by the mention-based network.

Figure 7.2 highlights the interests of the model for identifying the structure of interactions. For example, one immediately sees the importance of user B in friend graph as well as the importance of user A in the mention graph. Under some specific hypothesis, these nodes may be referred to as more prestigious than others.

The graph model can also express the strength of relationships using weighted edges. For example, a weight can give more importance to a relationship between individuals who meet each other daily compared with individuals who meet weekly. When relationships are weighted, the graph is called a *weighted graph*; otherwise, it is called a *binary graph*.

A single graph may have different representations. Figure 7.3 illustrates the same graph in four ways: the visual representation, the adjacency matrix, the edges, and adjacency lists.

The *adjacency matrix*, denoted A, is a mathematical representation of a graph. The adjacency matrix representing a four-node graph is composed by four rows and four columns. The element of the ith line and j^{th} column denoted $a_{i,j}$ equals one if node i is connected to node j, and 0 otherwise. When edges are weighted,

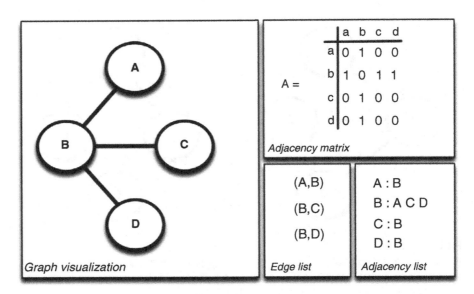

FIGURE 7.3

Four types of graph representations: visualization, adjacency matrix, adjacency, and edge lists. The graph is unweighted, undirected, and composed of four nodes and three edges.

the elements $a_{i,j}$ are equal to the strength of the relationship between i and j – the weight. Such matrix representation is used by many algorithms, and allows capturing some graph properties such as shortest paths, Eigenvector centrality, etc.

The visual representation of a small graph is easily readable and analyzable by human. For example, one immediately captures the importance of node B in Figure 7.3 with the visual representation that can be much less intuitive with other representations. Visual attributes, such as node size, link thickness, labels, and colors, can represent multidimensional data. Many graph visualization algorithms exist (Force atlas and Fruchterman Reingold are used in this chapter), and they all aim to provide an efficient way of visually representing potential information related to the entities and to the nodes. Pajek, Gephi, and Vizster are examples of graph visualization software (Batagelj, 2002; Heer & Boyd, 2005; Bastian, Heymann, & Jacomy, 2009; Van Landesberger, 2011). A proper visualization should respect a set of conditions to insure the graph readability: nodes must not hide each other, crosses between edges must be prohibited, short angles between edges must not exist, etc.

The *edge list* is a set of couples of nodes that represent the edges. In such representation, each line represents an edge that is expressed by the form: (*source*, *target*). The adjacency list indicates on every line the list of nodes that are adjacent to a given node. It is usually in the following form – *source_1: target_1 target_2 target_3*.

The adjacency list is more efficient for computations than the adjacency matrix in the case of very *large graphs* (graphs with millions of nodes) and *sparse graphs* (graphs with a low density): a simple *edge list* only captures the existing edges, while adjacency matrix stores all nonexisting links as 0s. For this reason, adjacency list is often preferred to adjacency matrix when dealing with *sparse* and *large graphs*.

This chapter presents *simple graphs* whose nodes model a unique type of entities and edges model a unique type of relationships. Many other types of graphs exist: bipartites, multimodes, multilayers, etc. They could simultaneously represent multiple types of entities or relationships but are not treated in this chapter.

Several questions would help efficiently model data as a graph:

What are the entities to analyze?
What types of relationships are relevant to this analysis?
What type of data is required?
Where and how can I access these data?
How can I capture and measure the relationships in an efficient way?
What are the key entities in my analysis?
What properties exist between my entities?

Many methodologies, tools, and resources address each of these issues. In the next section, we will provide some clues for answering these questions.

GRAPH CREATION TECHNIQUES

Graph theory is a powerful tool for modeling and analyzing things and their interactions. However, before obtaining a graph representation associated with a given research issue, such as open source intelligence, one has to go through the data gathering and cleaning, define entities and relationships, and also resolve the entity disambiguation problem. Each of those steps would be briefly explained in this section.

Data Gathering

The global amount of digital data is now counted in Zettabytes[1] and this number regularly increases. A reference for measuring the amount of data is the International Data Corporation (IDC). Data are produced everyday by enterprises' information systems, mobile users, sensors, robots, journalists, bloggers,

---

[1] A zettabyte equals to 10^{21} bytes.

social network users, etc. Many domains such as health, network science, sociology, management, etc., evolved thanks to these data. We identify two main data-gathering techniques: application programing interfaces (API) and web crawlers.

APIs are services that give an access to the built-in functionalities of an online platform. Sometimes, such services require an authentication for the harvester and can be limited to a number of data access (rate limits). Among the most commonly used API, one can quote Google Search, Google Map, Twitter, Accuweather, Facebook, etc. The APIs are accessed by a client via a query that is transmitted to a server, which provides an answer usually in an XML, JSON, or ATOM file format. The link given here is an example of the API query for gathering tweets mentioning the OSINT acronym on Twitter: https://api.twitter.com/1.1/search/tweets.json?q=OSINT

This API call requires an OAuth authentication that can be obtained by creating a Twitter application to obtain valid authentication tokens. An example of the query output (json file) is presented in Figure 7.4.

The restrictions of APIs often lead data scientists to use *webcrawlers* for data gathering. Webcrawlers are a piece of software that loops through a large set of predefined websites and harvest their source code. The source code is then parsed (usually with regular expressions) and the harvested data are stored in a relational or NoSQL databases (*MongoDB*, *CouchDB*, etc.).

```
"created_at":"Tue Apr 28 06:27:54 +0000 2015",
"id":592938270490763265,
"id_str":"592938270490763265",
"text":"RT @CyberExaminer: #cybersecurity OSINT Alone Does NOT Equal Threat Intelligence
http://t.co/PX29w4hh7C #infosec",
"source":"href=\"http://twitter.com/download/iphone\" rel="nofollow" Twitter for iPhone",
"truncated":false,
"user":{
    "id":2171079699,
    "id_str":"2171079699",
    "name":"Romuald Szkudlarek",
    "screen_name":"RomualdSzk",
    "location":"France",
    "description":"CISSP, CSSLP, CEH. #AppSec, #DataPrivacy. Cyber Security & Digital Risk
    Management. Passionate about software! Golf, Squash. Views are my own.",
    "followers_count":210,
    "friends_count":550,
    "listed_count":48,
    "created_at":"Wed Nov 06 17:35:11 +0000 2013"
    ...
    }
```

FIGURE 7.4

Sample of output related to the Twitter API search query. @RomualdSzk mentioned @CyberExaminer in a tweet, therefore the parsing of this file for creating a mention graph will produce two nodes @CyberExaminer and @RomualdSzk, and one edge between them (@CyberExaminer, @RomualdSzk).

Usually, a simple Python script is sufficient for gathering data via APIs or via a webcrawler. However, many tools, such as *DeixTo (a data extraction tool)*, *Talend Open Studio (TOS, an Extract Transform and Load software)*, *NodeXL (social network analysis and visualization template for Excel)* permit to crawl and to parse web pages and/or to perform API queries to collect data. TOS also includes components generating a graph type of file using different sources of data (*Gephi* plugin). When dealing with social networking sites data and graphs, the *NodeXL* plugin combined with *SocialNetImporter* for Excel is an example of tools that allows both collecting and modeling social data as a graph without any coding skills. Also, many social network applications such as *Netvizz* for Facebook allow collecting/visualizing data from social media. *Netvizz* generates a Graph Modeling Language (GML) file that can be directly read by any social network analysis tools (e.g. *Pajek*, *NetworkX*).

Defining and Computing Relationships

Defining nodes and relationships from raw data are certainly one of the most important steps when dealing with graphs. Although the entities we want to observe and analyze are often known, the types of interactions we are interested in are often not trivial. Moreover, the way one computes links will determine what aspects of entities will be highlighted and is directly related to the potential outcomes of the study.

User profiles are often the entities that we aim to analyze for social networks. Regarding relationships, the traditional social graph proposes to create links between two profiles u and v if either u belongs to v contacts list or if v belongs to u contacts list but many different relationships also exist.

This binary vision of the social graph can be improved by considering the measured number of interactions between two profiles (strength of ties). Examples of measured interactions are the number of messages/phone calls between u and v, the ratio of actions/time u has devoted to v, etc. Note that all of these relationships are not necessarily symmetrical (e.g., an SMS has a sender and a receiver) and this may lead to *directed weighted graphs*. Figure 7.5 indicates some traditional ways of computing adjacency matrices of a graph.

Despite the simple count or ratio for evaluation of the strength of relationships, the pointwise mutual information (PMI) metric provides an interesting alternative when we may or may not observe conjointly two entities in a same particular context. Such metric is calculated based on the probability of observing conjointly ($p(i, j)$) the two entities with respect to their own probability of being observed ($p(i)$, $p(j)$). As an example, this solution has been used for building an ingredient network from a large set of recipes (Teng, Lin, & Adamic, 2012).

$$A_{binary}(i,j) = \begin{cases} 1 & if\ i\ is\ friend\ with\ j \\ 0 & otherwise \end{cases}$$

$$A_{weighted}(i,j) = \#\ of\ interactions\ between\ i\ and\ j$$

$$A_{ratio}(i,j) = \frac{\#\ interactions\ of\ i\ with\ j}{\#\ interactions\ of\ i}$$

$$A_{PMI}(i,j) = log\left(\frac{p(i,j)}{p(i)p(j)}\right)$$

$$A_{TFIDF}(i,j) = tf_{i,j} * idf_i$$

$$A_{Similarity}(i,j) = S(i,j)$$

FIGURE 7.5

Common computation techniques of graph relationships between two nodes *i* and *j*. *tf* is the text frequency; *idf* is the inverse document frequency (Ramos, 2003); *S* can be any personalized similarity measure (usually normalized); *p(i, j)* the probability of observing conjointly *i* and *j*; *p(i)* are the overall probability of observing *i*.

In general, it is also possible to combine multiple aspects of relationships into a unique similarity metric that will weigh the relationships of the graph. For example, one can define a multidimensional similarity between Twitter profiles to identify malicious campaigns. As stated in Perez, Birregah, Layton, Lemercier and Watters (2013), such weight is measured as a linear combination of temporal similarity of sent tweets and the authorship attribution score related to the senders' profiles.

Despite the fact that traditional graph metrics and algorithms were only built for unweighted networks, many works have now adapted the metrics and algorithms to weighted graphs (e.g., Opsahl, Agneessens, & Skvoretz (2010) for node centrality measures).

Disambiguation Techniques

While working with social entities, one may encounter the problem of entity disambiguation. This problem is observed whenever two nodes refer to the same entity. Such a phenomenon is usual in social networks as a person may be identified with distinct names o n distinct databases. This issue often occurs in coauthorship graphs where authors of publications are identified using distinct names. For example, the mathematician Leonhard Euler may be spelled as L. Euler, Leonhard Euler, L Euler, etc. If a unique identifier such an email or a platform Id is available, the entity disambiguation problem may be circumvented.

The field of entity resolution when applied to social networks aims to determine whether two different profiles correspond to the same entity (Raad, Chbeir, & Dipanda, 2010; Raad, Chbeir, & Dipanda, 2013).

The direct approach is based on unique identifiers (e.g., mail). These approaches are generally related to the profiles representation. Among the most common representations of the profiles, resource description framework (RDF) is a metadata model that describes any type of information as a subject–predicate–object triples (Brickley & Guha, 2004). This model has been enhanced in the field of social relations by two ontologies: friend of a friend (FOAF) and semantically-interlinked online communities (SIOC) (Bojars, Passant, Cyganiak, & Breslin, 2008). These ontologies contain rich specifications that identify the relationships between individuals and their profiles. Such description formats contain unique identifiers that can be used to directly identify an entity across multiple platforms and are named "inverse functional property" (IFP) (Figure 7.6).

The work of Ding, Zhou, Finin and Joshi (2005) is based on the use of "foaf: mbox_sha1sum," "foaf: homepage," and "foaf: name" to match profiles. The foaf attribute "mbox_sha1sum" is the result of the mathematical function SHA1 applied to the email address. The underlying assumption is that the profiles of the same person refer to the same email address. The homepage ("foaf: homepage") is also used as an identifier to perform a direct correspondence between several entities. A strong disadvantage of this approach relies on the

```
<foaf:Person rdf:about="#danbri" xmlns:foaf="http://xmlns.com/foaf/0.1/">

 <foaf:name>Dan Brickley</foaf:name>

 <foaf:homepage rdf:resource="http://danbri.org/" />

 <foaf:openid rdf:resource="http://danbri.org/" />

 <foaf:img rdf:resource="/images/me.jpg" />

</foaf:Person>
```

FIGURE 7.6

Example of a FOAF profile. This profile represents a person and contains name, homepage, OpenID and image properties.

fact that users may not indicate their homepage on their multiple profiles and may use different emails.

Some social networks' users are identified by a pseudonym (e.g., on Twitter) that can also be used for the identification of links. The reader can refer to Damerau (1964), Jaro (1989), Levenshtein (1966), Kukich (1992), Porter and Winkler (1997), Yancey (2005) for more details. The issue of entity disambiguation in terms of username is in the nondetection of a match if the two names are slightly different. A set of measures can overcome this limitation. Some metrics aim to capture the degree of similarity not only between two strings in general (Ahmed, 2007) but more specifically, between two persons' names. A large set of different measures analyzes the similarity, for example using the phonetic of names (e.g. Soundex by Zobel (1996)). The reader may refer to Christen (2006) and Elmagarmid (2007) for a complete list of measures.

GRAPH ANALYSIS FOR OSINT

This section presents some introductory concepts of social network analysis and will cover a set of metrics that applies at different scales. First, we will present metrics that reveal structural properties of networks. Then, we will cover metrics that characterize positions of nodes into the network, and third we will discuss measures to detect communities.

Structural Observations
Density of a Graph
A graph is basically composed of N nodes connected by L edges. The *density* of a graph is a measure of connectedness of nodes in the graph. It is often viewed as a metric of efficiency since a high-density network has more connections and thus better exploits the total number of possible interactions. In some contexts, a high density may allow diffusing information faster. Density is equal to the ratio of the number of observed links divided by the total number of possible links between the nodes. For undirected graphs, it is calculated as follows:

$$d = \frac{L}{(N \times (N-1))/2}$$

Neighborhood, Degree, Average Degree, and Degree Distribution
The neighborhood of a node refers to the set of nodes that are connected to it. The neighborhood of a node u is denoted as $N(u)$. In the example of Figure 7.3, $N(A) = \{B\}$; $N(B) = \{A,C,D\}$; $N(C) = B$; $N(D) = B$. The size of the neighborhood of a node is defined as the *degree* of a node. It is the number of edges that are linked to the node. In social networks, this usually corresponds to the number of contacts (e.g., friends). On Facebook, the degree is equal to the number of friends

of a given profile. On directed graphs, the nodes have *in-degrees* and *out-degrees*. The in-degree of a node u is denoted $d_{in}(u)$ and corresponds to the number of edges that arrives at the node u. The out-degree of a node u denoted $d_{out}(u)$ is the number of edges that leave the node u. On Twitter, the in-degree refers to the number of followers and the out-degree to the number of followees. In Figure 7.7, the node B has a degree of 3 while nodes A, C, and D have a degree of 1.

The *average degree* of a graph corresponds to the average number of connections that have a node in the graph. For undirected graph the average degree, denoted $\langle k \rangle$, is defined as $\langle k \rangle = \dfrac{2L}{N}$. This measure corresponds to the average in-degrees or out-degrees for the directed graphs. Figure 7.7 shows the undirected graph and its average degree equals to $(2*3)/4 = 1.6$.

The average degree is an aggregated metric. As a result, the average degree of a graph may be high because of the existence of hubs (nodes with very high number of links) despite the fact that most of nodes have a low degree. This property is not shown by the average degree, but the difference in the degree of nodes is highlighted by the *degree distribution* graph metric.

The degree distribution captures the probability that a given node has a degree of k. Given the number of nodes that has a degree of k (denoted N_k), the probability of a node to have a degree of k is given by: $p_k = \dfrac{N_k}{N}$. By calculating this ratio over k one can plot the degree distribution of a graph. On the degree distribution plot, the x-axis represents the degree k and the y-axis represents the

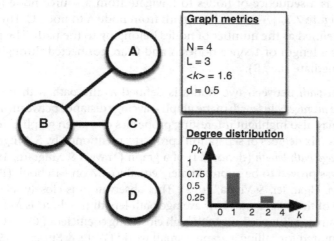

FIGURE 7.7

An example of undirected graph of size 4. The number of nodes $N = 5$ and the number of edges $L = 4$. The average degree equals 1.6. The degree distribution indicates that 75% of nodes have a degree of 1 and 25% of nodes have a degree of 3.

number (or ratio) of nodes having that degree. Figure 7.7 shows an example of degree distribution of a simple graph of size 4. Nodes A, B, and C have a degree of one and node B has a degree of 3. Thus, $p_{k=1} = \dfrac{3}{4}$ and $p_{k=3} = \dfrac{1}{4}$.

The degree distribution of social networks often follows the power-law (e.g., Internet graphs, Facebook, Hollywood actors). The power-law distribution of the degree illustrates that few nodes have a very high degree (called Hubs), but that most of nodes have a low degree. This is expressed by the formula $p_k = \alpha k^{-\beta}$, where Beta is the exponent of the power-law. Such graphs are called scale free because the shape of the distribution is invariant to the scale we look at it. On Facebook this expresses the fact that many individuals have a few friends and only a few have a very high number of friends (thousands).

This surprising finding led researchers to wonder what common ingredients may be at the origin of such phenomenon. The Barabási-Albert (Albert & Barabási, 2002) model provides an insight into this question by highlighting two essential ingredients for producing power-law distribution: growth and preferential attachment. Growth expresses the dynamics of the network; this means that not all actors are present from the start; other nodes may join the graph over time. The preferential attachment reveals that whenever a new node has a choice to create connection, it may prefer the nodes with a higher degree rather than nodes with low degree.

Paths and Average Path Length

The concept of *path* allows exploring the structure of a given graph. A path is described as a sequence of nodes to navigate from a source node to a target node. In Figure 7.7, $\{A \rightarrow B \rightarrow C\}$ is a path from node A to node C. The length of a path is defined as the number of nodes belonging to the path. The path from A to C has a length of 1 since nodes A and C are connected through the only one intermediate (i.e., B).

The *shortest path* between two nodes is defined as the path with the minimal length. The *average path length* in the graph – average distance between any couples of nodes may also highlight interesting properties of a given graph. For example, the famous "six degrees of separation" property, mentioned by S. Milgram, refers to the *average path length* (denoted l) of a graph (Travers & Milgram, 1969). This property was proven to be approximately equal to 4.7 on Facebook (Backstrom, Boldi, Rosa, Ugander, & Vigna, 2012). This observation is closely related to the expression of the *small world*. Low average path length ($l \sim \ln n$) is indeed one of the two main conditions along with high clustering coefficient ($C \gg C_{\text{random graph}}$) that are required for calling a graph a small world (Watts & Strogatz, 1998).

Many algorithms remain on the concept of paths (e.g., diffusion, influence, trust, contagion). Referring to a business application, LinkedIn users are identified as belonging to the first, second, or third circle of a contact by the length of the shortest path between them.

Components

A graph is usually composed of nodes that are not all connected together. It is indeed composed of a set of *components:* a set of nodes where each node can be reached by every other node in the component. We distinguish *strongly connected components* from *weakly connected components* depending on whether we take or not into account the direction of the edges. When the largest component occupies a large portion of the nodes it is referred to as the *giant component* of the graph.

Beyond the general observations and characteristics of graphs, a key interest of social network analysis is to identify actors (nodes) that appear "more important" than others. Those key players in the graph may exhibit specific characteristics and may influence in different ways the structure and other actors in general. The next section presents a set of metrics used to characterize the importance of a node in a given graph structure.

Characterizing Position of Nodes

Freeman (1979) observed a *star network* as shown in Figure 7.8 and identified the main question to answer: What are the key advantages of the node A comparing to nodes B, C, D, and E?

Freeman identified three main advantages of the node A compared with the other nodes:

1. Node A has more ties than nodes B, C, D, and E
2. Node A is closer to the other nodes
3. Node A is an intermediate between B, C, D, and E

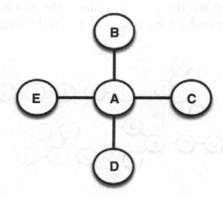

FIGURE 7.8

Star network of size 5 illustrating three centrality measures: degree, betweenness, and closeness.

The first observation is referred to as the *degree* of the node presented earlier. It follows the basic assumption that people with more connections are more important. The second observation is referred to closeness centrality. It assumes that proximity to the other is the criterion for importance. The last point is referred to as *betweenness* centrality and assumes that being in between others is important. Both betweenness and closeness centrality measures are discussed above.

Betweenness Centrality

The betweenness centrality captures how much a given node (hereby denoted u) is in-between others. This metric is measured with the number of shortest paths (between any couple of nodes in the graphs) that passes through the target node u (denoted $\sigma\sigma_{v,w}(u)$). This score is moderated by the total number of shortest paths existing between any couple of nodes of the graph (denoted $\sigma\sigma\sigma_{v,w}$). The target node would have a high betweenness centrality if it appears in many shortest paths.

$$B(u) = \sum_{u \neq v \neq w} \frac{\sigma_{v,w}(u)}{\sigma_{v,w}}$$

Naturally, in a star network presented in Figure 7.8, node A has a higher betweenness centrality than nodes B, C, D, and E. Node A belongs to all shortest paths while nodes B, C, D, and E belong to none of the shortest paths.

Figure 7.9 presents four different typologies of graphs and the betweenness centrality for each node.

Closeness Centrality

The *closeness centrality* is tightly related to the notion of distance between nodes. The distance between two nodes is defined as the length of the shortest path between two nodes. The *farness* is equal to the sum of the distance from a node to all the other nodes. Closeness centrality is the reciprocal of the farness.

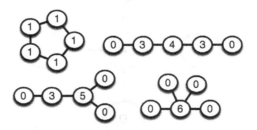

FIGURE 7.9
Betweenness centrality illustrated for different network configurations. For clarity, the centrality is here not normalized by the number of shortest path.

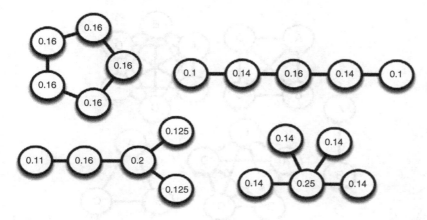

FIGURE 7.10

Closeness centrality is illustrated for four network configurations. Higher scores are given to the nodes that appear more central in terms of distance (they can reach other in a few hops).

It highlights nodes that may reach any other nodes within a few hops and nodes that may be very distant in the graph (Figure 7.10).

$$C(u) = \frac{1}{\sum_{y} d(u, y)}$$

Many other centrality metrics exist, such as Eigenvector, PageRank (Page, Brin, Motwani, & Winograd, 1999) and Katz centrality measures. Each of these measures represents the importance of nodes in the graph regarding some specific assumptions regarding the topological properties of nodes. For example, Eigenvector centrality assumes that having more contacts is not the main criterion of importance, instead having important contacts better reveals the centrality of a node. Under this assumption the centrality of a node is related to the sum of the centrality of its neighbors.

The metrics presented above captured the "importance" of nodes. The next section opens the discussion about the question of communities and the clusters' identification.

Structures and Communities of Nodes
Structural Patterns: Cliques and Cores

Cliques are examples of communities whose nodes are all connected together (everyone knows each other in the community). Figure 7.11 illustrates a set of cliques of different size (2 to 6). Note that, by construction, the number of links of a clique of size N is equal to $(N \times (N - 1))/2$.

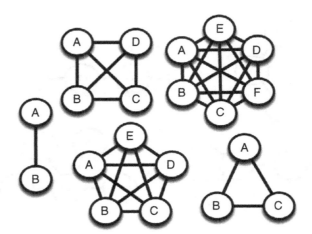

FIGURE 7.11

Cliques of size 2 to 6. Each clique is characterized by the fact that every node is connected to every other nodes of the clique. Each clique has a density of 1.

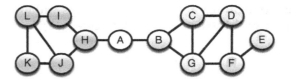

FIGURE 7.12

A graph composed of 12 nodes and 17 edges. This graph exhibits two communities that one can capture visually.

Although cliques may be good candidates to community detection a main issue when looking for such type of patterns is that *cliques* of large size may be very seldom in a graph. Indeed, any missing tie in a given set of nodes may misclassify a clique as a community.

The graph of Figure 7.12 is composed of five cliques of size 3 (closed triangles). The cliques are $\{L,K,J\};\{B,C,G\};\{C,D,G\};\{G,D,F\};\{D,F,E\}$. Note that the subgraph $\{C, D, G, F\}$ has one missing tie $\{C,F\}$ in order to be considered a clique. As one may observe, the cliques do not allow capturing the two communities that exist in the graph. This is mainly due to the fact that the constraint is too strong.

Alternatives to cliques are *N-cores* and *p-cliques* that respectively remain on the number and frequency of ties into communities. *N-cores* are a set of nodes whose each member connects to at least *N* other members of the community.

P-cliques are communities whose members connect to at least *p* percent of the other member of the same community.

Note that the community highlighted on the left-hand side of the graph in Figure 7.12 is a 2-core. Every node belonging to the set {*L, I, H, J, K*} is connected to at least two other nodes of the core.

Communities

Note that cliques and cores of large size may be rare in real-life graphs such as social networks that are often *sparse*. Therefore, less restrictive assumptions should be used to better identify communities. When considering communities, a largely accepted definition is *"a set of nodes that have a higher likelihood of connecting to each other than to the nodes of other communities."* Two main points arise for defining a community:

1. Connectedness: nodes of a community must be connected
2. Density: the nodes of a community must be highly connected

A typical example in community detection in graphs is the Zachary Karate club (see Figure 7.13). The sociogram of the club captures the relationships between the 34 members outside the club observed between 1970 and 1972 (everyone

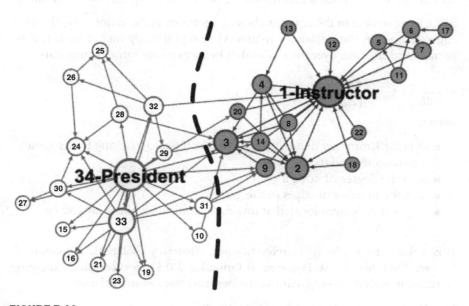

FIGURE 7.13

Social network of the Zachary Karate club before the club split. Two key players the president and the instructors have a high degree in the graph. They both appear to be at the core of a community (resp. in white and in gray).

knows each other in the club). The main interest for the sociologist was in the fact that this club was split after a conflict between two main players (the instructor and the president). Half of the members formed a club around the instructor (node 1) and the rest either found a new instructor or stopped the practice of the sport. With the "maximum flow – minimum cut" the Ford–Fulkerson algorithm applied to the social graph, Zachary was able to predict with very high accuracy which member will belong to which group after the club separation (Zachary, 1977). This example highlights how graph theory can allow capturing, understanding, and predicting evolution of real-world processes.

One of the most famous metrics when trying to identify community structure in graphs is called *modularity*. We later define this metric and present a broadly used algorithm that remains in this metric for community detection.

Modularity

The *modularity* is a number that illustrates how much a given graph may be organized into communities. The *modularity* (Newman, 2006) captures how good is a given partition compared with a randomly wired network. The random network is here calculated based on a randomization of the original graph, while keeping the degree of each node unchanged. Under this constraint, the probability of observing a link between a node i and j equals $\frac{k_i \times k_j}{2L}$. Modularity Q, as expressed in the equation below, increases as the number of observed edges (stored in the adjacency matrix A) is significantly higher than the expected random ratio over the nodes that belongs to the same community.

$$Q = \frac{1}{2L} \sum_{vw} \left[A_{vw_{vw}} - \frac{k_i \times k_j}{(2L)^2} \right] \delta(c_v, c_w)$$

where:

- δ is the Kronecker delta, it equals to one if u and v belong to the same community and 0 otherwise.
- k_i is the degree of node u
- L is the number of edges in the graph
- A_{vw} is the element located at row v and column w of the adjacency matrix A

This value can be used as reference for clustering (Clauset, Newman, & Moore, 2004; Shiokawa, Fujiwara, & Onizuka, 2013) by successively merging communities that allow obtaining the best increases in modularity.

The iterative process has the five following steps:

1. Each node belongs to a unique community.
2. Consider each community pair, and evaluate the modularity score Q that could be obtained by merging them.

3. Merge the communities that allow the highest variation in modularity (ΔQ).
4. Repeat the steps (2 and 3) until only one community remains.
5. Return the partitions that have allowed obtaining the highest modularity score.

Note that many clustering approaches exist (e.g., Girvan–Newman algorithm, CFinder algorithm, Markov Cluster Algorithm). When trying to identify communities, one should consider the benefits and drawbacks of each method in order to apply the most appropriate one. Examples of comparison criteria are: the computation costs and capacity of the algorithm to scale on large dataset; the capacity of the approach to identify the best number of communities; the possibility of identifying some overlapping communities; etc.

TWITTER CASE STUDY

The Twitter Dataset

This section discusses social network analysis methods using a real-life data extracted from Twitter. The data were collected via Twitter Application Programming Interfaces; the API call was presented in Figure 7.4. The query was set up to collect tweets that mentioned the OSINT keyword during the 3-month period from January 26, 2015 to April 26, 2015. The final database contains approximately 100,000 tweets that were generated by up to 20,000 profiles. Using this dataset we will show how ours interactions on a social network can be relevant and can generate added value for an observer on a dedicated subject.

Before analyzing the data by graph, we investigated the keywords used in the database of tweets. Figure 7.14 illustrates the most important keywords; the size of the word is proportional to the occurrence of the topic in the database.

The cloud of words in Figure 7.14 highlights the importance of *security* and *cyber criminality* issues related to OSINT. This content analysis points the trends topics for this community during the specified timeframe. This allows providing a clear picture of the concerns of the OSINT community and key theme. For example, malware, botnet, and hacking are often referred and reveal the importance of the cyberspace. We also observe the interest on particular geographical areas such as Ukraine, China, India, Egypt, and Russia. The OSINT community is more focused on subject relative to global security. With this analysis we concentrate on the major hot news during this period. We further investigate the dataset using the mention graph.

General Graph Metrics

Figure 7.15 shows a visual representation of the Twitter mention graph created using the harvested data. For the reminder, the nodes of such a graph represent

FIGURE 7.14

Keywords mentioned in the tweets database related to the OSINT topic. The size of the words is proportional to their occurrence in the dataset. English linking words are filtered from the visualization.

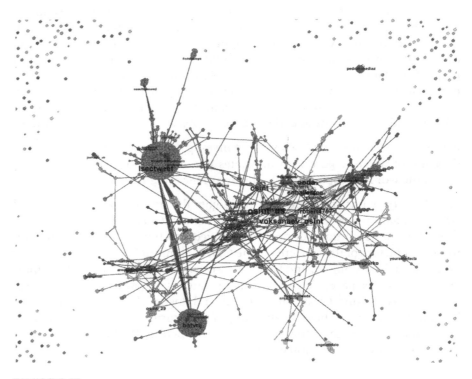

FIGURE 7.15

Twitter mention graph related to the OSINT topic. The graph is composed of 12,406 profiles connected by 14,451 mentions. All disconnected nodes are profiles that have published tweets related to the OSINT without mentioning any profile.

Twitter profiles identified by screen name, and edges between two profiles exist if a given profile has mentioned another profile in a tweet. The edges are weighted by the number of mentions.

The graph is composed of 12,406 profiles connected by 14,451 mentions.

An interactive version of the graph can be accessed online.[2] This interactive online graph is performed by Scott A. Hale, Oxford Internet Institute. The full dataset can be accessed by requesting the corresponding author.

The density of the graph equals 0.001, which is quite low: two given profiles of the graph have only 0.1% probability of being connected. This density indicates that mentions are not widely used by the Twitter OSINT community, and may also highlight the fact that OSINT profiles do not necessarily know each other on the Twitter network.

The mention graph has an average degree of 2.4. This means that a profile, during the specified time frame, refers in an average to two or three profiles.

Figure 7.15 depicts the degree distribution of the investigated graph. The figure plots for each value of k the associated probability p_k of observing nodes of degree k. The graphic shows that more than 80% of the nodes of the graph have a very low degree (below two) and only few nodes have a very high degree. About 10 nodes have a degree that is greater than 80 (they are called Hubs). This means that these profiles are often mentioned or often mention many profiles. Such degree distribution may highlight some graph properties such as the speed of information spreading (Figure 7.16). For more information, the reader can refer to Barabási and Albert (1999).

The modularity of the graph equals 0.883, which is rather large. Note that a modularity value higher than 0.3 is usually considered significant. This number shows that communities exist in the graph: some nodes share more connections with each other than with the rest of the network.

In Figure 7.15, we observe that communities appear as star networks around the hubs. This observation also shows that nodes with a very high degree tend to connect to nodes with a very low degree. This phenomenon is known as *degree correlation* and influences the spread of ideas over the network. For example, in the OSINT community, the topology indicates how easily an OSINT contributor may spread and access information. Despite the information diffusion aspect, the presence of Hubs may reveal actors that are references/facilitators in the domain.

This section discussed general graph metrics and its application to Twitter mention graph. The next section inspects the "importance" of nodes.

---

[2] The graph is accessible at the back of the following web page: http://goo.gl/Xdj5dj.

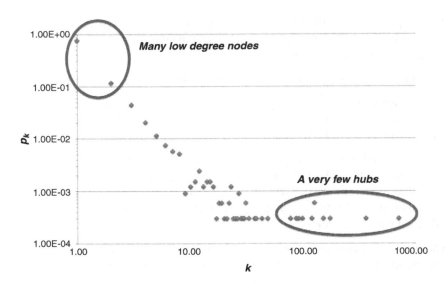

FIGURE 7.16
Degree distribution of the mention graph. This distribution highlights that most of the nodes have a very low degree and that a few hubs with very high degree.

Node Metrics and Profiles' Centrality
The top five profiles regarding their degree are listed in Tables 7.1 and 7.2 along with the description of their Twitter profiles.

Communities
On the Twitter mention graph, we have applied a weighted modularity-based clustering algorithm. This has led to the identification of two main clusters whose size is greater than 10% of the nodes. The color of the nodes in Figure 7.15 represents the cluster to which a node belongs. The first community is composed of 20.44% of the nodes that correspond to nodes that have mentioned or have been mentioned by @IsecTweet. The second community is composed of 10.92% of the nodes that have mentioned the following profiles: @botvrij. We noted that these two profiles are very active and generate many messages in specific destination of a set of given profiles.

CONCLUSION
The development of online social networks has changed the face of the Internet. These transformations conduct to a more and more collaborative environment. Every day, billions of users participate in social networks. They share, produce, consume media; form communities; collaborate to solve complex

Table 7.1 TOP 5 Twitter Profiles Regarding the Node Degree (Profiles With the Highest Number of Mentions Related to OSINT)

Profile	Degree	Description
@lsectweet	704	LSEC – leaders in security is a not for profit association focused on ICT security. Bringing together research, security providers, and enterprise users.
@botvrij	358	Botvrij.be is the Belgian support center of the European antibot pilot ACDC
@ooda	175	Identify, manage, and respond to global risks and uncertainties while exploring emerging opportunities and developing robust and adaptive future strategies.
@rdsweb	152	Entusiasta da INFOSEC and OSINT
@robert4787	127	Adjunct professor – write about U.S. and Foreign spy agencies-Member Ass. Of Former Intelligence Officers (AFIO)

Table 7.2 TOP 5 Twitter Profiles Regarding Betweenness Centrality

Profile	Betweenness	Description
@lsectweet	2,711,805	LSEC – leaders in security is a not for profit association focused on ICT Security. Bringing together research, security providers and enterprise users.
@rdsweb	1,382,305	Entusiasta da INFOSEC & OSINT.
@osint	1,366,001	Paulo Félix, OSINFO open source information.
@botvrij	1,132,604	Botvrij.be is the Belgian support center of the European antibot pilot ACDC
@osintcrime	946,272	@DrEricGrabowsky Utilizing Open-Source Intelligence (OSINT) to Discover Criminal Activity and to Find Wanted Fugitives #crime #tcot #OSINT #Internet

issues; exchange goods and services. Social Network Analysis allows getting a more efficient phenomenon-based point of view of all of these interactions. This discipline is important for many areas of research like sociology, social psychology, anthropology, or business management. It is multidisciplinary field that bridges social and technological perspectives. Due to the large quantity of data produced, the web provides a large landscape to explore for data scientists. We have presented some introductory concepts related to graphs and more specifically social network analysis. We have discussed a few main issues when trying to analyze data as a graph: graph creation, relationship weighting, and entity disambiguation and graph analysis. We believe that social networks analysis opens a large scope of perspective in various areas.

References

Albert, R., & Barabási, A. -L. (2002). Statistical mechanics of complex networks. *Rev. Mod. Phys.*, *74*(1), 47–97.

Alhajj, R., & Rokne, J. G. (2014). *Encyclopedia of social network analysis and mining*. Berlin: Springer, ISBN 978-1-4614-6169-2.

Backstrom, L., Boldi, P., Rosa, M., Ugander, J., & Vigna, S. (2012). Four degrees of separation. In *The 3rd annual ACM web science conference* (pp. 33–42). New York: ACM.

Barnes, J. A. (1954). Class and committee in a Norwegian island parish. *Human Relations, 7*, 39–58.

Bojars, U., Passant, A., Cyganiak, R., & Breslin, J. (2008). Weaving SIOC into the web of linked data. In *Proceedings of the WWW 2008 workshop linked data on the web (LDOW)*, Beijing, China, 2008.

Barabási, A. -L., & Albert, R. (1999). Emergence of scaling in random networks. *Science, 286*, 509–512.

Bastian, M., Heymann, S., & Jacomy, M. (2009). Gephi: an open source software for exploring and manipulating networks. In E. Adar, M. Hurst, T. Finin, Natalie, S., Glance, N. Nicolov, Belle, L., & Tseng (Eds.), *ICWSM*, The AAAI Press.

Batagelj, V., & Mrvar, A. (2002). Book section, Graph drawings, Volume 2265 of the series Lecture Notes in Computer Science. *Pajek – Analysis and Visualization of Large Networks*. Berlin: Springer, pp. 477–478.

Brickley, D., & Guha, R.V. (2004). RDF Vocabulary Description Language 1.0: RDF Schema. Rapport technique, février.

Christen, P. (2006). A comparison of personal name matching: Techniques and practical issues. In *workshop on Mining Complex Data (MCD)*, held at IEEE ICDM'06, Hong Kong, pp. 290–294.

Clauset, A., Newman, M. E. J., & Moore, C. (2004). Finding Community Structure in Very Large Networks. Physical Review E-PHYS REV E 70:066111.

Damerau, F. J. (1964). A technique for computer detection and correction of spelling errors. *Communication of the ACM, 7*(3), 171–176.

Ding, L., Zhou, L., Finin, T. W. , & Joshi, A. (2005). How the semantic web is being used: an analysis of FOAF documents. In *Hawaii international conference on system sciences (HICSS)*.

Easley, D., & Kleinberg, J. (2010). *Networks, crowds, and markets: reasoning about a highly connected world*. New York: Cambridge University Press.

Elmagarmid, A. K., Ipeirotis, P. G., & Verykios, V. S. (2007). Duplicate record detection: a survey. *IEEE Transactions on Knowledge and Data Engineering, 19*(1), 1–16.

Euler, L. The Konigsberg Bridge problem, Commentarii academiae scientiarum Petropolitanae 8, 1741, pp. 128–140.

Freeman, L. C. (1979). Centrality in social networks: conceptual clarification. *Social Networks, 1*(3), 215–239.

Granovetter, M. (1973). The strength of weak ties. *The American Journal of Sociology, 78*(6), 1360–1380.

Heer, J., & Boyd, D. (2005). Vizster: Visualizing online social networks. In *Proceedings of the 2005 IEEE symposium on information visualization* (INFOVIS'05). Washington, DC: IEEE Computer Society, 5-.

Huberman, B. A., Romero, D. M., & Wu, F. (December 5, 2008). Social networks that matter: Twitter under the microscope. *SSRN Electronic Journal* http://ssrn.com/abstract=1313405.

Jaro, M. A. (1989). Advances in record-linkage methodology as applied to matching the 1985 census of Tampa, Florida. *Journal of the American Statistical Association ,89*, 414–420 Key: citeulike:1820064.

Kukich, K. (1992). Techniques for automatically correcting words in text. *ACM Computing Surveys, 24*(4), 377–439.

Levenshtein, V. (1966). Binary codes capable of correcting deletions, insertions, and reversals. *Soviet Physics Doklady*, *10*(8), 707–710.

Moreno, J. L. (1934). 1953 Who Shall Survive? Foundations of Sociometry, Group Psychotherapy and Sociodrama. Rev. & enl. ed. Beacon, NY: Beacon House.

Milgram, S. (1967). The small world problem. *Psychology Today*, *2*,6067.

Newman, M. E. (2006). Modularity and community structure in networks. *Proc Natl Acad Sci U S A*, *103*(23), 8577–8582.

Opsahl, T., Agneessens, F., & Skvoretz, J. (2010). Node centrality in weighted networks: generalizing degree and shortest paths. *Social Networks*, *32*(3), 245–251.

Page, L., Brin, S., Motwani, R., & Winograd, T. (1999). The PageRank citation ranking: bringing order to the web. Technical Report. Stanford InfoLab.

Perez, C., Birregah, B., Layton, R., Lemercier, M., & Watters, P. (2013). REPLOT: REtrieving profile links on Twitter for suspicious networks detection (pp. 1–8). Presented at the 2013 international conference on advances in social networks analysis and mining (ASONAM 2013).

Porter, E. H., & Winkler, W. E. (1997). Bureau of the census et bureau of the census : approximate string comparison and its effect on an advanced record linkage system. In *Advanced record linkage system*. U.S. Bureau of the Census, Research Report, pp. 190–199.

Raad, E., Chbeir, R., & Dipanda, A. (2010). User profile matching in social networks. In *13th International conference on network-based information systems (NBiS)* (pp. 297–304). IEEE.

Raad, E., Chbeir, R., & Dipanda, A. (2013). Discovering relationship types between users using profiles and shared photos in a social network. *Multimedia Tools Appl*, *64*(1), 141–170.

Ramos, J. (2003). Using TF-IDF to determine word relevance in document queries. Technical report, Department of Computer Science, Rutgers University, Piscataway, NJ.

Scott, J. (2000). *Social network analysis: a handbook* (2nd ed). Sage Publications.

Simmel, G. (1955). *Conflict and the web of group affiliations*. New York: Free Press.

Shiokawa, H., Fujiwara, Y., & Onizuka, M. (2013). Fast algorithm for modularity-based graph clustering. In AAAI.

Teng, C.-Y., Lin, Y.-R., & Adamic, L. A. (2012). Recipe recommendation using ingredient networks. In The 3rd annual ACM web science conference (pp. 298–307). New York: ACM.

Von Landesberger, T., Kuijper, A., Schreck, T., Kohlhammer, J., Van Wijk, J., et al. (2011). Visual analysis of large graphs: state-of-the-art and future research challenges. Computer Graphics Forum, Wiley-Blackwell, 30(6), pp.1719–1749.

Travers, J., & Milgram, S. (1969). An experimental study of the small world problem. *Sociometry*, *32*(4), 425–443.

Wang, A. (2010). *Detecting spam bots in online social networking sites: a machine learning approach* (pp. 335–342). Rome, Italy: Springer Verlag.

Watts, D. J., & Strogatz, S. H. (1998). Collective dynamics of 'small-world' networks. *Nature*, *393*(6684), 440–442.

White, H. C., Boorman, S. A., & Breiger, R. L. (1976). Social structure from multiple networks. *American Journal of Sociology*, *81*, 730–780.

Yancey, W. E. (2005). Evaluating string comparator performance for record linkage Institution: Bureau of the census.

Zachary, W. W. An information flow model for conflict and fission in small groups. University of New Mexico, 1977. JSTOR 3629752.

Zobel, J., & Dart, P. (1996). Phonetic string matching: lessons from information retrieval. In *Proceedings of the 19th annual international ACM SIGIR conference on research and development in information retrieval* (SIGIR) (pp. 166–172), New York, NY: ACM.

CHAPTER 8

Ethical Considerations When Using Online Datasets for Research Purposes

Christian Kopp, Robert Layton, Iqbal Gondal, Jim Sillitoe
Internet Commerce Security Laboratory, Federation University, Australia

INTRODUCTION

The Internet has become an important community communications platform, supporting a range of programs and virtual environments. While there are many ways in which people choose to develop personal interactions over the Internet, one of the most popular manifestations is the creation and mainte- nance of social relationships using social and dating websites (Alam, Yeow, & Loo, 2011). When used in this way, the virtual world can reflect, to some degree, the development of intimate personal relationships in the real world. People can exchange messages that were previously exchanged privately off- line, such as local news, recent experiences, invitations to meet, and even more personal matters. An important difference that has arisen with the use of virtual space is that while such information may be of a personal nature, it can be shared more widely rather than maintaining the essential one-to-one nature of private interactions. This sharing can vary from restricted access to certain people who have been accepted as "friend" contacts, or it can be disseminated quite publicly. As a result of this sharing, it has been observed that on social websites, a wide range of topics are discussed, and, as such, the sites record a significant part of the social lives of persons in a community (Ellison, 2007).

Another common form of virtual community on the Internet are forum pages. In such an environment, governments and public or private organizations can provide information about a topic of special interest to the community. In ad- dition, these pages can provide additional support in the form of an interactive forum, where Internet users can share their perspectives on topics of interest, or seek advice or counselling for issues of concern. Community users are en- couraged to provide posts based on their own experience or understandings, with the discussions usually being guided by experienced moderators who also maintain the web page and the forum. In this way, the Internet has be- come one of the most important sources of contemporary information. People

131

who are looking for material of any kind, at least in the very early phases of an investigation or interest, can be guided by comments and data recorded on these public sites. The topics available are extraordinarily multifarious, including questions related to health, behavior, education, hobbies, or interests; indeed, almost any other issue that can be imagined is available (Bickart & Schindler, 2001).

As a consequence of the interactive nature of these sites, be they relatively private in nature or more public forums, they accumulate a significant amount of primary information that are increasingly being used for a variety of research purposes (Haker, Lauber, & Rössler, 2005; Wesemann & Grunwald, 2008).

At this point, the question of ethical use of the available data arises – is it to be treated as publicly available material which can be freely quoted or are there some implied restrictions on the use of comments and personal revelations? Our contention is that even if data are technically widely accessible to the public, it still needs to be treated in an ethical manner, which implies that ethical considerations of research using online data from social media and forums need to be explicitly undertaken. In this chapter, the authors consider how approaches to ethical practice might be conceptualized when related to the separate elements of sourcing material, storage of relevant research data, and analysis of data which are drawn from websites based on personal communications from users which have been published in free accessible social web pages and Internet forums.

The most critical ethical issues that arise are those related to potential risk or harm for the research participants. These possibilities require the researcher to at least inform the participant about any risks in relation to the intended research and to make sure that the participant understands all aspects of potential negative consequences in relation to the proposed research targets to give them an opportunity to consider their options and to ultimately provide consent for use of the material in a different milieu.

The aim of this chapter is to introduce and discuss what we see as the risks and ethical considerations that need to be undertaken when publicly accessible data are used for research. Our concerns stem from two factors

- First, just because data are publicly accessible does not necessarily mean that it can be used freely for purposes that were not foreseen by the respondent;
- Second, it is not always possible to contact the original authors or data custodians responsible for these datasets to obtain explicit permission for the data's use for research purposes. With the increasing popularity and use of online material, this concern is going to become more pressing (Eysenbach & Till, 2001).

Our focus here is predominately on the "Principals" related to the dataset. These Principals are the users of the websites, the owners of the social media profiles, and the authors of the forum posts. We consider that there may be significant impacts on these people which may arise from research conducted either about the contained information or about the circumstances that caused the social forum to be created.

In doing this, we accept there will be normal conditions associated with the use of the websites themselves, where owners and creators may have placed explicit restrictions on use of the data. For instance, some websites explicitly state that they own any data on their site, and that any usage needs to be formally approved by the website operator (Diaz, 2013). Discussion of these restrictions is not addressed in this chapter, as we assume that any researcher working with ethical intent will naturally apply these restrictions. Clearly, if approval is required by the website operator for use of the data, then explicit approval is needed by the researcher to pursue ethical research on that website.

We also have not considered the role that common law has instituted in regard to these concepts (Diaz, 2013), for much the same reason. While privacy-related laws may change over time, together with how they can be applied within different jurisdictions, it is assumed that any researcher will make themselves familiar with the restrictions pertaining to specific material. Also, although we realize that common law and ethical requirements cannot always be cleanly separated, in this chapter we have chosen not to focus specifically on what issues might be raised when thinking about the effect of legal requirements on the ethical use of data.

EXISTING GUIDELINES

As a starting point to our considerations regarding ethical considerations when using online datasets for research purposes, we have looked at existing guidelines that refer generally to work done with potentially sensitive material. As Thomas (1996) has outlined, all researchers have the obligation to protect the dignity, privacy, and well-being of human subjects during research investigations that use informant's private material. This requirement materially affects how the researcher (i) gathers and selects relevant data, (ii) treats the personal exposure of subjects' private communications, and (iii) makes the synthesized results suitable for display in a public forum.

In this respect, Thomas refers to two conventional sources for Ethical Guidelines, whose considerations inform the ethical policies and standards of most universities. These sources derive from two documents; the Belmont Report (Belmont, 1979) and the Federal Register (Federal, 1991). In the paragraphs that follow, these two key documents will be summarized to highlight specific issues that will be of importance when we begin to consider web-based material.

It appears that the Belmont Report implies a "teleological" perspective on ethical stances that are recommended for research purposes. In this respect, Thomas says that such a teleological perspective follows the premise that appropriate ethical behavior (carried out in the present) is determined by the moral consequences (in the future) of an act. Further, this position implies that recommendations based on a teleological perspective should be interpreted to mean that at the end of the research, the results should contain the best possible balance between greatest social good (in terms of knowledge generation) and the least social harm (in terms of the dignity and well-being of the informants).

As a consequence of following this teleological perspective, the Belmont Report specifies three broad principles for practice. These are (i) Respect for Persons (Autonomy), (ii) Beneficence, and (iii) Justice, and each of these key concepts will be elaborated as follows.

First, the notion of "Respect for Persons" must always play a central part in determining ethical research behavior. The Belmont report comments explicitly that: "Respect for persons incorporates at least two ethical convictions: first, that individuals should be treated as autonomous agents, and second, that persons with diminished autonomy are entitled to protection" (Belmont, 1979).

The important term here is "autonomous agent" which clearly demands that the researcher must ensure that an informant is not under any duress, and is capable of making personal actions, often in the form of written or spoken words, which are explicitly understood to not cause harmful repercussions at any future time. Inherent in this understanding is that persons with "diminished autonomy," who may be important informants to many studies, must be carefully protected. This situation will occur in the case of minors, those with impaired mental capabilities, or possibly those of advanced age. A pertinent comment, made in the Belmont report, indicates how a researcher should go about ensuring autonomy when it says: "In most cases of research involving human subjects, respect for persons demands that subjects enter into the research voluntarily and with adequate information" (Belmont, 1979).

Thomas (1996) specifically commented that that this guideline is intended primarily to protect those persons, who are not fully capable of making an informed decision to participate in research, from any form of physical or psychological abuse. The guidelines also require all participants who provide information to the researcher to be given adequate information, usually in the form of a plain language statement, about the nature of the project. They should also be informed of their right to be able to withdraw from the project at any time without penalty. In practice, this principle is reflected in the process of informed consent, in which the risks and benefits of the research are disclosed to the subject (Frankel & Siang, 1999).

In considering this issue, we have to look first at the question what is informed consent. Thomas, referring to the Belmont Report (Belmont, 1979), notes that there is widespread agreement that the consent process can be analyzed as containing three elements: information, comprehension, and voluntariness.

- *Information:* In regard to the handling and transmission of information, the Belmont Report states that: "Most codes of research establish specific items for disclosure intended to assure that subjects are given sufficient information. These items generally include: the research procedure, their purposes, risks and anticipated benefits, alternative procedures (where therapy is involved), and a statement offering the subject the opportunity to ask questions and to withdraw at any time from the research" (Belmont, 1979). In most traditional research instances, a plain language statement, authorized by a relevant Ethics Committee, is provided and explained to the research participants before the data collection stage starts. In an online situation, this is increasingly more difficult as is outlined later in this chapter.
- *Comprehension:* Considering the more problematic assurance of comprehension of relevant details of the intended research, the Belmont Report says that: "The manner and context in which information is conveyed is as important as the information itself. For example, presenting information in a disorganized and rapid fashion, allowing too little time for consideration or curtailing opportunities for questioning, all may adversely affect a subject's ability to make an informed choice" (Belmont, 1979). Thomas specifically comments further that, according the Belmont Report principles, the researcher needs to assure that research subjects comprehend the information and understand what they are consenting to, which again poses significant problems when using online data for research purposes.
- *Voluntariness:* Finally, in regard to coercion and influence, the Belmont Report says explicitly that: "This element of informed consent requires conditions free of coercion and undue influence. Coercion occurs when an overt threat of harm is intentionally presented by one person to another in order to obtain compliance. Undue influence, by contrast, occurs through an offer of an excessive, unwarranted, inappropriate or improper reward or other overture in order to obtain compliance." (Belmont, 1979). This means that the participants must give consent voluntarily for their responses to be used in a context other than that which they first were uttered, but, as will be discussed later in more detail, this apparently simple principle is more difficult to honor when material is on a web-based medium.

Second, while the concept of "Beneficence" is also widely agreed to be an essential ethical issue, in practice its application involves somewhat more complex understanding. In the Belmont report, it is outlined that: "Persons are treated in an ethical manner not only by respecting their decisions and by protecting them from harm, but also by making efforts to secure their well-being. Such treatment falls under the principle of beneficence. The term 'beneficence' is often understood to cover acts of kindness or charity that go beyond strict obligation. In this document, beneficence is understood in a strong sense, as an obligation. Two general rules have been formulated as complementary expressions of beneficent actions in this sense: (1) do no harm and (2) maximize possible benefits and minimize possible harms" (Belmont, 1979).

Thomas indicates that this principle is meant to extend the physical Hippocratic maxim familiar to medical personnel of "do no harm" to the ethical obligations of a researcher. The principle of beneficence thus requires that researchers need to think carefully through the implications of the outcomes of their research, especially in sensitive areas where the participants could face unanticipated physical, social, or legal risks from publication of research material.

The final principle, Justice, also involves some unexpectedly complex issues. The Belmont report provides an interesting comment that introduces this discussion. It states that it is important to determine: "who ought to receive the benefits of research and bear its burdens" (Belmont, 1979).

Thomas (1996) opines that this statement outlines a principle of justice which obligates the researcher to balance the benefits and risks "fairly" between the greater social interests and the interests of the research subjects. The Belmont report goes further in saying that "An injustice occurs when some benefit to which a person is entitled is denied without good reason or when some burden is imposed unduly," and "the principle of justice is that equals ought to be treated equally." This raises the question who is "equal" and who is "not equal," particularly in an online context. Common consent between commentators is that there can be important differences in position based on experience, age, deprivation, competence, merit, and position. Such considerations go some way toward constituting criteria for justifying differential treatment for certain purposes. As a consequence, the Belmont report lists five formulations regarding the distribution of burdens and benefits. These formulations are:

1. to each person an equal share;
2. to each person according to individual need;
3. to each person according to individual effort;
4. to each person according to societal contribution; and
5. to each person according to merit.

These formulations have been put forward in an attempt to avoid an unequal balance of burdens and benefits. Situations of inequity have happened in the past where impecunious patients carried the burdens of research by being used for medical experiments while only rich patients stood to benefit from the results of the work. It follows from the Belmont formulations that, whenever research is supported by public funds, nobody should be assumed to be able to participate on the basis of being poor, a member of an ethnic minority, or just conveniently available. In addition, it should be an outcome of natural justice that any developed therapeutic devices or treatment arising from such work should be accessible to anybody and not only to those who can afford it (Belmont, 1979).

In concert with the Belmond Report, which is, as we have seen, a list of recommendations for ethical research behavior, the Federal Register (Federal, 1991) specifies those specific rules and obligations that oversee ethical behavior (Thomas, 1996). This Federal Policy for the Protection of Human Subjects, which is also known as the "Common Rule," was published in 1991 and codified into separate regulations by 15 Federal departments and agencies. It is one of the four subparts of the US Department of Health and Human Services (HHS) regulations, and is identified by the code 45 CFR part 46. The "45 CFR part 46" contains subpart A "Common Rule," subpart B, which contains additional protections for pregnant women, human foetuses, and neonates; subpart C, additional protections for prisoners; and subpart D, additional protections for children (HHS, 2015a). Some of these subparts have obvious relevance for our considerations of online research.

Furthermore, the Federal Policy includes reference to a number of international agreements such as the Nuremberg Code and the Declaration of Helsinki (Williams, 2005), as well as being clearly influenced by the Belmont Report. But while the Belmont Report provides recommendations for research which can be interpreted in an online context, Common Rule (45 CFR 46, Subpart A) sets the rules for research when it is being funded by one of the 18 Federal agencies. As part of the checks and balances, this formulation requires a review of the proposed research by an Institutional Review Board (IRB), the informed consent of research subjects, and institutional assurances of compliance with these regulations (Williams, 2005).

INTERPRETATION OF EXISTING GUIDELINES FOR ONLINE PURPOSES

Considering that existing ethical guidelines emerging from these sources (Belmont, 1979; Federal, 1991) are generally meant for off-line research, it raises the obvious question of whether they can be applied to online research as they stand, or whether they can be easily modified to take cognisance of the changed circumstances.

As a starting point, we note that according to Knobel (2003), as early as 2001 the Association of Internet Researchers (AOIR, 2001, p. 1) had identified a number of important differences between online and off-line research. These are:

- A greater risk to individual privacy and confidentiality. The risk is greater because the online information about individuals faces a greater accessibility compared with off-line information. This would increase the likelihood that subjects are not aware that their behaviors and communications are being observed and recorded (e.g., in a large-scale analysis of postings in a chatroom or an online forum).
- A greater challenge to researchers regarding the obtaining of informed consent. As discussed later in this chapter, obtaining informed consent from an online participant involves significantly more problems compared with off-line participants. This raises questions related to how to obtain ethical consent and how to validate the consent in the anonymized online world.
- A greater difficulty in ascertaining subjects' identity. Online users overwhelmingly use pseudonyms and therefore do not reveal their real identity. This raises questions related on how to validate the consent in the anonymized online world. In many cases, an online user can employ multiple identities, a problem that needs to be carefully considered by the researcher.
- A greater difficulty in selecting the correct ethical approach. Due to the rich diversity of research venues (private email, chatroom, webpages, etc.) the researcher needs to be more careful in applying the right ethical approach for the particular context. It may be that one approach is not appropriate for a different situation that involves special issues or personnel, for example.
- A greater difficulty in discerning ethically correct approaches. The Internet allows engagement of people from multiple cultural backgrounds and from varying levels of autonomy, which implies we may need to institute different ethically approaches.

In summary, Knobel (2003) suggests that: (i) it is more difficult in the online world to the distinguish between public and private spaces; (ii) obtaining informed consent from study participants is much more problematic; and (iii) the assurance of participants' anonymity in research publications can be very difficult to ensure if the material is in the public sphere.

Whereas these points are a generally useful beginning platform, Trevisan in Trevisan and Reilly (2014) has concluded that the "universal" ethical guidelines, provided in the early years of the 21st century, have become rapidly outdated, as both new media technologies and user behaviors have evolved. New technologies have made it easier to create web pages with interactive functions that can be used as user forums or chat rooms. This flexibility and ease of access allows more universal involvement with chat room, since while these functions are not only easier and cheaper to implement they are also, when created, easier to use. Hence, more people with less technical skills (elderly or handicapped people and children) are able to access the online world and participate in it.

The increasing population involved in online groups has a significant impact on the behavior of the group and the people who contribute to it. We can assume that the increased population on a site develops a higher and more complex dynamic in behavior change, as is seen in real world situations. For example, some extreme behavior patterns can be developed and copied by other users. The boundaries of accepted and expected behavior therefore are constantly changing. This can be seen in the common use of some words or phrases that were not acceptable in a conversation some years ago because they appeared to be vulgar or politically incorrect but now they have become accepted vocabulary (Tudor, 2010). A similar development happens in the online world, where behavior that initially was not acceptable in the society has now become acceptable. This is clearly seen in the range of topics that emerge in online discussions. Topics that were not open for discussion some years ago are now appearing and receiving open acceptance. This has a significant impact on the ethical considerations given to use of the material, since an issue that previously needed carefully ethical consideration is now being discussed openly.

Trevisan and Reilly (2014) discuss these changes that relate to the boundaries between personal and political content on social websites. They particularly mention ethical questions related to the protection of the privacy of disabled participants in this content. On the one hand, disabled participants require a level of protection, but, on the other hand, the availability of a social web page offers them a liberating forum in which they can find an equal voice.

Roberts' (2015) observation is that ethical discussions related to conduct qualitative research stem from 2001. This work was initially provided by Eysenbach and Till (2001) and Roberts feels it would be timely to now revisit ethical issues associated with conducting qualitative research within Internet communities. As a consequence, Roberts identifies and discusses added guidelines regarding conducting ethical research in online communities, suggesting that the following works need to be consulted:

1. The National Health and Medical Research Council, the Australian Research Council, and the Australian Vice-Chancellors' Committee, 2007.

2. The American Psychological Association Report of Board of Scientific Affairs' Advisory Group on the conduct of research on the Internet (Kraut et al., 2004).
3. The British Psychological Society (2007), *Guidelines for ethical practice in psychological research online*.

Based upon these guidelines, Roberts indicates that ethical research balances potential benefits from research against potential harm. However, now that qualitative psychological research is increasingly conducted online, the question of what constitutes harm and who has the "right" to define harm within online communities, has become somewhat contentious (Hair & Clark, 2007). In a similar vein, Thomas (1996) illustrates the variety of positions about guidelines in online social research to illustrate the complexity of this area, Thomas has identified (i) deontological, (ii) teleological, and (iii) postmodern approaches to this issue. However, notwithstanding the variety of positions about guidelines, there seems to exist some common agreement that online research also needs to follow the general and fundamental principles of the Belmont report, these principles need additional interpretation related to the differences between online and off-line research as discussed above. In the following section, we revisit the three principles and discuss their interpretation for online research.

THE THREE PROPOSED PRINCIPLES APPLIED TO ONLINE RESEARCH

Based on the available perspectives on ethical research behavior which were previously presented, there appears to be common agreement in the area that online research also needs to follow the three Principles proposed by the Belmont Report (Belmont, 1979), each of which will be considered as follows.

AUTONOMY

As indicated earlier, the first principle requires that subjects be treated with respect as autonomous agents. In practice, this principle manly focuses on the processes related to informed consent (Frankel & Siang, 1999). In this respect, it is important to note that obtaining informed consent is more complex in online research compared with conventional research. It requires the researcher to consider, in addition to the question of what is informed consent, to address the questions of: (i) when it is required, (ii) how it can be obtained in the online world, and (iii) how it can be validated in the online world. Each of these questions will be explicitly discussed as follows.

What Is Informed Consent in the Online Research?

In Thomas' (1996) opinion, informed consent regarding online research remains the same as in the conventional research. It naturally contains the three elements: information, comprehension, and voluntariness as discussed earlier in this chapter. However, while the notion of informed consent is interpreted in the same way as in conventional research, there is nevertheless an implication that more discussion may be required, and if so, the method of how it may be obtained and validated needs to be explicitly addressed.

When Is Informed Consent Required?

Some opinions say consent is always required. King (1996) sees a potential harm for authors of messages in cyberspace forums when they remain unaware that their messages are being analyzed until the results of the research are published. There is a risk that messages may be misinterpreted, leading to wrong and damaging interpretations being presented in the research results.

Other opinions say for the use of publicly available material, informed consent is not generally required, but then this decision may finally depend on the context in which the message has been posted (Frankel & Siang, 1999). It appears that, to decide if informed consent is required, a distinction between the public and private domains is important. The public domain commonly refers to information-generating institutions and repositories such as television, public records, radio, printed books, or conferences, and data collected from these public domains might not need the consent of the author to be used in research. The question of interest here is whether the same considerations can be applied to data from online newsgroups and online support groups that, ostensibly at least, are openly accessible to anyone and which can be accessed by anyone, many months or years after the messages were initially posted. Put in other words, does this feature of accessibility make these postings a public domain and therefore open to widespread use?

Liu (1999) says, regarding data handling and data reporting, no ethical issues arise as long as direct quotation is avoided and it is not possible to relate the work to any particular participant. In this view, the only issue up for debate is regarding the method of data collection, and it is here that ethical issues may arise. According to Waskul (1996), online interaction is neither public nor private, and he uses the notions of being "publicly private and privately public." Particular cases need to be seen in the context of the forum in which it has been published. In this respect, Liu distinguishes three different kinds of online communications, suggesting that there are (i) postings in public channels, (ii) postings in private channels, and (iii) private one-to-one exchanges.

According to the views of Liu (1999), public channels are those avenues with no restrictions on who can view the data. The implication here is that there would be no consent required for research use of data help in such a format since they are explicitly meant for public consumption, and these postings would be open for recording, analyzing, and reporting as long as the identities are shielded. Further, it would imply that it would be not necessary to inform the author or to obtain their consent for use of the data before collecting the postings for research purpose (Liu, 1999; Paccagnella, 1997). It would therefore remain the author's responsibility to filter out the messages that they might consider revealing or constitute a misuse of private information (Frankel & Siang, 1999). As an example, Rodriquez (2013) considers that even websites related to sensitive online communities, such as those focused on Alzheimer's disease, will fall into the category of public spaces on the basis that they are not password protected.

Some researchers have gone so far as to say that even sites that require registration may be viewed as public spaces. Schotanus-Dijkstra, Havinga, van Ballegooijen, Delfosse, Mokkenstorm, and Boon (2014) analyzed postings to online support groups for persons-at-risk regarding tendencies to commit suicide. These sites required registration, and the researchers requested, and obtained, permission to use recorded data from the owning organizations. They did not, however, seek permission from participating individuals. The authors argued that the groups were in the public domain, despite the registration-restricted process, and therefore informed consent was not required at the individual level.

We find that these two examples raise an important secondary consideration. Should the sensitivity of the topic or setting need to be considered in determining whether an online community should be regarded as public or private, notwithstanding the mode or ease of access to the information?

An interesting perspective has been given by the Association of Internet Researchers (AoIR) (Buchanan, 2012, p. 4), who have a guiding principle that the researcher's obligation to protect the individuals' well-being and privacy increases as the individual's vulnerability increases. Trevisan and Reilly (2014) looked at this first guiding principle carefully and argued that it would be difficult to identify and verify the members of a potential "vulnerable online group" as being really vulnerable people. This is based on the understanding that the identity of individual members of online communities is, as is usual in the online world, anonymous. This anonymity means it would be practically impossible to verify if a particular member or members chosen for research purposes are really representatives of a "vulnerable online group."

A second issue that arises is that disability scholars have criticized the default categorization of disabled people as "feeble" and "vulnerable" (Finkelstein, 1980). They argue that when experiences of disabled people which have been reported in postings are treated too cautiously, it would disempower the posters and reinforce the "experts know best" approach. This characterization of posters involved in digital disability rights groups as being "vulnerable" by default and thus holding back important information from the reports would, in many instances, jeopardized the very nature of the study.

These author's caution that "special treatment" can be seen as *de facto* "silencing" of disabled people's voices which, in their opinion, would result in more harm than good. The challenge is to ensure a fair representation of participants' voices without violating personal rights, and instead of focusing on "who" presented the content in a particular argument, the focus should be rather on what was said. In this respect, Trevisan and Reilly (2014) identified a list of examples of "sensitive topics" which needs to be handled with additional care:

- Personal daily routines;
- Individual details about impairment and/or medical records;
- Emotional accounts of pain and chronic illness;
- Financial information about income and/or welfare payments;
- Discrimination and abuse episodes;
- Criticism/praise of individual providers of healthcare and support services;
- Suicidal thoughts.

Private channels are those avenues where permission needs to be granted before an external person can gain access, either by being invited or being granted access to the avenue after a request. The process for approval can be manual, where a site administrator determines whether the person is eligible to view the content, or automatic, such as with those websites that require registration before viewing the content. Often, this latter option does not require any other proof of identity. Of relevance here is that, while obtaining access to the information is relatively straightforward, the use of data from these channels for research purposes becomes more complicated. It would, for example, depend on the number of participants involved in the channel. If there are a large number of participants in the communication it could be argued that it is as a public channel, while if there are only two or three participants it needs to be considered as a private channel (Liu, 1999; King, 1996; Herring, 1996). Determining the threshold between these definitions is not an easy task, and needs to be properly considered for each context.

Private one-to-one messaging is always regarded as private communication. Its use as research material would require informed consent from the messaging participants before any recording of their private communications, or gathering personal information, is to be instituted (Liu, 1999). A prime example of such a channel is email, where the sender only intends for the recipient to receive and have access to the message, but it is technically possible for a third party to gain a copy of the material.

How Can Informed Consent Be Obtained and From Whom?

If the researcher comes to the conclusion that informed consent is required for use of online material, then it immediately raises the question of from whom the consent needs to be required (Roberts, 2015). This is also one of the Internet-specific ethical questions raised by the Association of Internet Researchers (AoIR) (Buchanan, 2012). Consent may be requested from the individual poster, the group who have hosted the forum, the web page moderators, or from a combination of these sources. Rodriguez, for example, in his research asked the web page owners for consent but not the individuals (Rodriquez, 2013). In contrast, Roberts (2015) advises following a very strict regime, where informed consent from individual research participants would generally be required for data collection on private spaces of online settings. Further, informed consent should be required regarding data collection on public online settings in the case that some individuals indicate they want permission sought before their quotes are used (Bond, Ahmed, Hind, Thomas, & Hewitt-Taylor, 2013). However, in addition to the consent of individual research participants, Roberts advises that the researchers also need to provide notifications to the community and community gatekeepers for the group, and, further, repeated notifications would be necessary as membership of online communities changes over time. Roberts (2015) has also outlined that often members of online communities react negatively to having research conducted within their community. Eysenbach and Till (2001) analyzed newsgroup comments in response to research requests. They identified concerns relating to researcher unfamiliarity with the online contexts studied and found examples of resentment when the research is conducted by an existing member of the group.

However, not all community members have negative reactions to being researched. According to a study by Moreno, Grant, Kacvinsky, and Fleming (Moreno, Grant, Kacvinsky, Moreno, & Fleming, 2012), more than a half of 132 interviewed 18–19-year-old Facebook users accepted the study while 28.8% were neutral, and only 15.2% expressed concerns. While only a small number of community members in this study articulated concerns, they nevertheless cannot be ignored. This brings the discussion back to the dilemma between "disturbing the integrity of Internet communities by seeking consent, or violating privacy by not seeking consent" (Heilferty, 2011, p. 949). Both horns of this dilemma need to be balanced in the context of online research.

OBTAINING CONSENT

This foregoing discussion raises the question of how intending online researchers might go about obtaining meaningful consent for the use of web-based data. There are three immediately obvious ways to proceed: (i) to ask directly for consent, (ii) to look for implied consent in the culture of the data source, and to look for clues in the report that might include consent.

Asking for Consent

The first way to obtain the consent would be to ask for it. In the online world this can be difficult, impossible, or sometimes potentially harmful. In many cases, the discussion was undertaken months or years ago and the author does not longer participate in the forum. In addition, many websites do not require formal identification for accounts, allowing users to be registered under alias names with no personally identifying information. In some cases, even the email address used to register may no longer be in use, making it nearly impossible to contact the author of older posts.

Harm can happen to the researched online community. In Bradley and Carter's (2012) study, the ethics committee advised the researcher should not misrepresent themselves in the interactive "chat room." This would disturb the natural flow of the discussion. As a consequence, the Association of Internet Researchers (AoIR) (Buchanan, 2012) asks that the researcher needs to be able to change research procedures or requirements in the case that the desired consent cannot be obtained.

Also, King (1996) sees a disturbing problem in the analysis of online communications. Requesting permission from the group to undertake a study will possibly influence the behavior of the members and impact the result of the research. One way out of this "Hawthorne effect" dilemma would be to wait till the end of the study and ask for consent before publication. This would run the risk for the study that the researcher might not get permission to publish their results and ruin the efforts of the research. This possibility highlights the significance of the dilemma of the conflict between ensuring the legitimacy of the results, while respecting the considerations of the author of the data.

Implied Consent
Culture

One way of looking at implied consent is the culture in which the data is given. For example, the online microblogging website "Twitter" encourages openness between its users. Twitter's "About page" contains the following statement, front and center:

> "Twitter helps you create and share ideas and information instantly, without barriers" (Williams, 2005). In addition, Twitter's privacy page contains the following tip:
>> "What you say on Twitter may be viewed all around the world instantly" (Twitter, 2015b).

More explicitly, their privacy statement contains the following information:

> "Our Services are primarily designed to help you share information with the world. Most of the information you provide us is information you are asking us to make public. This includes not only the messages you Tweet and the metadata provided with Tweets, such as when you Tweeted, but also the lists you create, the people you follow, the Tweets you mark as favorites or Retweet, and many other bits of information that result from your use of the Services" (Twitter, 2015b).

Information on Twitter is more than the basic content of the messages (or tweets). It automatically includes location information, which is added. For instance, when a user tweets from their smartphone the automatic adding of location information is, as the above statement says, considered public information. Users have the option of not sharing their location information but they have to change the settings on their Twitter account.

Looking at the Twitter's "About page" and the above tip, it could be reasonably assumed that if information is on Twitter, there is an implied consent that the information is publicly available. Of course, as we have discussed, publicly available is not the same permission for using the data in a research study. There is still a significant risk for harm to the involved posters by publication of the analysis results and their interpretation. As discussed later in this chapter, the publication of misinterpreted results, which can be applied to an individual or a group of individuals, can put them in an unfavorable light. They might be embarrassed, exposed, or even experience social disadvantages due to these damaging interpretations.

In contrast, consider the online profile website Facebook. Facebook information is, by default, available only to friends of the given user. There are settings to make posts public included in the options. It is interesting to note that this has not always been the case, where earlier versions of Facebook were much more open by default. The posts' default privacy setting was public, and consequently there was a lot of information available generally. This has been significantly restricted in recent years (from 2012 to the present). Facebook, in this way, is implied to be "not public," and one could argue that even if posts are set to be publicly available, this may be more as a result of technical error than intent on the user's behalf.

Facebook's privacy website focuses on how users can select who can see particular data. Its operation focuses on restricting access to data and allaying concerns that people may have about who can have access to what they post. By couching access in these terms, Facebook is implied to be "not public," and care should be taken to obtain consent before using data from Facebook, even though data may be labeled as being "publicly available."

Trevisan and Reilly (2014) question to what extent Facebook pages and social media platforms can be treated as "public" spaces. They opine that it would be a question that could never be finally answered because both the technology and the user habits change constantly. This situation allows only a case-by-case approach that must consider simultaneously features of individual online platforms, experiences in comparable off-line spaces, and the topic to which the individual is trying to contribute. As discussed earlier in this chapter, the sensitivity of the topic and the nature of the group needs to be carefully considered.

While Facebook hosts both public and private groups, it also requires users to register to access its services (Sveningsson Elm, 2008) in Markham and Baym (2008). By looking at this from this site it could be categorized as a public space because the user voluntarily did not uses the offered privacy settings for his account during the registrations process or later and remained public (Zimmer, 2010). Indeed, most Facebook pages are set up in such a way so as to allow any Facebook user to freely view their content, and since the owner of the pages is aware of this, it might be reasonable to consider Facebook to be seen as a "semi-public" space. This reinforces the need for the researcher to consider whether to obtain informed consent or possibly to merely inform the users that research is being conducted. In these cases, there should be a statement of what measures will be taken to ensure that users' privacy and anonymity will be protected.

Another difference between Facebook and Twitter (and the vast array of other social media websites, each with their own nuances), a difference that is also reflected in other social websites, is that while Twitter allows people to use pseudonyms, Facebook explicitly forbids this practice and will ban users who do not use their real names. This distinction is probably one of the most critical in deciding whether implied public permission is given to outside persons wishing to use the site for other purposes. If the website has a policy that forces the use of a real name, then users probably need to be asked about the sensitivity of the data they are sharing, and who they might authorize to see it. While people can, and do, share their real names on Twitter, this is by choice and is not being enforced as a requirement of using the service – this possibly implies wider access consent.

Other Ways of Implied Consent

The University of Newcastle in the UK writes on their "Research and Enterprise Services" page that implied/implicit consent can be provided by an act that shows that the person knowingly provides consent. Such consent to participate in a study might be implied by, for example, completing a questionnaire (Newcastle, 2015). The author of a posting can express consent for further publication directly or indirectly in the posting. It can be expressed directly by saying, "I want people to know about this experience," or indirectly it can be said that "I want to inform and warn people about this situation or experience." Further, it can be argued that some Internet forums imply consent for wider usage through the nature of the topic. A forum that offers to share information about experiences related to potential danger can be seen as a forum where users make a post explicitly in order to have a voice and to warn other people.

How Can Provided Consent Be Validated?

Finally, there is the nature of the consent form and the validity of the process. In the physical world, informed consent is either secured with a written signature on a consent form, or with telephone surveys there is reliance on verbal consent. Online, the equivalent would be a click to a statement such as "I agree to the above consent form." A significant problem here, though, is the question of how valid is such consent may be when the age, competency, or comprehension of the potential subject is unknown? The key issue therefore is to resolve how informed consent can be authenticated online. As indicated earlier in this discussion, special considerations are needed for vulnerable members of the community, such as children and persons of diminished mental capacity. In this respect, the use of pseudonyms leads to the possibility that vulnerable populations not normally recruited for a study could be included without the researcher's knowledge (Frankel & Siang, 1999). Further, most "vulnerable persons" by this definition are quite capable (and often do) click through these consent forms without being aware of the implications.

If, in a particular instance, there is no evidence available for consent or that validation of consent is not possible, the researcher will need to carefully consider requirements under which the data can be ethically used. The identity of the initial author will need to be protected by anonymization of the data, and there should be no use of direct citations. This issue will be revisited later in this chapter.

BENEFITS AGAINST RISKS

There is widely common consent in the literature that an elementary principle of research ethics is to minimize potential harm for the people involved in the research.

Waskul (1996) says that the researcher must take great care not to harm the participants in any way or to skew the context of the research. Liu (1999) follows this opinion and says further that, related to research ethics, while it does not essentially matter if codes are not explicitly followed, it is most important to protect the participants for any potential harm.

In contrast, Frankel and Siang (1999) see the situation more in relation to the outcome of the research, and states that research ethics requires researchers to maximize the possible benefit from the research and minimize the harm and risk to the participants. This can be interpreted that a certain risk or even small harm can be accepted if it is balanced with the research outcome, which can be an important contribution to knowledge (Frankel & Siang, 1999). It can be argued this must be a significant benefit for the research, which can be generally recognized by the society as being more important than the violation of the integrity of the participating individual. It could also be argued that the individual could accept the small risk or harm in order to gain a personal benefit. This personal benefit could be an improvement of well-being, obtaining a voice to articulate an issue, or even a direct financial reward.

Benefits

Benefits can be defined as gain to the individual through improved well-being, or empowerment of the individual by giving him or her voice (Frankel & Siang, 1999). Well-being can be gained by supporting the author's intention to send a message to people with a similar background or to contribute to find a solution for a certain problem. The second aspect, which is related to giving a voice, appears to be very important in this respect when it is realized that it can help people who have difficulties in accessing real public forums due to illness, remote living conditions, or lack of verbal communication skills, to be heard.

Benefits can also be defined as gain to the society or science through a contribution to the knowledge base (Frankel & Siang, 1999). In this context, it can be seen as a benefit to be able to collect data from widely dispersed populations at relatively low cost and in less time when compared with similar efforts in the physical world. In this way, the use of online datasets can increase the successful outcome of the research. Also the fact that an increased use of cyber communities, where people from all geographical areas are able to communicate and discuss any subject, increases the research options and contributes to a potential successful research outcome in a reasonable short time with less effort when compared with the real world.

On the other hand, these benefits need to be balanced with any potential risks or harm that may arise for the respondents, a discussion of which follows.

Risks

The utility of publicly available datasets is quite extensive, with an increasing number of studies using datasets of this nature. This increasing number of studies increases the potential for harm which can be caused through the study.

Harm to Participant

Harm, in general, usually refers to the possibility of serious injury or psychological abuse and may not only affect individuals, but specific population subgroups as well (Frankel & Siang, 1999). While these forms of harm are obviously significant, they are not likely to occur in online research.

The most likely harm to research participants in online research is the loss of privacy and public exposure, which may include the loss of reputation of the poster's virtual identity in the virtual world. Many Internet users build and maintain carefully their virtual identity in online environments and this identity often becomes as important as a real identity. The damage or loss of the reputation of this identity represents a significant harm in the personal life of the individual.

Loss of privacy can be particularly troublesome in cases where different databases are linked together. For instance, a small amount of information shared on one website can be linked with other small amounts of information on other websites. For instance, a user may reveal their country of origin on one site, and complain about the weather on another site. Together, these could quickly tell someone which city the person lives in by matching this against weather records on that day. More nuanced cases could even reveal much more detailed information. Data contained on digital photos could contain location information, leading to the exact whereabouts of a person. Linking this with data on other websites could reveal exactly who and where a person is.

Zimmer (2010) undertook research on the social website Facebook. Despite taking care to protect privacy, significant violations occurred through the project. After analyzing the violations Zimmer identified two elementary ethical problems that led, in their project, to violations of the integrity of website members whose data were analyzed. These were:

1. Failure to mitigate what leads to privacy violation;
2. Failure to adhere to ethical research standards.

These observations allowed Zimmer to identify the following factors that can cause privacy violation. First, the collection and storage of extensive large amounts of personally identifiable data inevitably increases the risk of privacy violation (Smith, Milberg, & Burke, 1996). Large amounts of data make it hard for researchers to properly manage and disguise personally identifiable information. An example of this is the release of the "Enron emails." Enron was a very large multinational corporation in the 1990s, with a reported revenue at the time of over $100 billion. It was revealed in 2001 that there were widespread fraudulent practices within the company, a revelation that would eventually bankrupt the company and lead to substantial criminal charges. As part of the investigation, the regulator released a large number of emails that are believed to number more than 600,000. This resulting dataset is now used by researchers across the world in many different domains, as it is a rich source of information. However, it also contained personally identifiable information, including social security numbers, addresses, medical files, and other information. Some of these data has been retracted in common sources of the email dataset, but is nevertheless still widely available in older versions. A researcher collecting information of this scale would not be able to manually process each to determine if personal information is involved.

Ethical concerns from citizens in Pennsylvania, USA, lead to the call for a moratorium on data collection (Hoge, 2014). On January 3, 2012, new FERPA regulations went into effect that allowed contractors to access personally identifiable information in a student's record. After investigation, Hoge identified significant problems in the regulations which could lead to privacy violations. This led to a request to Governor Corbett to place a moratorium on the data collection in the Pennsylvania Information Management System and to rescind all contracts with outside contractors who can access personally identifiable information.

The second factor identified by Zimmer which can cause privacy violation was that the risk of privacy violations increases when information about individuals is accessible to persons who are not properly, or specifically, authorized to have access to that data. Third, unauthorized secondary use of personal information is a concern in that information collected from individuals for one purpose might be used for another secondary purpose without authorization from the individual, thus the subject loses control over their information. Within Smith (1996) framework, this loss of control over one's personal information is considered a privacy violation.

Fourth, errors in the dataset which can lead to a wrong interpretation can constitute a privacy violation. It not only leads to a wrong conclusion, but also has the risk of applying the wrong attributes to individuals or a group of individuals who cannot identify themselves having these characteristics. It can also lead to undue embarrassment of the individuals if the identification is possible. This has resulted in various policies ensuring individuals are granted the ability to view and edit data collected about them to minimize any potential privacy violations.

The resulting harm that can emerge from deliberate or unintentional misuse of data can take a number of forms, which are individually noted as follows:

Harm for the Online Group

The sense that their group is no longer anonymous will negatively affect the interpersonal dynamics among group members and adversely impact the level of intimacy among participants. The risk exists for the research to damage the very phenomena of cyberspace interpersonal dynamics that one is intent on exploring. It has been claimed that such naturalistic observations can irrevocably damage the community studied (King, 1996).

Roberts (2015) outlined that when a study is undertaken related to online communities, all members of the community may be affected and not only the members who choose to participate. For example, not only could the author of a piece be affected, but also the entire online group may suffer since they all might be presented in a wrong light, creating distress, social exposure, or embarrassment. Moreover, if the results are published in such a way that members of a virtual community can identify their community as the one studied without their knowledge, psychological harm may result.

Harm for the Researcher

Revealing research can also cause harm for the researcher. This can happen by receiving distressing information, virtual, or real threats. Besides the normal academic or nonacademic critical comments that the researcher needs to address in an academic way through additional publication or presentations, they may need do deal with unjustified written or verbal attacks. In many cases, it is enough not to merely respond to these charges, but the researcher will need to be prepared to cope personally with them so that it does not do any harm to his own psyche.

When Can These Risks Happen?

This lack of understanding by participants, and sometimes researchers as well, of the technical and storage capabilities of Internet technologies may elevate these risks. The risk of exposure can surface at different stages of research, from data gathering, to data processing, to data storage, and dissemination. These stages can include one case where datasets that are not normally public being made available by researchers, or a second case where data are reused when it is publicly available.

In the first case, there are often ambiguous problems arising with the aggregation of data. For instance, if the linking of databases allows for the identification of individuals, either directly through personally identifiable information, or indirection through the use of informed guesses. In these cases, those databases should not be allowed to be released together, and this is so important that the Australian government, for instance, contains laws that prohibit certain databases being linked for this reason. The research advantages would be beneficial though, from both a knowledge generation and public policy perspective. Being able to link health databases to social services databases would allow for improved services, more efficient social infrastructure, and better outcomes. This must be balanced with the loss of privacy, and the potential for noncleared employees to see confidential data, where, for example, a social worker might be able to see or infer knowledge about a person's health from their benefits.

It is the second case, where publicly available data are collected "first hand" by a researcher or an analyst, which this chapter particularly focuses upon. In these cases, it is often not clear where a database will lead the research until it is analyzed. Any loss of privacy may be able to be estimated up-front, but may change as the data are collected. Further, there is the possibility for the data collection or collation processes to be incorrect, leading to an excess of data being collected. Another related concern is security. While very large online data sources, such as Facebook or Twitter, have good security mechanisms in place for instance to stop people viewing information marked as private, not all sources as well as this would be protected. As an example, a hotel app was found to leak the booking details of other customers, a normally private piece of information. If the data sources cannot be trusted to keep these data secure, this may lead to a loss of privacy. However, it cannot be denied that the benefit to, for instance, an intelligence agency would be significant if they could know who is staying in which room, contributing to knowledge of the movements of people of interest.

Furthermore, as data are accumulated and stored over the years, outdated or poorly designed security measures may create more opportunity for the risk exposure to a later time. *The Internet does not forget*, and information that finds its way online can frequently be retrieved many years later. With the development of improved search engines, data become even more accessible. In addition to individual record files, data can be copied through automated processes and redundantly stored on several sites. As a consequence, even if the information was deleted from the original page, it might still be available on different web pages. For example, people who added a photo in their profile on LinkedIn can often find that picture elsewhere online.

JUSTICE

Justice, the third principle according the Belmont report discussed earlier, seeks a fair distribution of the burdens and benefits associated with research. The Belmont report introduced this principle when it was found that, after research in health area was undertaken, certain individuals were seen to bear disproportionate risks in medical experiments without getting consequent benefits. This happened during World War II (Annas & Grodin, 1995), in prior experiments (Lederer & Davis, 1995), and later, for example, in the Milgram experiments (Badhwar, 2009).

While in online research we do not expect this type of physically harm to occur to an individual, as discussed earlier the concern is with privacy violation and its potential for harm. When we look a fair and equal balance of risk it goes back to the selection process of the data which belong to the individuals. Applying the Belmont principle of justice to the online world, it can be interpreted that the selection of participant data must ensure that subjects' data are selected for reasons directly related to the problem being studied instead of for their easy availability. This principle of justice in the online world is mainly related to a fair selection process of the data and the involved process to obtain consent as discussed earlier.

Flicker (Flicker, Haans, & Skinner, 2004) follows Frankel (Frankel & Siang, 1999) opinion that sees the ethical principle of justice in health research being interpreted as "fair, equitable, and appropriate treatment in light of what is due or owed to persons." The principle of justice comes to life during analyzing messages from their message board. The dilemma here is that messages are posted in ongoing conversations, and the posts where the researcher has consent to use, are mixed with posts where they have no consent (Flicker, Haans, & Skinner, 2004). These authors discuss the question of justice in relation to justification of selection of the posts and a justified usage of postings where no consent was obtained.

Frankel follows the opinion that justice in the online research is mainly related to the selection process and adds that the application of justice would be complicated due to the feature of anonymous and pseudonymous communications (Frankel & Siang, 1999). In the physical world, researchers need to consider factors as gender, race, and age in the selection process, but this is obviously more difficult in the Internet environment as many people protect their anonymity and this information is not available.

SUMMARY

The Internet offers a large amount of data that are public accessible, and these data offer a convenient and reliable source of research which is currently being more and more used. For ethical reasons, guidelines for research use are clearly essential, and the Belmond report is important because it provides three principles that are generally used as guideline for conventional research. The principles of "Autonomy, Benefits, and Justice" also provide a good ethical basis for online research but need additional, sensitive interpretation because the conditions of the medium are very different. It depends on the topic, the online community, the access requirements to the forum and the research which level of ethics clearance are required. Sensitive areas need to be looked at case by case to make a decision related to ethical questions.

One important issue that continually arises is that personal reports from some vulnerable groups are meant to, and possibly want to, be heard by the public. This implies that just because information comes from a recognizable vulnerable group, it does not mean that research must necessarily ignore or alter it significantly. It needs to be treated with ethical consideration and can be included in a study to provide these groups with a voice. The Internet might be the only chance to tell the public about the topic.

Ethical considerations in online research are significantly more complex and require a more sensitive case-by-case decision than traditional research. In addition to this complexity, Internet technology develops rapidly, and the user behavior changes so quickly that the researcher will be forced to revisit their ethical consideration regularly. In addition, online sources of information lack to maturity in research-collection methods that off-line data sources have.

Researchers aiming to use online data need to take into considerations the issues presented in this chapter, as well as interpreting those within the legal and ethics frameworks imposed upon their research.

This means that in addition to the existing guidelines, as per the Belmond report, they need to consider two main differences between online and off-line research and apply it to their research. First, there is a greater risk to privacy and confidentiality in online research, as opposed to physical harm normally associated with conventional research. As a consequence, the researcher needs to plan the project in a way to limit this risk and avoid any violation. Second, it is a greater challenge to obtain informed consent of research participants. Researchers need to look at ways how to obtain this informed consent and need to have a strategy to deal with data where it is not possible to obtain it. While informed consent is difficult to achieve, it is a cornerstone to ethical research.

References

Alam, S. S., Yeow, P. H. P., & Loo, H. S. (2011). An empirical study on online social networks sites usage: online dating sites perspective. *International Journal of Business and Management, 6*(10), 155.

Annas, G. J., & Grodin, M. A. (1995). The Nazi doctors and the Nuremberg code. *Journal of Pharmacy and Law, 4*, 167–245.

Association of Internet Researchers (AOIR) (2001). AOIR Ethics Working Committee: a preliminary report. aoir.org/reports/ethics.html (accessed 7 April 2015).

Badhwar, N. K. (2009). The Milgram experiments, learned helplessness, and character traits. *The Journal of Ethics, 13*(2–3), 257–289.

Belmont, R. (1979). *Ethical principles and guidelines for the protection of human subjects of research.* Washington, DC: Department of Health, Education, and Welfare. Retrieved from http://www.hhs.gov/ohrp/policy/belmont.html.

Bickart, B., & Schindler, R. M. (2001). Internet forums as influential sources of consumer information. *Journal of Interactive Marketing, 15*(3), 31–40.

Bond, C. S., Ahmed, O. H., Hind, M., Thomas, B., & Hewitt-Taylor, J. (2013). The conceptual and practical ethical dilemmas of using health discussion board posts as research data. *Journal of Medical Internet Research, 15*(6), e112.

Bradley, S. K., & Carter, B. (2012). Reflections on the ethics of Internet newsgroup research. *International Journal of Nursing Studies, 49*(5), 625–630.

Buchanan, E. (2012). *Ethical decision-making and Internet research.* Retrieved from http://pure.au.dk/portal/files/55543125/aoirethics2.pdf

Diaz, A. A. (2013). "Getting Information off the Internet Is like Taking a Drink from a Fire Hydrant" - The Murky Area of Authenticating Website Screenshots in the Courtroom. *American Journal of Trial Advocacy, 37*, 65.

Ellison, N. B. (2007). Social network sites: definition, history, and scholarship. *Journal of Computer-Mediated Communication, 13*(1), 210–230.

Eysenbach, G., & Till, J. E. (2001). Ethical issues in qualitative research on Internet communities. *BMJ (Clinical Research Ed.), 323*(7321), 1103–1105.

Federal, R. (1991). *Part II: Federal policy for the protection of human subjects; notices and rules.* Washington, DC: U.S. Government Printing Office.

Finkelstein, V. (1980). *Attitudes and disabled people: Issues for discussion.* New York: World Rehabilitation Fund. Retrieved from http://disability-studies.leeds.ac.uk/files/library/finkelstein-attitudes.pdf.

Flicker, S., Haans, D., & Skinner, H. (2004). Ethical dilemmas in research on Internet communities. *Qualitative Health Research, 14*(1), 124–134.

Frankel, M. S., & Siang, S. (1999). Ethical and legal aspects of human subjects research on the Internet. *Published by AAAS Online.*

Hair, N., & Clark, M. (2007). The ethical dilemmas and challenges of ethnographic research in electronic communities. *International Journal of Market Research, 49*(6), 781–800.

Haker, H., Lauber, C., & Rössler, W. (2005). Internet forums: a self-help approach for individuals with schizophrenia? *Acta Psychiatrica Scandinavica, 112*(6), 474–477.

Heilferty, C. M. (2011). Ethical considerations in the study of online illness narratives: a qualitative review. *Journal of Advanced Nursing, 67*(5), 945–953.

Herring, S. (1996). Linguistic and critical analysis of computer-mediated communication: some ethical and scholarly considerations. *The Information Society, 12*(2), 153–168.

HHS, U. (2015). Federal policy for the protection of human subjects ('common rule'). Retrieved from http://www.hhs.gov/ohrp/humansubjects/commonrule.

Hoge, A. (2014). Consent frequently asked questions. Retrieved from http://www.newswithviews.com/Hoge/anita111.htm.

King, S. A. (1996). Researching Internet communities: proposed ethical guidelines for the reporting of results. *The Information Society, 12*(2), 119–128.

Knobel, M. (2003). Rants, ratings and representation: ethical issues in researching online social practices. *Education, Communication & Information, 3*(2), 187–210.

Kraut, R., Olson, J., Banaji, M., Bruckman, A., Cohen, J., & Couper, M. (2004). Psychological research online: report of board of scientific affairs' advisory group on the conduct of research on the Internet. *American Psychologist, 59*(2), 105.

Lederer, S., & Davis, A. B. (1995). Subjected to science: human experimentation in America before the Second World War. *History: Reviews of New Books, 24*(1), 13–113.

Liu, G. Z. (1999). Virtual community presence in Internet relay chatting. *Journal of Computer-Mediated Communication, 5*(1), 0–10.

Markham, A. N., & Baym, N. K. (2008). *Internet inquiry: Conversations about method.* Thousand Oaks, CA: Sage Publications.

Moreno, M. A., Grant, A., Kacvinsky, L., Moreno, P., & Fleming, M. (2012). Older adolescents' views regarding participation in Facebook research. *Journal of Adolescent Health, 51*(5), 439–444.

Newcastle, U. (2015). Consent frequently asked questions. Retrieved from http://www.ncl.ac.uk/res/research/ethics_governance/ethics/toolkit/consent/consent_faqs.htm.

Paccagnella, L. (1997). Getting the seats of your pants dirty: strategies for ethnographic research on virtual communities. *Journal of Computer-Mediated Communication, 3*(1), 0–10.

Roberts, L. (2015). Ethical issues in conducting qualitative research in online communities. *Qualitative Research in Psychology, 12*(3), 314–325.

Rodriquez, J. (2013). Narrating dementia: self and community in an online forum. *Qualitative Health Research, 23*(9), 1215–1227.

Schotanus-Dijkstra, M., Havinga, P., van Ballegooijen, W., Delfosse, L., Mokkenstorm, J., & Boon, B. (2014). What do the bereaved by suicide communicate in online support groups? A content analysis. *Crisis: The Journal of Crisis Intervention and Suicide Prevention, 35*(1), 27.

Smith, H. J., Milberg, S. J., & Burke, S. J. (1996). Information privacy: measuring individuals' concerns about organizational practices. *MIS Quarterly, 20*(2), 167–196.

Sveningsson Elm, M. (2008). How do various notions of privacy influence decisions in qualitative Internet research? In: Annette Markham and Nancy Baym (eds.), *Internet Inquiry: Dialogue among Researchers*. Sage Publications, Los Angeles, CA, pp. 69–87.

Thomas, J. (1996). Introduction: a debate about the ethics of fair practices for collecting social science data in cyberspace. *The Information Society, 12*(2), 107–118.

Trevisan, F., & Reilly, P. (2014). Ethical dilemmas in researching sensitive issues online: lessons from the study of British disability dissent networks. *Information, Communication & Society, 17*(9), 1131–1146.

Tudor, L. (2010). LANGUAGE IN ACTION: SLANG. *Interstudia (Revista Centrului Interdisciplinar De Studiu Al Formelor Discursive Contemporane Interstud)*(6), 253–262.

Twitter, P. (2015b). *What you say on twitter may be viewed all around the world instantly*, Retrieved from https://twitter.com/privacy.

Waskul, D. (1996). Considering the electronic participant: some polemical observations on the ethics of online research. *The Information Society, 12*(2), 129–140.

Wesemann, D., & Grunwald, M. (2008). Online discussion groups for bulimia nervosa: an inductive approach to Internet-based communication between patients. *International Journal of Eating Disorders, 41*(6), 527–534.

Williams, E. (2005). *Federal protection for human research subjects: an analysis of the common rule and its interactions with FDA regulations and the HIPAA privacy rule*, Retrieved from https://www.fas.org/sgp/crs/misc/RL32909.pdf.

Zimmer, M. (2010). "But the data is already public": on the ethics of research in Facebook. Ethics and information technology. *Journal of Experimental Social Psychology, 16*(12), 313–325.

CHAPTER 9

The Limitations of Automating OSINT: Understanding the Question, Not the Answer

George R.S. Weir

Department of Computer and Information Sciences,
University of Strathclyde, Glasgow, UK

INTRODUCTION

Answering key questions on matters of fact, such as whether a particular individual was employed by a named organization at a specific point in time, is easy if one has access to relevant data, for example, company financial records, income tax returns, or details of bank account transactions. For good reasons, such data are not widely accessible without authorization. In contrast, open source information may be unrestricted and free to access by interested parties. Whether such readily accessible data will prove helpful in determining an answer to such questions of fact as our aforementioned employment query is far from certain. The availability of relevant data is not assured. The desired information may simply be unavailable. If it is available, there is no assurance that the enquirer can successfully negotiate the required technology, adequately specify the desired information, and retrieve the data.

In contrast, we might anticipate an automated information retrieval system that can elicit the desired information from the investigator and query all openly available data sources in order to establish the best possible response to the searcher's information requirements (cf. Studeman, 2002). The increasing availability and ease of searching open source information might lead one to expect highly fruitful applications that are attuned to users' information requirements, interests, and associated data (e.g., Best, 2008). This chapter considers the viability of such an automated application of open source information toward answering the intelligence requirements of assumed investigators. In what follows, we raise a series of issues that can affect the search for intelligence in any investigation and thereby expose limitations or obstacles to the prospect of effective automated open source intelligence.

FINDING ANSWERS TO QUESTIONS

Anyone who has engaged in research or factual enquiry will appreciate that locating relevant information can be time-consuming and often frustrating. Retrieving information may be regarded as finding answers to questions (e.g. Jouis, 2012, Chapter 15) and these questions are often enquiries about matters of fact (such as the employment details mentioned above). When we seek definitive answers to specific questions we presume that there is a one-to-one correspondence between question and answer, for example, if the question has the form, "Did George Washington cross the Delaware in 1776?", the logically appropriate answer is either "yes" or "no".[1] Answering such questions should be a simple matter of locating the corresponding answer to the question. Yet, this may still be a hit or miss affair. Although the query format is simple, with its one-to-one relationship between question and answer, there can be no guarantee that available information resources actually contain the required answer to this question. So we meet the first obstacle to automating open source enquiries: availability of definitive answers. In principle, if a question cannot be answered using manual interrogation of available resources, then it cannot be answered using automated interrogation of available resources. But this is surely an unfair charge against the automation movement. Perhaps our automated information retrieval system would indicate the absence of the answer in a shorter time and with greater credibility. So, we might have greater confidence that the answer cannot be found manually, if it cannot be found automatically. Even in cases where the definitive answer is not available, the automation agenda could enhance our search process and more efficiently establish the end point in our enquiry.

Of course, many information requirements are more complex than such binary questions. Some enquiries require multiple data points in order to establish a plausible conclusion, or even to formulate a coherent hypothesis. In this vein, we find Sherlock Holmes crying out "Data! Data! Data! I can't make bricks without clay" (Conan Doyle, The Adventure of the Copper Beeches). Holmes recognizes the importance of relevant data when seeking to establish facts and regards data is the clay that we need to make the bricks that support our hypotheses and build our theories. But not all data are equally available or equally useful and not all information requirements are well specified.

As well as the search for specific detailed information, there are many speculative or exploratory enquiries that upon realization may contribute significantly toward the individual's goal. In such cases, the search may commence with no

---

[1] In response to such an enquiry, we are not willing to entertain Lewis Carroll style answers such as "a teapot."

clearly defined information target but with a view to "shedding light" on the subject matter and this, in turn, may initiate a perpendicular chain of thought that redirects the search focus. A common characteristic of academic research is the exploration of extant-related research publications with a view to establishing the landscape of work that has already been undertaken. In doing so, the researcher may seek to identify significant gaps in work to date, in terms of focus, methods, or objectives. But there is no way to specify this objective directly, as a basis for information retrieval. Instead, such high-level information objectives have to be realized as a series of searches for constituent data.

CREDIBILITY AND THE QUALITY OF RESULTS

In light of such easily expanding information needs, there is considerable appeal in the prospect of adding automated intelligence to identify and address the appropriate information resources, specify the breadth of associated queries, and subsequently coordinate, synthesize, and report on the results. These are the prospective benefits of having one or more "personal assistants" to address individual aspects of the complex information retrieval task. Perhaps this is where we might best benefit from automating the process.

Over the past few decades, numerous so-called "intelligent personal assistants" have been developed and discussed. These are usually allocated a particular task domain, such as appointments and schedule management (e.g., Modi, Veloso, Smith, & Oh, 2005; Myers et al., 2007), or email management (e.g., Segal & Kephart, 1999; Li, Zhong, Yao, & Liu, 2009). Others are directed at decision support and information retrieval (e.g., Hsinchun, Yi-Ming, Ramsey, & Yang, 1998; Klusch, 2012). Central to such systems is the need to characterize the aims and objectives of the user and decompose these into a specific related set of information management tasks. Often, heuristics and statistical probabilities are employed to determine likely associations between user interests, for example, if the searcher is interested in aspect a then they are likely to be interested in aspect b.[2] In a more elaborate form, association measures in data mining or knowledge discovery algorithms provide a basis for enhanced information systems, such as automated OSINT (cf. McCue, 2014; Dawson, 2015; Bayerl & Akhgar, 2015).

Open source investigations are often complex, time consuming, and limited in achievement. Of course, many issues can be resolved, clarified, proved, or

---

[2] This associative approach is also fundamental to "recommender systems" that use insight on the information-seeking behavior of many users' to shed light on the likely interests of new enquiries (cf. Pazzani & Billsus, 2007; Manouselis, Drachsler, Verbert, & Duval, 2012; Bobadilla, Ortega, Hernando, & Gutiérrez, 2013; Kim, 2014; Berkovsky & Freyne, 2015).

disproved by reference to openly available information resources but much will depend upon the desired information and this, in turn, is predicated upon the specific questions being raised in the investigation and the manner in which these are specified and addressed via the information search and retrieval facility.

In most cases that include an online investigation, when we search for information, we have a specific information need. This is often associated with a named entity (cf. Artiles, Amigó, & Gonzalo, 2009; Bhole, Fortuna, Grobelnik, & Mladenic, 2007). Named entities are people, places, or events and these entities are uniquely distinguishable from other entities. For instance, we may seek biographical details on Bruce McInnes[3] and initiate a search on public information space such as Web search engines, social networks (such as Facebook, Twitter, and LinkedIn, or consolidated search sites such as Wink), and other people-related open-source data sets (such as Zabasearch or Pipl). In this instance, we are quickly rewarded by relevant details sourced from LinkedIn. Bruce is a LinkedIn member who has provided sufficient personal information in his profile to satisfy our search and establish that he is the individual whose details we seek. We might end our search once we have achieved sufficient relevant details.

Inevitably, there are possible problems or limitations in this scenario. The search objectives are quite specific and relatively easily satisfied. A single information source proves sufficient to recover the required information, but how do we establish that we have found the correct Bruce McInnes?

Prudence dictates that we consider the *provenance* of the data that we have located. We may presume that our Bruce McInnes actually provided the located information to LinkedIn, but we have no means of confirming this assumption. Perhaps someone acting on behalf of Bruce uploaded the details that we encountered on LinkedIn. More worryingly, someone masquerading as Bruce may have established the LinkedIn account. The provenance issue may be clear cut if the retrieved biographical data were found to have originated on a previously unfamiliar foreign website, rather than LinkedIn.

Ultimately, we give some sources of information greater weight than others because we are acquainted with a particular information resource and consider it authoritative. When we consider the provenance, we are seeking further reason to believe what we have found. In this way, provenance contributes to credibility.

The likelihood is that we already possess some information – in which we have confidence – that matches details in our search results. Yet, we may be foolish

---

[3] In fact, Bruce is fictional and serves purely as an illustration.

to conclude quickly that there is a unique individual identified by our search. Some degree of *corroboration* is required to establish credibility and conclude that we have indeed found information on our target individual.

If Bruce did indeed provide the information, we presume that he would not falsify any details, but we may have no means of confirming this assumption either. Once again, we may reduce such concerns by seeking *corroboration* from other sources. If numerous different information sources offer consonant details this adds to their credibility; we are more inclined to believe what we have found and may consider the results more *authoritative* than a single source of results.[4] Such cross site contrasts and comparisons are increasingly employed as a basis for weighting the credibility or relevance of results (cf. Brin & Page, 2012; Kumari, Gupta, & Dixit, 2014; Whang, Lenharth, Dhillon, & Pingali, 2015). Of course, this increases the complexity and overheads on our search through the need for more behind-the-scenes computation, evaluation, and synthesis of results.

While credibility is considered an essential quality for retrieved results, this does not establish the truth of any returned details. Veracity is a stronger and more desirable quality but may prove impossible to establish. In this case, we often have to treat data with considerable credibility as if it were true (or proceed with this assumption until proved false).

These insights allow us to identify a minimum set of related requirements for information integrity that should be considered in any intelligence gathering endeavor.

- Provenance
- Corroboration
- Credibility (veracity)

Meeting these requirements gives the enquirer confidence in matching the retrieved information with the posed query and underpins the supposed veracity of that information. This is especially important when sourcing information from sites that are provided at no cost or to which anyone may contribute information. In the first case, there may be little incentive for the site to verify the information it provides and in the second case, individuals may compete to influence the content and tenor of social networking sites.

Such considerations must also apply and be explicitly addressed in the context of automated enquiry, since explanations and justification for decisions taken by

---

[4] There remains a risk that erroneous information is repeated without correction across multiple available sites. In this case, the preponderance of sources lends misleading credibility to the false data.

the automated intelligence must be available to convince the investigator (and any third-party) that the proffered information has the required integrity. This set of explanations is analogous to the chain of custody maintained in forensic investigations. In the case of automatic open source investigation, details of each step in the automated process must be available to substantiate the chain of reasoning. This amounts to "explaining the questions being answered"!

RELEVANCE

Provenance and corroboration with their contribution to credibility are a minimum set of requirements on any retrieved information, in order that it have sufficient integrity to be acceptable. These requirements must be supplemented by one further condition that renders the information useful. This is the essential requirement that the retrieved information be *relevant* to the user's enquiry.

Relevance is a slippery concept. Deciding whether some information retrieved in a search is relevant requires a cogent grasp of the underlying purpose of the associated enquiry. The key to employing conventional Web search engines such as Goole, Yahoo, Bing, etc., lies in being able to formulate queries in a manner that minimizes ambiguity and transparently expresses the searcher's objectives. Efficient search systems, including any prospective automated OSINT facility, interpret the user's objectives via the entered search query and may then add further sophistication in refining and ordering the results.

Most information retrieval facilities are still heavily syntax based. This means that the retrieval system will seek exact and partial matches across its data set for specific terms in the search query. More sophisticated systems add further insights to refine the search interpretation. For instance, maintaining a record of previous searches from the same user as a basis for disambiguation. Beyond this, there are moves to add greater knowledge to the interpretation of search expressions. The so-called "semantic web" describes attempts to add classification and contextual mark-up to conventional syntax-based data sets. One method is to develop ontologies that represent relationships between concepts (actually, syntactic components). Thereby, a query in a specific knowledge domain can be interpreted in the light of the "domain knowledge" that is encoded in one or more related ontologies (cf. Jain & Singh, 2013; Song, Liang, Cao, & Park, 2014; Sayed & Sankar, 2014).

Undoubtedly, adding such contextual knowledge can enhance the search process by narrowing the interpretation of the user's search and returning more results that are more closely focussed on the intended query. But we should note that the emphasis in these developments is to "better interpret the user's query"; in other words, aiming to better understand the question that the user is posing. This is the key to returning information that is relevant to the user's purpose.

Traditional information retrieval concentrates on finding documents[5] that contain the terms employed in the user's search. Suppose that I want information on publications by Bruce McInnes. I execute a search using this author's name and obtain 800 hits. Depending upon the nature of my search domain (e.g., web search as opposed to IEEExplorer[6]), some of these hits will identify publications but others may be references to web pages that mention this author or web pages that contain one or more of the terms in the author's name.

From the retrieval system perspective, my search has been poorly specified. Simply giving the string "Bruce McInnes" gives little scope for disambiguation (in terms of search objectives). Some search engines may track my link selection from the returned hits and use this insight as a basis for refining subsequent searches with the same search terms. If I was able to indicate that my search term is a person's name and that my focus of interest is their role as an author, this could serve to clarify my purpose and allow the information retrieval facility to filter results accordingly. Plausibly, this filtering could employ semantic web technologies to locate contexts in which the search terms represent an author and thereby provide results that are directly focussed on my search objectives. Once more, this highlights the importance of understanding the nature of the user's query in order to establish relevance.

While advances in semantic web and ontologies make such refinement a realistic prospect, at present, most available information is not structured or marked semantically to indicate the nature of the data or its role in a specific knowledge domain. Any automation introduced in support of refined search must work with the nature of available data and this primarily means retrieval through syntax-matched search. Until freely available information facilities are enriched with contextual, domain, and related semantic mark-up, the "knowledge processing" load on any automated OSINT information retrieval system will be significant. Since the "conversion" from simply matched text results to contextually relevant focussed information must be accomplished through application of local OSINT algorithms or third-party online services.

Establishing relevance is a major requirement for effective information retrieval but is subject to the quality of available data and also to the searcher's ability to formulate a suitable search query. The query formulation provides the basis for any subsequent retrieval, including the application of any automation or filtering techniques that aim to enhance the relevance of results.

---

[5] The term "documents" is used broadly here to cover collections of data, such as published papers, catalogue entries, and web pages.
[6] A digital library of IEEE publications (at http://ieee.org/ieeexplore).

OSINT systems may alleviate some uncertainty by building specific varieties of search into the user interface. For instance, a query that seeks information on a named individual could be initiated by entering the name (as the search text) and clicking a button for "Named Individual." Similar options may be included for "Named organization," "Events on specified date in specified location." In each case, the nature of the search is conveyed to the retrieval system and adds context information to the search envelope. This is one approach to easy expression of the user's "cognitive search intent" (Kato, Yamamoto, Ohshima, & Tanaka, 2014; White, Richardson, & Yih, 2015) that tries to avoid ambiguity and other possible misinterpretation of the user's objective. Avoiding the need to make assumptions about the user's search intent will go some way toward reducing mistakes.[7] This measure can also reduce the overhead of postprocessing the results, since less reasoning about likely user intention will be required.

When designing an automated system for OSINT, useful functionality may be added through application of Natural Language Processing algorithms (cf. Noubours, Pritzkau, & Schade, 2013). There are at least three contexts in which such technology may assist. First, the nature of the search query may be elucidated (Buey, Garrido, & Ilarri, 2014; Ma et al., 2014). This may improve interpretation of user intent and so reduce ambiguity. Second, in contexts where open source data are unstructured, NLP could add insight on named entities (Di Pietro, Aliprandi, De Luca, Raffaelli, & Soru, 2014), such as determining which diverse referents apply to a specific individual. Third, automatic translation may remove language barriers to data synthesis (Neri, Geraci, & Pettoni, 2011). Each of these measures may assist by extending the result set or by improving result relevance.

THE LIMITATIONS OF AUTOMATING OSINT

In the foregoing, we have considered obstacles to effective information retrieval in general and OSINT in particular. The primary factors that influence the value of any retrieved data are relevance and credibility. Ideally, credibility will be coupled with veracity, since we prefer to work with information that is factually correct and not simply plausible, but we may only be able to add to credibility the assumption of truth unless contradicted by other credible information.

Automated OSINT may fail on four common grounds. First, the desired and sought information may simply be unavailable from any accessible source

---

[7] In some contexts, the predictable manner in which search engines "interpret" queries may be used to avoid revealing the searcher's true intention (cf. Weir & Igbako, 2013).

(*availability*). Second, the user's intention (as expressed by the search terms) may be misread by the retrieval system (*interpretation*). Third, the search formulation may fail to return the required information (*formulation*). Fourth, the information seeker may fail to recognize the relevance and significance of returned data (*confusion*). Each of these failings may be influenced by the subtle and complex relationship between question and answer. Poorly formulated queries may result in low availability. While poorly aggregated responses may create confusion on the part of the searcher.

The considerable challenge facing automated OSINT is to interpret the user's query correctly, locate relevant information from open source data sets, amalgamate the results, and present responses in a coherent and comprehensible fashion. None of these steps is easy or guaranteed of success.

We have stressed the importance of relevance. The enemy of relevance is ambiguity so our OSINT system needs to be capable of disambiguating the user's query and also the content of results. While automated NLP systems can assist with ambiguity, we might expect information query systems to be no better than the best human ability to recognize such ambiguities. This simply reflects the inherently entropic nature of natural language.

CONCLUSIONS

In considering the prospects for automated OSINT, we have identified the key ingredients and potential issues that are common in any information retrieval system. Advances in technology can help to address these issues and move toward fully automated OSINT. The greatest challenge is to correctly interpret the user's intended search in the face of ill-formulated search expressions and ambiguity. We may hope that this technical challenge can be met. Perhaps practical insight may be sought in the view of Marshall McLuhan: "Anybody who begins to examine the patterns of automation finds that perfecting the individual machine by making it automatic involves "feedback." That means introducing an information loop or circuit, where before there had been merely a one way flow or mechanical sequence" (McLuhan, 1964, p. 354).

Realistically, we might aim for an information loop rather than a one-way flow to attain a practical middle ground in which an interactive semiautomated system allows users to pose queries and respond to intermediate results as a means of refining and reexpressing their information objectives (cf. Moussa, et al., 2007; Kovashka et al., 2012). Employing a feedback loop to refine an information envelope could meet the dual problems of ill-defined search and poorly formulated information needs. In this fashion, we may have a system that is properly focussed on understanding the question, not the answer.

References

Artiles, J., Amigó, E., & Gonzalo, J. (2009). The role of named entities in web people search. In *Proceedings of the 2009 conference on empirical methods in natural language processing: Volume 2* (pp. 534–542). Association for Computational Linguistics.

Bayerl, P. S., & Akhgar, B. (2015). Surveillance and falsification implications for open source intelligence investigations. *Communications of the ACM, 58*(8), 62–69.

Berkovsky, S., & Freyne, J. (2015). Web personalization and recommender systems. In *Proceedings of the 21th ACM SIGKDD international conference on knowledge discovery and data mining* (pp. 2307–2308). ACM.

Best, C. (2008, July). Web mining for open source intelligence. In *12th IEEE International conference on information visualisation, IV'08* (pp. 321–325).

Bhole, A., Fortuna, B., Grobelnik, M., & Mladenic, D. (2007). Extracting named entities and relating them over time based on Wikipedia. *Informatica, 31*(4), 463–468.

Bobadilla, J., Ortega, F., Hernando, A., & Gutiérrez, A. (2013). Recommender systems survey. *Knowledge-Based Systems, 46*, 109–132.

Brin, S., & Page, L. (2012). Reprint of: the anatomy of a large-scale hypertextual web search engine. *Computer Networks, 56*(18), 3825–3833.

Buey, M. G., Garrido, Á. L., & Ilarri, S. (2014). An approach for automatic query expansion based on NLP and semantics. In *Database and expert systems applications* (pp. 349–356). Berlin: Springer International Publishing.

Dawson, M. (2015). A Brief Review of New Threats and Countermeasures in Digital Crime and Cyber Terrorism. New Threats and Countermeasures in Digital Crime and Cyber Terrorism, 1.

Di Pietro, G., Aliprandi, C., De Luca, A. E., Raffaelli, M., & Soru, T. (2014). Semantic crawling: an approach based on Named Entity Recognition. In *2014 IEEE/ACM international conference on advances in social networks analysis and mining (ASONAM)* (pp. 695–699).

Fernández, M., Cantador, I., López, V., Vallet, D., Castells, P., & Motta, E. (2011). Semantically Enhanced Information Retrieval: an ontology-based approach. *Web Semantics: Science, Services and Agents on the World Wide Web, 9*(4), 434–452.

Hsinchun, C., Yi-Ming, C., Ramsey, M., & Yang, C. C. (1998). An intelligent personal spider (agent) for dynamic Internet/Intranet searching. *Decision Support Systems, 23*(1), 41–58.

Jain, V., & Singh, M. (2013). Ontology based information retrieval in semantic web: a survey. *International Journal of Information Technology and Computer Science (IJITCS), 5*(10), 62.

Jouis, C. (Ed.). (2012). *Next generation search engines: advanced models for information retrieval.* IGI Global.

Kato, M. P., Yamamoto, T., Ohshima, H., & Tanaka, K. (2014). Investigating users' query formulations for cognitive search intents. In *Proceedings of the 37th international ACM SIGIR conference on research and development in information retrieval* (pp. 577–586). ACM.

Klusch, M. (Ed.). (2012). *Intelligent information agents: agent-based information discovery and management on the Internet.* Berlin: Springer Science & Business Media.

Kim, Y. S. (2014). *Advanced intelligent systems* (Vol. 268). Y. J. Ryoo, M. S. Jang, & Y. C. Bae (Eds.). Berlin: Springer.

Kovashka, A, Parikh, D., & Grauman, K. (2012). WhittleSearch: image search with relative attribute feedback. In *Proceedings of the IEEE conference on computer vision and pattern recognition (CVPR)*, Providence, RI, June 2012.

Kumari, T., Gupta, A., & Dixit, A. (2014). Comparative study of page rank and weighted page rank algorithm. *Proceedings of International Journal of Innovative Research in Computer and Communication Engineering, 2*(2).

Li, W., Zhong, N., Yao, Y., & Liu, J. (2009). An operable email based intelligent personal assistant. *World Wide Web, 12*(2), 125–147.

Ma, Y., Zhong, Q., Mehrotra, S., & Seid, D. Y. (2004, November). A framework for refining similarity queries using learning techniques. In *Proceedings of the thirteenth ACM international conference on information and knowledge management* (pp. 158–159). ACM.

Manouselis, N., Drachsler, H., Verbert, K., & Duval, E. (2012). *Recommender systems for learning*. Berlin: Springer Science & Business Media.

McLuhan, M. (1964). *Understanding media: the extensions of man*. London: Routledge & Kegan Paul.

McCue, C. (2014). *Data mining and predictive analysis: Intelligence gathering and crime analysis*. London: Butterworth-Heinemann.

Modi, P. J., Veloso, M., Smith, S. F., & Oh, J. (2005). Cmradar: A personal assistant agent for calendar management. In *Agent-oriented information systems II* (pp. 169–181). Berlin, Heidelberg: Springer.

Moussa, M. B., Pasch, M., Hiemstra, D., Van Der Vet, P., & Huibers, T. (2007). The potential of user feedback through the iterative refining of queries in an image retrieval system. In *Adaptive multimedia retrieval: user, context, and feedback* (pp. 258–268). Berlin, Heidelberg: Springer.

Myers, K., Berry, P., Blythe, J., Conley, K., Gervasio, M., McGuinness, D. L., & Tambe, M. (2007). An intelligent personal assistant for task and time management. *AI Magazine, 28*(2), 47.

Neri, F., Geraci, P., & Pettoni, M. (2011). Stalker: overcoming linguistic barriers in open source intelligence. *International Journal of Networking and Virtual Organisations, 8*(1–2), 37–51.

Noubours, S., Pritzkau, A., & Schade, U. (2013). NLP as an essential ingredient of effective OSINT frameworks. In *Military Communications and Information Systems Conference (MCC)* (pp. 1–7), 2013. IEEE.

Pazzani, M. J., & Billsus, D. (2007). Content-based recommendation systems. In *The adaptive web* (pp. 325–341). Berlin, Heidelberg: Springer.

Sayed, A., & Sankar, S. (2014). From XML to RDF: a new semantic information retrieval system. *International Journal of Electronics Communication and Computer Engineering, 5*(1), 85.

Segal, R. B., & Kephart, J. O. (1999). MailCat: an intelligent assistant for organizing e-mail. In *Proceedings of the third annual conference on Autonomous Agents* (pp. 276–282). ACM.

Song, W., Liang, J. Z., Cao, X. L., & Park, S. C. (2014). An effective query recommendation approach using semantic strategies for intelligent information retrieval. *Expert Systems with Applications, 41*(2), 366–372.

Studeman, A. W. (2002). International Views of OSINT. Open Source Intelligence Reader, 56.

Weir, G. R. S., & Igbako, D. (2013). Strategies for covert web search. In *Fourth cybercrime and trustworthy computing workshop (CTC)* (pp. 50–57). IEEE.

Whang, J. J., Lenharth, A., Dhillon, I. S., & Pingali, K. (2015). Scalable data-driven pagerank: algorithms, system issues, and lessons learned. In *Euro-Par 2015 parallel processing* (pp. 438–450). Berlin, Heidelberg: Springer.

White, R. W., Richardson, M., & Yih, W. T. (2015). Questions vs. queries in informational search tasks. In *Proceedings of the 24th international conference on World Wide Web companion* (pp. 135–136). International World Wide Web Conferences Steering Committee.

CHAPTER 10

Geospatial Reasoning With Open Data

Kristin Stock*, Hans Guesgen**

**School of Engineering and Advanced Technology, Massey University, New Zealand
(Albany, Auckland campus); **School of Engineering and Advanced Technology, Massey
University, New Zealand (Palmerston North campus)*

INTRODUCTION

Geospatial data is data about objects, events, or phenomena that have a location on the surface of the earth. The location may be static in the short-term (e.g., the location of a road, an earthquake event, children living in poverty), or dynamic (e.g., a moving vehicle or pedestrian, the spread of an infectious disease). Geospatial data combines location information (usually coordinates on the earth), attribute information (the characteristics of the object, event, or phenomena concerned), and often also temporal information (the time or life span at which the location and attributes exist).

Much geospatial data is of general interest to a wide range of users. For example, roads, localities, water bodies, and public amenities are useful as reference information for a number of purposes. For this reason, whether collected by public or private organizations, large amounts of geospatial data are available as open data. This means that it can be accessed freely by users, and is made available through open standards. The development and use of open standards within the geospatial community have been heavily supported because of the wide range of uses to which geospatial data can be applied, and because of the large numbers of agencies both globally and locally that are involved in collecting such data.

In this chapter, we discuss the ways in which geospatial reasoning has been applied to open data. We define geospatial reasoning as both reasoning about the location of objects on the earth (e.g., relating to inference of spatial relationships) and reasoning about geospatial data (e.g., relating to the attributes of data that is geospatial in nature). We begin by describing specific aspects of the open geospatial data environment as background, and then we discuss a number of different types of reasoning that have been applied to geospatial data, including classical reasoning and probabilistic, fuzzy, rough, and heuristic reasoning approaches. We then present two specialized case studies to

171

illustrate the use of geospatial reasoning with open data: (1) the use of fuzzy reasoning for map buffering and (2) the automated learning of nonclassical geospatial ontologies.

THE OPEN GEOSPATIAL DATA ENVIRONMENT

Traditionally, geospatial data was collected mainly by government departments, often involving several departments within any given jurisdiction. For example, one department may be responsible for collecting land boundary (cadastral) data, another for roads and transport data, another for environmental data, and another for health data, etc., according to their departmental portfolios. Integration of data from different departments was often difficult because of the use of different formats, data models, and semantics. For example, the department responsible for land boundaries may have collected data about roads in terms of the legal road reservation, while the department responsible for road maintenance may have collected data about the constructed road: the materials, surface, and physical area of the road itself, and the department concerned with conservation may have collected data about wildlife road crossings. In each case, "road" means different things (has different semantics), is likely to have different attributes, different data structures, and different identification mechanisms. Furthermore, this situation was repeated in each different jurisdiction, so that departments maintaining the same kind of data (e.g., land boundaries) in different jurisdictions used different formats, structures, and semantics for their own data. In situations in which data was to be shared between jurisdictions, this caused problems. For example, in Australia, each of the states and territories used their own system, formats, and structures for each of the different geospatial datasets, making it very difficult to create unified data across state and territory borders or to create a national dataset for issues that were countrywide. In Europe, similar challenges occurred with the addition of language differences. For example, data about protected sites often requires a cross-border approach as species habitats do not stop at national boundaries, but each nation maintains its own datasets with different formats and structures.

As a result of these data integration challenges, open geospatial data has been an important goal within the geospatial community for some years. The Open Geospatial Consortium (OGC) has developed a number of standards to enable the open sharing of data, not least of which is the Web Feature Service (WFS) Specification, which defines a web service request and response format to allow data providers to make their data available to data users. This standard and other OGC standards are mainly focussed on data format, and do not address the data model or the semantics of the data content.

In order to resolve the issue of semantic data integration, a number of national and international efforts have been made to define standard data models that can be used to create unified datasets. For example, Australia has created the Harmonized Data Model[1], and more recently, the European Union (EU) INSPIRE Directive[2] has involved the definition of a suite of data standards in which Member States will be required to provide their data to enable integration across the EU. Other efforts to make geospatial data more open include the Global Earth Observation System of Systems (GEOSS[3]) which has the goal of enabling access to environmental data globally; and linked data initiatives, in which geospatial data is made available through RDF using linked data principles of unique identification of resources (for example, in the United Kingdom[4]).

Through all of the efforts to integrate geospatial data and provide open access over recent decades, semantic issues have been recognized as important in enabling successful sharing of geospatial data. To this end, a number of ontologies of thematic concepts used for geospatial data have been developed, and this is one of the main areas in which geospatial reasoning is used with open data. A second broad area of interest for geospatial reasoning is that of qualitative spatial reasoning, in which methods are developed to reason about the relationships between geospatial objects in space. These and other topics are discussed in the remainder of this chapter.

REVIEW OF REASONING METHODS WITH GEOSPATIAL DATA

Geospatial Domain Ontologies

One of the main applications of classical geospatial reasoning has been through ontologies describing particular domains that use geospatial data. Ontologies based on classical logic define the concepts that are of interest within a domain using clearly specified axioms, which enable the semantics of data to be understood by users. Ontologies also enable various kinds of reasoning that can be used to infer to which concept an instance belongs according to the axiomatic definition of the concept, for example. Most recently, OWL (W3C OWL Working Group, 2012) description logics have been used, enabling subsumption hierarchies to be inferred using the specifications of individual concepts to aid in resource discovery (Janowicz, Scheider, Pehle, & Hart, 2012; Neuhaus & Compton, 2009; Lutz & Klien, 2006).

In recognition of the growing proliferation of domain ontologies and the need to allow these ontologies to be related to each other, upper level ontologies have

---

[1] http://www.icsm.gov.au/hdm/
[2] http://inspire.ec.europa.eu/
[3] http://www.earthobservations.org/geoss.php
[4] http://data.gov.uk/linked-data

been defined to provide fundamental ontological concepts that are domain neutral. Examples include DOLCE (Borgo, Carrara, Garbacz, & Vermaas, 2009) and SUMO (Niles & Pease, 2001). Domain ontologies that describe concepts in a geospatial domain and application ontologies that describe the way in which a domain ontology may be used to achieve a particular purpose can then be defined and connected to these upper level ontologies. SWEET is a large example of an OWL geospatial domain ontology, covering 4100 concepts and combining 125 modular ontologies (Raskin & Pan, 2005). A myriad of small ontologies have been created for particular purposes[5], some of which connect to upper-level ontologies, others of which exist in isolation.

The purpose of many of these ontologies is to define a common set of concepts to support data sharing, integration, or reuse, in accordance with the definition of an ontology as a specification of a shared conceptualization (Studer, Benjamins, & Fensel, 1998). For this purpose, reasoning is not always required. In addition to ontologies such as OWL, it is common to define ontology-like structures (vocabularies or thesauri, in varying positions along the semantic spectrum (McGuinness, 2003)) to specify the semantics of concepts in a geospatial application using a language that carries limited or no reasoning, like RDF, SKOS, etc., GEMET is an example[6].

In those cases in which an ontology has been reasoned over, a common purpose is to improve the results from querying of geospatial data, ensuring that in addition to an originally selected term, terms referring to semantically related concepts can also be retrieved. This approach has been applied to both domain ontologies (Klien, Lutz, & Kuhn, 2006); domain and geographic ontologies (Fu, Jones, & Abdelmoty, 2005) and domain and scientific method ontologies (Stock et al., 2013).

Geospatial Service Ontologies
A branch of research that applies ontologies to the description of geospatial processes implemented as web services has also employed reasoning, mainly with the OWL-S web service ontology and developing mechanisms to support web service orchestration. This work particularly focusses on some of the challenges presented by the goal of automatically plugging geospatial web services together, and determining whether those services are appropriate for use with certain data, and with other services. For example, data resolution may be relevant in determining whether it should be used with a certain process, and if so, which other processes might subsequently be appropriate (Hobona, Fairbairn, Hiden, & James, 2010; Granell, Díaz, & Gould, 2010).

---

[5] For example, http://ontolog.cim3.net/cgi-bin/wiki.pl?OpenOntologyRepository
[6] GEMET: http://www.eionet.europa.eu/gemet.

Qualitative Spatial Reasoning

Qualitative spatial reasoning (QSR) has been a fruitful research field for some decades, specifically addressing the recognition that reasoning about relationships of objects in space (including geographic space) is better handled qualitatively rather than quantitatively. Geographic information systems, which have been the main method for working with geographic information, are quantitative and work with data using metric coordinate systems. However, human reasoning about spatial relationships is able to handle notions of vagueness and uncertainty in a way that quantitative reasoning cannot.

Seminal work in QSR was conducted on topology (one of the most important types of spatial relation): the Region Connection Calculus and the 9 intersection model. The Region Connection Calculus (RCC) (Cohn, Bennett, Gooday, & Gotts, 1997; Cohn & Hazarika, 2001) defines a series of 12 relations (e.g., within, touching) and a subsumption lattice indicating how the relations are related to each other. As well as topological relations between regions, the RCC addresses the topological shape of regions, providing mechanisms for identifying different multipart shapes (doughnuts, etc.), and defines a predicate signifying the convex hull of a geometry (conv(x)). This can then be used to perform various kinds of reasoning to determine, for example, whether one geometry is inside the convex hull of another, while not overlapping with the geometry itself. The whole of RCC is undecideable, but subsets can be defined that are decideable. This work also illustrates the use of geospatial reasoning with intuitionistic first-order logic, a type of propositional logic in which statements preserve verifiability rather than truth.

The 9-intersection model is another approach to describing and reasoning about topological relations (Egenhofer & Herring, 1991). It describes relations in terms of the interior, exterior, and boundary of the objects, and the 9 intersection is a matrix relating those three aspects of two regions to each other, to describe their topology. The model describes 8 relations between pairs of regions; 19 between a simple line and a region and 33 between pairs of lines.

Other significant work has addressed different types of spatial relations, including distance (Aurnague & Vieu, 1993; Zimmermann, 1994; Liu, 1998), nearness (Clementini, Di Felice, & Hernández, 1997; Hernandez, Clementini, & Felice, 1995; Schockaert, De Cock, Cornelis, & Kerre, 2008; Du, Alechina, Stock, & Jackson, 2013), orientation (Mukerjee & Joe, 1990; Zimmerman & Freksa, 1996; Clementini, Skiadopoulos, Billen, & Tarquini, 2010), and direction (Moratz & Wallgrun, 2012), among others. The QSR work generally focusses on defining the properties of spatial relations amid compositions and transformations, and has provided a basis for applications in natural language querying (Shariff, Egenhofer, & Mark, 1998) among other things.

Ontologies have also been created to define spatial relations, including GUM-Space (Hois, Tenbrink, Ross, & Bateman, 2009), the Ordnance Survey Spatial Relations Ontology,[7] and the NeoGeo spatial ontology.[8] While reasoning over these ontologies has been limited, Hois and Kutz (2008) connect GUM-Space to the Double Cross Calculus (Freksa, 1992) to support spatial reasoning.

Probabilistic Geospatial Reasoning

While classical geospatial reasoning defines concepts using axioms that are either absolutely true or absolutely false, probabilistic reasoning allows for degrees of certainty of truth. In this case, concepts are defined as probabilistic sets, in which the values for the properties that define the sets have probabilities attached, and probabilistic reasoning (e.g., Bayesian inference) is used to determine the probability of an individual being a member of a concept given the probabilities of the property values. Probabilistic ontologies allow uncertainty in membership (likelihood or certainty of truth), but the concepts themselves have a clear definition (Costa & Laskey, 2006; Stuckenschmidt & Visser, 2000), unlike fuzzy reasoning, which permits degrees of truth.

Probabilistic reasoning combines probability with deductive logic, and is often used in the geospatial context for environmental modeling (e.g., Pérez-Miñana, Krause, & Thornton, 2012), as many environmental parameters are uncertain, so decision making supported by reasoning that incorporates that uncertainty is more appropriate than axiomatic reasoning. For example, the likelihood of a flood event occurring depends on a number of factors, all of which have varying degrees of uncertainty attached to them (e.g., the likelihood of a particular volume of rain). Dynamic Bayesian networks are also used to allow a probabilistic model to also be modeled temporally, creating time slices that are connected to each other via probabilistic reasoning (Jha & Keele, 2012).

Uncertainty is an important issue for geospatial reasoning, as all locational measurements have some degree of uncertainty attached to them. Probabilistic ontologies (e.g., PR-OWL[9]), which augment classical ontologies with mechanisms to represent probability distributions, have been used to represent this uncertainty, and to reason with multientity Bayesian networks (Laskey, Wright, & da Costa, 2010).

Beyond the use of probabilistic reasoning to assist in applied decision making in a geospatial context, other applications of probabilistic reasoning in the geospatial field include Winter and Yin (2011), who describe a method for probabilistic spatio-temporal reasoning using time geography, and Bitters (2009),

---

[7] http://data.ordnancesurvey.co.uk/ontology/spatialrelations/

[8] http://socop.oor.net/ontologies/1021

[9] http://www.pr-owl.org/

who uses the probabilities of spatial relations between particular types of geographic features (e.g., the likelihood that a house will have an *on* relation with a land parcel is very high) to predict the location of features whose position is not known.

Fuzzy Geospatial Reasoning

While probabilistic reasoning models the likelihood (or degree of uncertainty) of particular relations between concepts, or of concept membership; fuzzy reasoning caters for degrees of truth. The true–false dichotomy of classical reasoning is replaced by the ability to specify that a concept is true to a certain degree. For example, we may use probabilistic geospatial reasoning to express how certain we are that the statement "Orewa is in Auckland" is true (because perhaps our data has come from an unreliable source), and we may use fuzzy geospatial reasoning to express that Orewa is somewhere around the border of Auckland, and by some definitions may be considered in Auckland, and by others out of Auckland (it is considered part of greater Auckland).

Fuzzy reasoning is often used to model concepts that are designed as sets with vague definitions (e.g., qualitative measures like large cities, wide rivers, warm weather). Concept membership may be given a degree of truth, to indicate the degree of largeness, wideness, or warmness, etc. Fuzzy ontologies allow vagueness in concept definition (Bobillo & Straccia, 2011).

Fuzzy geospatial reasoning has been applied in a number of different ways, including as part of the qualitative spatial reasoning field. For example, a fuzzy connection calculus has been defined to model fuzzy topological relations (Schockaert, De Cock, Cornelis, & Kerre, 2008; Guesgen, 2005) and fuzzy models of nearness (Schockaert, De Cock, Cornelis, & Kerre, 2008; Gahegan, 1995; Worboys, 2001) and direction (Petry et al., 2002) have been developed.

As with probabilistic reasoning, fuzzy reasoning has been used in a domain context, to support decision making. Examples include fuzzy reasoning to support assessment of road danger (Effati et al., 2012), management of typhoons (Chen, Sui, & Tang, 2011), and assessment of landscape morphometry (Fisher, Wood, & Cheng, 2004). Most of these cases apply fuzzy reasoning to geospatial features and phenomena, but are mainly focussed on attribute rather than geometric data, in contrast to the examples in which fuzzy reasoning is used to perform geospatial reasoning about spatial relations.

Geospatial Reasoning With Multivalue Logics

In addition to the graded approaches offered by fuzzy and probabilistic reasoning, three-valued logic has been used, in which either regions or concepts like "nearness" are conceptualized as having broad boundaries, so a given point can be inside a region, outside a region, or in an intermediate broad boundary region (Clementini, Di Felice, & Hernández, 1997), based on the notion of rough set theory developed by Pawlak (1991). Egg-yolk theory extends RCC to deal with vague boundaries, dealing with degrees of membership like fuzzy logic, but in a noncontinuous way (Cohn & Gotts, 1996). "Nearness" has also been addressed with four-value logic (Worboys, 2001).

Heuristic Geospatial Ontologies

Another approach to nonclassical geospatial reasoning has been developed by Stock et al. (2015), in which concepts are defined in terms of heuristics (rules of thumb), rather than axioms. Concept membership can then be determined by evaluating an instance against these heuristics and by calculating a degree of truth, or degree to which the instance meets a given heuristic. Heuristic ontologies also incorporate probabilistic reasoning in that they apply measures of the predictive power of a heuristic (likelihood that the truth value of the heuristic indicates a valid concept membership). This approach employs aspects of fuzzy and probabilistic reasoning, but differs from both in that it defines the notion of a collection of heuristics that each have an established predictive power (being the frequency with which an instance meeting the heuristic is actually a valid sequence) that, combined with the degree to which those heuristics are met by an instance, can be used to establish whether an instance is a valid member of a concept.

Contextual Reasoning in the Geospatial Context

The importance of context for geospatial reasoning has been recognized for some years, as the interpretation of spatial concepts is often dependent on the ways in which those concepts are used. For example, geographic features such as mountains and rivers may be defined using criteria that depend on their geographical and cultural context: a mountain in Australia is quite different from a mountain in Switzerland. Similarly, the interpretation of spatial relations is dependent on the context of use. For example, in *the house is on the island*, the spatial relation *on* is interpreted very different from its use in *the house is on the main street*. Work on context has thus far been largely confined to specific projects addressing contextual issues. Examples include the extension/ definitions of ontologies that include concepts to describe the context in which concepts are defined (Frank, 2001) and the use of context (defined in terms of goals, situations, events, and actions) as a bridge across ontologies (Cai, 2007).

Standpoint Semantics for Geospatial Reasoning

Bennett (2001) approaches the issues of context using standpoint semantics. This approach considers that a given geographic concept (e.g., desert) may have several different definitions, each corresponding to different interpretations of the concept. Each of these definitions is referred to as a precisification, and may be modeled using classical semantics. A standpoint is a collection of precisifications held by some agent (e.g., a person). This work is mainly aimed at addressing the issue of vagueness in terms of geographic features.

CASE STUDIES IN GEOSPATIAL REASONING

In this section, we present two case studies in geospatial reasoning by way of providing more detailed examples. The first applies fuzzy reasoning to the map buffering, and the second addresses the challenge of automated learning of nonclassical geospatial ontologies.

Case Study 1: Geospatial Reasoning for Map Buffering

In the 1980s, Tomlin introduced map algebra (Tomlin, 1990), the concepts of which found their way into a number of geographic information systems. Some of the operations suggested by Tomlin inspired the work that is discussed in this chapter. However, the origin of it is map buffering, which is a commonly used technique in geographic information systems.

Map buffering is a tool commonly used in geographic information systems to increase the size of an object. For example, declaring all buildings on a university campus as smoke-free does not necessarily achieve the desired effect of having no smoke in buildings, because smoking close to buildings might still cause smoke to get into the buildings. The addition of a zone of, say, 10 m around the buildings might solve this problem. In terms of map buffering this means that we take a map of the campus and buffer all buildings by 10 m.

Together with other map operations such as intersection, union, and complement, map buffering offers a powerful tool to reason about geospatial information. To illustrate this form of reasoning, we will use the example published in Guesgen and Histed (1996).

The city council needs to find a location for a new dump. To limit the cost of transporting garbage and to maximize the useful life of the new dump, they have decided the following:

- The dump must be within 500 m of an existing road.
- The dump must have an area of more than 1000 square meters.

Environmental legislation has further limited the possible locations for the new dump:

- The dump must be at least 1000 m from residential or commercial property.
- The dump must be at least 500 m from any water.
- The dump must not be situated on land covered in native vegetation.

Assuming that we have maps showing property, water areas, road networks, and vegetation, we can perform the following map operations:

- Take the property map and select all property that is residential or commercial.
- Buffer the property selections by 1000 m.
- Apply the complement operation to select everything outside this area.
- Apply similar actions to the map showing water areas.
- Use the map showing the road network and buffer the road data by 500 m.
- Use the vegetation and select all vegetation that is not native.

The property and vegetation maps are then intersected with each other to produce a map showing all areas that are more than 1000 m from residential or commercial property and that do not contain native vegetation. After that, the water and road maps are merged to produce a map showing all areas within 500 m of a road that are also more than 500 m from water. Finally, the resulting two maps are merged to produce a map showing all possible locations for the city dump. A selection can then be made from all locations that are more than 1000 square meters in area.

When specifying a problem in the way illustrated earlier, it might happen that the problem becomes over-constrained, which means that the final map does not show any suitable area. In this case, one might attempt to relax the problem. For example, instead of requiring the dump to be within 500 m of an existing road, one might allow the dump to be as far as 600 m away from the road. The question, of course, then arises to find the best relaxations for the problem, without dropping requirements unnecessarily.

A straightforward solution to overcome the problem of over-constrained problems is to encode possible relaxations into the problems themselves. If, for example, a location for the dump within 500 m of a road is the preferred option, we can annotate these locations with a high preference value, but at the same time, we would annotate all locations within 600 m of road (but more than 500 m away) with a slightly smaller preference value.

An often used formalism to express preferences is fuzzy set theory. In fuzzy set theory, a classical subset A of a domain D is replaced with a fuzzy set $\tilde{A}$, which associates membership grades with the elements of A. Rather than deciding whether an element d does or does not belong to the set A, we determine for each element of D the degree with which it belongs to the fuzzy set $\tilde{A}$. In other words, a fuzzy subset $\tilde{A}$ of a domain D is a set of ordered pairs, $(d, \mu_{\tilde{A}}(d))$, where $d \in D$ and $\mu_{\tilde{A}}: D \in [0, 1]$ is the membership function of $\tilde{A}$. The membership function replaces the characteristic function of a classical subset $A \subseteq D$.

Given a number of fuzzy sets, we can use the same operations as for classical sets to combine the fuzzy sets: intersection, union, and complement. In the context of fuzzy sets, these operations are defined pointwise by combining the fuzzy membership functions, which can be done in various ways. The original combination scheme proposed by Zadeh (1965) is based on using the minimum and maximum of the membership functions. Given two fuzzy sets $\tilde{A}1$ and $\tilde{A}2$ with membership functions $\mu_{\tilde{A}1}(d)$ and $\mu_{\tilde{A}2}(d)$, respectively, the membership function of the intersection $\tilde{A}3 = \tilde{A}1 \cap \tilde{A}2$ is pointwise defined by

$$\mu_{\tilde{A}3}(d) = \min\{\mu_{\tilde{A}1}(d), \mu_{\tilde{A}2}(d)\}$$

Analogously, the membership function of the union $\tilde{A}3 = \tilde{A}1 \cup \tilde{A}2$ is pointwise defined by

$$\mu_{\tilde{A}3}(d) = \max\{\mu_{\tilde{A}1}(d), \mu_{\tilde{A}2}(d)\}$$

The membership grade for the complement of a fuzzy set $\tilde{A}$, denoted as $\neg\tilde{A}$, is defined by

$$\mu_{\tilde{A}}(d) = 1 - \mu_{\tilde{A}}(d)$$

In 1965, Zadeh stresses that the min/max combination scheme is not the only scheme for defining intersection and union of fuzzy sets, and the most appropriate scheme depends on the context. While some of the schemes are based on empirical investigations, others are the result of theoretical considerations (Dubois & Prade, 1980; Klir & Folger, 1988). However, Nguyen, Kreinovich, and Tolbert (1993) proved that the min/max operations are the most robust operations for combining fuzzy sets, where robustness is defined in terms of how much impact uncertainty in the input has on the error in the output.

In the context of buffering maps, fuzzy sets can be used to gradually reduce the acceptability of an area, rather than stepping from a perfectly acceptable area to an area that is completely unacceptable. In the example of the dump, we might want to associate all locations within 500 m of a road with a membership grade of 1, but instead of associating all other locations with a membership grade of 0, we might want to associate those that are between 500 and 600 m of a road with a membership grade of 0.9, those between 600 and 700 m with a membership grade of 0.8, and so on.

Selecting the right membership grades is often a subjective matter, as they reflect how preferred an area is in the context of the given problem. This cannot always be expressed in a formula, unless the preference directly relates to some numerical measure. One example where this is the case is when the area becomes less preferred the further away we move from a core area (like the road network, for instance). In this case, we might define the membership function as a function of the distance to the core area:

$$\mu_{\tilde{A}}(d) = 1 / (1 + \text{dist}(d)^2)$$

The distance dist(d) can be the Euclidean distance between a location d and the closest point in the core area but it can also be some other distance measure, like estimated travel time for instance.

In some situations, it makes sense to define the membership function locally based on the membership grades of neighboring locations of the map, since this lends itself to an easy-to-implement, efficient buffering algorithm for raster maps. A neighboring location in a raster map can either be an edge-adjacent or vertex-adjacent location. Two locations of a raster map are edge-adjacent if and only if they have an edge in common, whereas they are vertex-adjacent if and only if they have a vertex in common.

To define the membership grades locally, we apply a buffer function to the membership grades of adjacent locations, as used before in Guesgen et al. (2003). A buffer function is a monotonically increasing function $\beta : [0, 1] \rightarrow [0, 1]$ with the following property:

$$\forall m \in [0,1] : \mu(m) \leq m$$

If d is adjacent to d', then the new membership grade of d' is determined by the maximum of the old membership grade of d' and the value of the buffer function applied to the membership grade of d:

$$\mu(d') \leftarrow \max\{\mu(d'), \beta(\mu(d))\}$$

Given a raster map D (i.e., a set of locations with an adjacency relation) and a membership function over D (which initially might be a two-valued function resulting in either 0 or 1), we can use a local propagation algorithm that applies a buffer function β to update the membership function of the map until a stable state is obtained. Such an algorithm is shown in Figure 10.1. The algorithm starts with an arbitrary location of the map and propagates the effects of buffering to its adjacent locations. Whenever the membership grade of a location is updated, the location will be revisited again in the future. The algorithm will eventually terminate when no membership grades are updated anymore.

There are various ways in which buffering algorithms can be implemented. In Guesgen, Hertzberg, Lobb, and Mantler (2003), we discussed various heuristics for achieving an efficient implementation of buffering, and also

Let μ be the membership function of the map D.

Let β be a buffer function.

While $L \neq \emptyset$:

    Select $d \in D$.

    $L \leftarrow L - \{d\}$

    For all adjacent locations d' of d:

        $\mu(d') \leftarrow \max\{\mu(d'), \beta(\mu(d))\}$

        If $\mu(d')$ has changed, then $L \leftarrow L \cup \{d'\}$

FIGURE 10.1

A local propagation algorithm for buffering raster maps.

suggested a hardware implementation of buffering. The hardware implementation utilizes a graphic card as it can be found in almost every modern computer. The idea behind the hardware implementation is to view a raster map as a two-dimensional pixel image in which the colors represent the different membership grades of the map. Using the z-buffer (or depth buffer) of the graphics card, we mimic the propagation of the membership grades. This way we can cut down the processing time for buffering to almost constant time.

Efficiency is certainly a crucial aspect when it comes to the implementation of buffering. However, equally important is ease of access to the algorithm. In recent years, web interfaces have become more and more popular, as they are almost independent of the computing platform (desktop, laptop, tablet, etc.) and its operating system. Especially in the context of open data, a web interface is appealing, as it makes access to the data seamless. With modern technology, such as JavaScript or HTML5 for instance, such an implementation is easy to achieve.

The map buffering algorithm discussed here may be used in a number of different contexts in combination with open data to perform analysis in cases in which black and white answers are either inappropriate or impossible. Many governments make datasets of the kinds illustrated in this case study openly available to support geospatial reasoning conducted by scientists, professionals, and members of the public. While the tools to do these kinds of analysis are not readily accessible, the combination of such tools and open data that is already available presents new opportunities for advanced analysis.

Case Study 2: Nonclassical Geospatial Ontology Learning from Data

Geospatial ontologies that describe geographic features, their characteristics, and relationships with other features are common, but are usually manually created. This is a lengthy and difficult process, as a full ontology requires specification of detailed axioms in order for reasoning to be possible. In fact, as mentioned in the section entitled Geospatial Domain Ontologies above Section 3.1, ontologies with limited axiomatic specification are frequently created as a means of supporting a common scheme of concepts to be used by an information community. Many geographic data sources do not use ontologies at all. Some adopt a standardized conceptual schema that is less semantically rich than an ontology. Examples include thesauri or taxonomies either defined specifically for the purpose or available as a general resources (e.g., GEMET[10]). When ontologies, thesauri, or other conceptual schema are adopted, data instances must be annotated to indicate the concept or concepts of which they are members, in order for the meaning of geographic features to be properly understood.

Some geographic data sources adopt unspecified semantics, and in particular the recent growth of volunteered geographic information has resulted in the creation of geographic features for which no particular conceptual schema is defined. While this makes data entry easier, as either no annotation or annotation according to the data entry operators' own notions may be used instead of adhering to an agreed scheme, it makes discovery of data more difficult, and reasoning almost impossible.

Various government initiatives combined with efforts driven by citizens, academics, and scientists are making data more accessible than ever before, but in order for this data to be most effectively utilized for a range of purposes (including those presented earlier in this chapter and illustrated in Case Study 1), information about the semantics of datasets must be available. In order to avoid the need to manually create ontologies to describe dataset semantics and to manually annotate data when it is created, in this case study we present a method for automated learning of geospatial ontologies from data instances. We provide a simple example that illustrates how ontology concepts and properties can be learnt from the geospatial characteristics of the features themselves.

Early work on ontology learning aimed to learn ontologies from text sources using computational linguistics methods to analyze text, extracting important lexical terms and identifying hierarchical structures among them to define concepts, and then identifying properties that linked these concepts from the

---

[10] https://www.eionet.europa.eu/gemet/

natural language text (Mädche, 2002). In addition to ontology creation, these methods have been used for ontology population, by harvesting information from text that can then be input into a structured ontology. For example, Carlson et al. (2010) start with an ontology and some examples of instances, and iteratively search for new ontology instances. Other approaches include learning axioms (including relations, subclass axioms, and disjointness), from RDF data instances, in recent years most commonly using inductive logic programming (ILP) (Bühmann & Lehmann, 2012; Bühmann & Lehmann, 2013; Völker & Niepert, 2011), and learning axioms from existing description logic ontologies (Lehmann, Auer, Bühmann, & Tramp, 2011; Lisi & Esposito, 2009; Lehmann & Hitzler, 2010).

In the geospatial arena, a method for extracting an application ontology from a database schema has been proposed, based on extraction rules (e.g., mapping database tables to ontology classes) and accommodating definitions of location that are represented in textual attributes as well as in the form of geometries. The application ontology is then enriched with a pre-existing domain ontology, by looking for concepts with the same name as those in the application ontology, and then importing all related concepts, properties, and relations (Baglioni, Masserotti, Renso, & Spinsanti, 2007).

While methods for automated learning of ontology concepts from data itself have been scarce (most work focussing on learning axioms once the concepts themselves have been identified), the problem of automated classification of data instances has been approached, mainly by defining a set of characteristics that can be measured in the raw data (often visual) for a given ontology concept, and by using these characteristics to determine to which ontology concept the instance belongs, by grounding the ontology concepts in raw data (Fiorini et al., 2013). This has some commonalities with the remote sensing land cover classification problem in which visual keys are used to identify particular land cover classes. An approach to the use of ontologies to aid in this classification has also been developed (Belgiu et al., 2014), and other work has explored the qualitative spatial relations that can be used to assist in interpretation of dynamic visual scenes (Cohn et al., 2003), and mechanisms for grounding ontologies in visual characteristics of concepts (Hudelot et al., 2005; Neumann and Moller, 2008).

In this case study, we attempt to learn ontology classes (we do not address axioms or ontology structure in the work described here) from geospatial data instances. In the geospatial domain, we have an opportunity that is not available in most other domains, in that all of the data we are dealing with has geographic location and extents. While attribute information may be expressed and interpreted in a variety of different ways (incorporating a range of semantics specific to the data creator) making the creation of a generic approach for attribute extraction across all datasets very difficult, the methods for representation of the geometric aspects of geospatial datasets have been sufficiently standardized (addressing differences in formats, projection systems, etc.) through open data initiatives to allow interpretation and analysis of geometric aspects across geospatial datasets from a wide range of different sources. In this work, we explore the feasibility of using geometric aspects of data instances to learn ontology classes in a generic approach that can be applied across a range of different geospatial datasets. We investigate the use of both the geometric characteristics of the data instances themselves, and also the relations between instances, adopting statistical approaches to create nonclassical (probabilistic) geospatial ontologies. Statistical approaches would not classically be considered geospatial reasoning, as classical ontologies employ logical reasoning approaches, but with the consideration of nonclassical ontologies, statistical and local approaches are combined in different ways. The ontology that results from the ontology learning process described here may also be subject to geospatial reasoning, as with any nonclassical geospatial ontology.

Case Study Data

We use data from Ordnance Survey's MasterMap product covering the northern part of Scotland to test the feasibility of the approach. We confine our attention to a database table containing Topographic Areas, incorporating a range of different geographic feature types, including water bodies (lakes, estuaries, etc), buildings, and natural features. The database table (Figure 10.2) has the following attributes and example data, and contains 12K features:

As can be seen, the majority of the attributes contain metadata and identifiers of various kinds, as well as an attribute containing the calculated area of the geometry. There are three attributes containing information about the types of features concerned:

- theme contains a high level category, with 16 distinct values (Figure 10.3):

	fid	featureCod	version	versionDat	theme	calculated	changeDate	reasonForC	descriptiv	make	physicalLe	descript_1
10	osgb1000000042	10056	9	2008-11-18	Land	4594.8273280000	(6:2001-02-01,2	(6:New,New,Rec	General Surface	Natural		50	NULL
11	osgb1000000042	10056	5	2008-11-18	Land	7071.994369999	(6:2001-02-01,2	(6:New,New,Rec	General Surface	Natural		50	NULL
12	osgb1000000042	10056	11	2008-11-18	Land	6741.4469440000	(6:2001-02-01,2	(6:New,New,Rec	General Surface	Natural		50	NULL
13	osgb1000000042	10111	12	2010-03-09	Land	74290.67750400	(7:1994-11-25,1	(7:New,New,Mo	Natural Environm	Natural		50	(1:Rough Grassla
14	osgb1000000042	10111	6	2008-11-18	Land	4656.803359999	(6:1994-11-25,1	(6:New,New,Attr	Natural Environm	Natural		50	(1:Rough Grassla
15	osgb1000000042	10056	8	2008-11-18	Land	224676.6636320	(8:1995-09-08,1	(8:New,Modified	General Surface	Natural		50	NULL
16	osgb1000000042	10111	12	2010-02-09	Land	15092.77209600	(7:1994-11-25,1	(7:New,New,Attr	Natural Environm	Natural		50	(1:Heath)
17	osgb1000000042	10056	10	2008-11-18	Land	2735.058751999	(6:2001-02-01,2	(6:New,New,Rec	General Surface	Natural		50	NULL
18	osgb1000000042	10111	19	2010-03-26	Land	20328.63020799	(7:1994-11-25,1	(7:New,New,Attr	Natural Environm	Natural		50	(1:Heath)
19	osgb1000000042	10203	8	2008-11-18	Water	9729.526015999	(6:2001-02-01,2	(6:New,New,Attr	Tidal Water	Natural		50	(1:Foreshore)
20	osgb1000000042	10203	7	2008-11-18	Water	63.755526399999	(6:2001-02-01,2	(6:New,New,Attr	Tidal Water	Natural		50	(1:Foreshore)
21	osgb1000000042	10056	6	2008-11-17	Land	4234.47955199	(6:1995-09-08,1	(6:New,Reclassifi	General Surface	Natural		50	NULL
22	osgb1000000042	10056	5	2008-11-17	Land	10112.83695400	(5:2001-02-02,2	(5:New,New,Rec	General Surface	Natural		50	NULL

FIGURE 10.2
Sample of case study data.

(1:Buildings)
(1:Land)
(1:Roads Tracks And Paths)
(1:Structures)
(1:Water)
(2:Heritage And Antiquities,Land)
(2:Land,Roads Tracks And Paths)
(2:Land,Structures)
(2:Land,Water)
(2:Roads Tracks And Paths,Structures)
(2:Water,Land)
Buildings
Land
Roads Tracks And Paths
Structures
Water

FIGURE 10.3
Values of theme attribute.

(1:Building)
(1:General Surface)
(1:Glasshouse)
(1:Inland Water)
(1:Landform)
(1:Natural Environment)
(1:Path)
(1:Road Or Track)
(1:Roadside)
(1:Structure)
(1:Tidal Water)
(1:Unclassified)
(2:General Surface,Structure)
(2:General Surface,Tidal Water)
(2:Historic Interest,Landform)
(2:Inland Water,Natural Environment)
(2:Landform,Road Or Track)

FIGURE 10.4
Sample values of descriptiv attribute

- descriptiv gives a more detailed feature type, with approximately 30 distinct values, including for example (Figure 10.4):
- descript_1 contains more detailed types in some cases, with about 80 distinct values, but only about 2000 of the 12,000 records in the dataset are populated (Figure 10.5).

The coding system used is not clean: there are some overlaps in the types used across these three attributes, and some similar/slightly varying values among and across the different coding systems (e.g., Buildings vs. 1:Buildings in theme, and 1:Buildings vs. 1:Building in theme and descriptive respectively).

```
(1:Cliff)
(1:Coniferous Trees)
(1:Foreshore)
(1:Heath)
(1:Marsh Reeds Or Saltmarsh)
(1:Multi Surface)
(1:Nonconiferous Trees)
(1:Pylon)
(1:Rock (Scattered))
(1:Rock)
(1:Rough Grassland)
(1:Scree)
(1:Slope)
(1:Track)
(2:Boulders (Scattered),Heath)
(2:Boulders (Scattered),Rough Grassland)
(2:Boulders,Heath)
```

FIGURE 10.5
Sample values of descript_1 attribute

In addition, the values contain repeating groups (in some cases more than one code is contained in a single attribute value).

We investigate the use of ontology learning in three stages. The first stage considers only geometric aspects of individual data instances. The second stage adds spatial relations between different groups of instances. Finally, in a third stage we include attribute values from the theme and descriptive attributes above. This latter stage was included simply to test whether this improved the results over the geometric aspects, as it is not consistent with our goal of creating a generic approach.

Stage 1: Provisional Class Learning from Geometry Data

Geospatial instances have the benefit of being represented with geometric extents which can be accessed and used to attempt to collect clues about the semantics of the instances. These geometric characteristics are not deterministic and cannot be used to determine with certainty whether or not an instance is a member of a given class, or the same class as some other instance, but they can be used as evidence of the likely membership of the instance, particularly in combination. For this reason, we adopt nonclassical ontologies to which a probability of membership may be attached.

Table 10.1 shows the specific geometric characteristics that we employ in the provisional class learning process. This first stage can be evaluated in terms of its success in ontology learning in its own right, and can also be used as an input into the second stage, which requires a provisional class for each instance to be known.

Table 10.1 Characteristics Used for Stage 1 Ontology Learning

Name	Description	Measures
Area	The size of the instance	Polygon area
Elongation	The degree to which the instance is elongated. For example, a river is likely to be more highly elongated than a house.	$e = \dfrac{perimeter\sqrt{\pi}}{2\pi\sqrt{area}} - 1$
Complexity	The number of different angles and bends in an instance. For example, a rocky outcrop is likely to be more complex than a house.	Number of vertices

The ontology learning process employs cluster analysis over the three geometric characteristics. We tested both hierarchical (average linkage UPGMA and centroid) and nonhierarchical (k-means) clustering methods. We also tested simple standardisation of input parameters, but found better results with approximate covariance estimation to deal with skewed clusters.

Stage 2: Class Learning from Geometry and Spatial Relations Data

In the second stage, we use the provisional clusters determined in the first phase to incorporate information about the spatial relations between instances within and between classes (provisionally represented as clusters from stage one). We conjecture that it is likely that in some cases, spatial relations between types of instances may assist us in learning ontology classes. For example, most buildings are close to roads; rivers usually run through valleys, certain types of buildings are more commonly found together (e.g., different types of shops) and jetties are normally on the edge of water bodies (note that none of these assertions are axiomatic, rather indicative). To incorporate this in the reasoning process, we include a measure to capture the spatial relation between a given instance and the closest member of an instance of each other class. This measure is based on distance, as a useful surrogate for spatial relation, which would require a much larger number of measures to consider each possible spatial relation type.

Second, we include a measure of isolation, based on the assumption that some object types might commonly occur in areas in which there is less density of features (e.g., a mountain top). This will depend to a large degree on the dataset, in that different datasets collect different types of geographic features, and to different levels of resolution. However, within a dataset, we include this as a potentially useful measure (Table 10.2).

Table 10.2 Characteristics Used for Stage 2 Ontology Learning

Name	Description	Measures
Spatial relation	The spatial relationship between the instance and the closest instance of each other provisional class.	Shortest distance from instance to closest member of each other class (number of measures = number of provisional classes – 1).
Spatial isolation	The degree to which the instance is isolated from other instances of any kind.	Shortest distance from instance to object of any kind. Mean shortest distance to closest five objects of any kind.
Spatial dispersion	The degree to which the instance is isolated from other instances of the same provisional class.	Shortest distance from instance to instance in the same provisional class. Mean shortest distance to closest five objects in the same provisional class.

Third, we include spatial dispersion as a measure of the closeness of other instances within the same provisional class. This is based on the assumption that different feature types may have different levels of closeness to other features of the same type. For example, buildings are often clustered together, while parks are less likely to be. Lakes and rivers may be clustered in some cases, but not others. This does not suggest spatial autocorrelation, as we want to avoid the assumption that classes should be defined by spatial regions (e.g., buildings may be scattered throughout an entire country, but still clustered in groups). It is possible that spatial autocorrelation may exist within classes (e.g., buildings may be more likely to occur in a particular region of a country), but we leave this for later work.

Stage 3: Class Learning from Attribute Data

Our goal is to develop a method that can be used generically across geospatial information, and as mentioned above, it is difficult to deal with attribute values without knowledge of the structure that is used (e.g., which attribute values should be included in an analysis). Nevertheless, we include the attribute data from theme and descripiv attributes simply to test how important this is in ontology learning, relative to geometric and spatial relation information. Since we know the structure of the theme and descriptiv attributes, this should be a useful input into the clustering process, and if successful, methods for generic handling of attribute values could be considered in future work.

The theme and descriptiv values for each instance were included in the cluster analysis using multidimensional scaling to convert a matrix of the semantic distance between pairs of values for those two attributes into two-dimensional space. The semantic distance matrix was calculated using WordNet with Wu and Palmer's measure of semantic similarity (Wu and Palmer, 1994).

Assigning Probabilities to Instances

Given that the classes using this method are defined statistically, it is appropriate that the resulting ontology be probabilistic rather than axiomatic. Each data instance is assigned a measure indicting the likelihood that it is a member of the assigned class, based on the distance of that instance from the cluster centroid (distance in the multidimensional space defined by the characteristics that were used in the clustering algorithm, rather than a distance in geographic space). The likelihood measure is the normalized inverse of the distance to the centroid. For clusters with only one member, the likelihood measure is 1, since the centroid distance is 0.

Results

Table 10.3 shows the results from the three stages of the analysis, using the known theme and descriptiv values to calculate precision and recall as shown later (precision and recall are calculated in the same way as for theme, but replacing the known descriptiv value for theme).

$$precision^{theme} = \frac{number\ of\ instances\ in\ cluster\ with\ most\ frequent\ theme}{number\ of\ instances\ in\ cluster}$$

$$recall^{theme} = \frac{number\ of\ instances\ in\ cluster\ with\ most\ frequent\ theme}{number\ of\ instances\ in\ entire\ data\ set\ with\ most\ frequent\ theme}$$

The hierarchical methods do not perform as well as k-means, and also have the disadvantage that they create clusters that are not disjoint, but range from the highest cluster which contains everything, to at the bottom level, clusters of only two instances. While this approach may have benefits in that ontologies are also hierarchical, the problem becomes one of selecting which clusters are the most suitable to be identified as classes in the ontology.

For k-means, the number of clusters tested was determined on the basis that there are approximately 16 distinct descriptiv values (after different expressions of the same descriptiv are considered) and approximately 80 distinct descript_1 values, giving a possible indication of the quantity of classes that might be contained in a formalized ontology that might reflect a similar level of granularity as the coding systems used for the data. We also tested with 30 clusters to determine whether a mid-point between the two schemes would yield different results.

Table 10.3 Results of Cluster Analysis

Method	Clusters	Theme				Descriptiv			
		p Mean	p Std Dev	r Mean	r Std Dev	p Mean	p Std Dev	r Mean	r Std Dev
STAGE ONE									
UPGMA with standardized data	500	0.82297	0.17978	0.00816	0.02411	0.67982	0.24556	0.01314	0.02722
UPGMA with approximate covariance estimation	500	0.88541	0.18071	0.00273	0.00549	0.73039	0.23210	0.00617	0.01055
Centroid linkage with approximate covariance estimation	500	0.88305	0.18161	0.00269	0.00570	0.72914	0.23459	0.00596	0.00963
k-means with approximate covariance estimation	80	**0.95222**	0.12744	0.01281	0.07653	**0.88522**	0.21183	0.01823	0.09328
k-means with approximate covariance estimation	30	0.94001	0.14924	0.03407	0.15408	0.87416	0.21670	0.04280	0.17058
k-means with approximate covariance estimation	16	**0.92831**	0.14893	**0.06257**	0.24032	0.83921	0.26980	**0.07152**	0.24578
STAGE TWO									
k-means with approximate covariance estimation all and same cluster	80	0.91186	0.16227	0.01265	0.08360	0.83566	0.21906	0.01760	0.09815
k-means with approximate covariance estimation all and same cluster	30	0.92576	0.11485	0.03342	0.16902	0.84502	0.22108	0.03975	0.17832
k-means with approximate covariance estimation all and same cluster	16	**0.92507**	0.11266	**0.06250**	0.24115	**0.84089**	0.21631	**0.06876**	0.24664
k-means with standardized data all and same cluster	80	0.89105	0.16186	0.01781	0.05750	0.79213	0.24139	0.02418	0.07028

k-means with approximate covariance estimation all, same and each other cluster	80	0.79795	0.18690	0.01428	0.03071	0.66942	0.25619	0.02145	0.03592
STAGE THREE (USING ONLY STAGE 1 MEASURES)								
k-means with approximate covariance estimation	80	0.93529	0.13622	0.01258	0.09367	0.84784	0.21359	0.01634	0.10357
k-means with approximate covariance estimation	30	0.92867	0.11119	0.03342	0.16878	0.82943	0.22512	0.03929	0.17786
k-means with approximate covariance estimation	16	0.90166	0.14237	0.06249	0.24423	0.82677	0.21804	0.06736	0.24787

In Stage 2, we conducted the cluster analysis with only spatial isolation and spatial dispersion (All and Same Cluster in Table 10.3), as well as with all three measures. The reason for this is that the inclusion of spatial relation adds 79 measures in addition to the 3 from Stage 1 and 4 others from Stage 2, so the spatial relation values tend to dominate the cluster analysis that includes the additional 79 measures. As can be seen, the resulting precision is somewhat lower when the larger set of 86 measures is included.

The best precision is obtained for the 80 cluster k-means in stage 1, with no improvement gained from the addition of spatial relation, isolation and dispersion measures, or attribute values for theme and descriptiv. Mean recall is poor for all cluster quantities (although some individual clusters have recall up to 0.82, but the mean recall across clusters remains low, mainly because there are a large number of clusters with only 1 member, representing extreme outliers), suggesting that potentially some of the clusters could be further combined, although even with only 16 clusters, the recall is still very poor. In fact, of the 5 possible theme values, only 2 are found as dominant values in the 80 clusters (Land with 70 clusters and Water with 10 clusters); and of the 16 possible descriptiv values, only 5 are found as dominant values in the 80 clusters (see Tables 10.4 and 10.5).

As can be seen from this data, the clusters are very skewed, with many clusters containing only a single instance, and one very large cluster containing two thirds of all the instances. This is not necessarily an issue. A dataset is certainly possible in which two thirds of the individuals are members of a single class, and in which there is only one individual in a class, particularly given that the data for this case study covers northern Scotland, and is only a fraction of the dataset covering the entire United Kingdom. Nevertheless, the large number of classes with single individuals that arises from a mapping directly from clusters into classes suggests that some of the clusters may be candidates for merging to create classes. Table 10.6 shows the distribution of descriptiv values across the case study dataset, giving an indication of the possible skewness of the data itself in terms of feature types.

If we are assuming that the desired ontology should match the descriptiv values used in the dataset, this table suggests that feature types with smaller numbers of instances are under represented in the clusters. This may be in part due to the use of the most dominant theme and descriptiv values within a cluster to calculate success measures (precision, recall), and in fact the clusters shown in Table 10.4 with 58 and 108 instances are both very borderline with only just over half of the instances having the same theme value, and less than half having the same descriptiv value. These two clusters contain a mixture of water features and landform features.

Table 10.4 Summary of Clusters Created by k-Means, Stage 1, ACE, 80 Clusters

Cluster Size	Freq.	Theme	Mean p	Max p	Min p	Mean r	Max r	Min r	Descripiv	Mean p	Max p	Min p	Mean r	Max r	Min r
1	32		1	1	1	0.000174	0.000558	0.000119		1	1	1	0.001036	0.005102	0.000186
2	13		1	1	1	0.000441	0.001117	0.000238		1	1	1	0.001727	0.010204	0.000371
3	6		0.944444	1	0.666667	0.000323	0.000357	0.000238		0.833333	1	0.333333	0.000894	0.001067	0.000371
4	3		1	1	1	0.000424	0.000476	0.000268		1	1	1	0.001267	0.001423	0.0008
5	2		1	1	1	0.000596	0.000596	0.000596		0.7	0.8	0.6	0.001245	0.001423	0.001067
6	2		0.833333	1	0.666667	0.000596	0.000715	0.000476		0.75	1	0.5	0.001601	0.002134	0.001067
7	2		0.857143	1	0.714286	0.000715	0.000834	0.000596		0.642857	1	0.285714	0.001601	0.00249	0.000711
8	1	Land	1	1	1	0.000953	0.000953	0.000953	Natural Environment	1	1	1	0.002846	0.002846	0.002846
10	1	Land	1	1	1	0.001191	0.001191	0.001191	Natural Environment	1	1	1	0.003557	0.003557	0.003557
12	1	Land	1	1	1	0.001429	0.001429	0.001429	Natural Environment	0.916667	0.916667	0.916667	0.003913	0.003913	0.003913
13	1	Land	1	1	1	0.001548	0.001548	0.001548	Natural Environment	0.923077	0.923077	0.923077	0.004269	0.004269	0.004269
15	1	Land	0.933333	0.933333	0.933333	0.001667	0.001667	0.001667	General Surface	0.4	0.4	0.4	0.001114	0.001114	0.001114
22	2		0.772727	1	0.545455	0.00466	0.0067	0.00262		0.772727	1	0.545455	0.009854	0.011881	0.007826
24	1	Land	1	1	1	0.002859	0.002859	0.002859	Natural Environment	0.833333	0.833333	0.833333	0.007115	0.007115	0.007115
35	1	Land	0.942857	0.942857	0.942857	0.00393	0.00393	0.00393	Natural Environment	0.828571	0.828571	0.828571	0.010317	0.010317	0.010317

(Continued)

Table 10.4 Summary of Clusters Created by k-Means, Stage 1, ACE, 80 Clusters *(cont.)*

Cluster Size	Theme											Descripiv
	Freq.	Mean p	Max p	Min p	Mean r	Max r	Min r	Mean p	Max p	Min p	Mean r	Max r	Min r	
43	1	Land	0.906977	0.906977	0.906977	0.004645	0.004645	0.004645	0.55814	0.55814	0.55814	0.008538	0.008538	0.008538	Natural Environment
48	1	Land	1	1	1	0.005717	0.005717	0.005717	0.895833	0.895833	0.895833	0.015297	0.015297	0.015297	Natural Environment
58	1	Water	0.517241	0.517241	0.517241	0.01675	0.01675	0.01675	0.482759	0.482759	0.482759	0.027723	0.027723	0.027723	Tidal Water
108	1	Land	0.509259	0.509259	0.509259	0.006551	0.006551	0.006551	0.351852	0.351852	0.351852	0.037624	0.037624	0.037624	Tidal Water
126	1	Land	0.992063	0.992063	0.992063	0.014888	0.014888	0.014888	0.761905	0.761905	0.761905	0.034152	0.034152	0.034152	Natural Environment
149	1	Land	0.966443	0.966443	0.966443	0.017151	0.017151	0.017151	0.785235	0.785235	0.785235	0.041622	0.041622	0.041622	Natural Environment
277	1	Land	0.99639	0.99639	0.99639	0.032873	0.032873	0.032873	0.574007	0.574007	0.574007	0.056564	0.056564	0.056564	Natural Environment
363	1	Land	0.575758	0.575758	0.575758	0.024893	0.024893	0.024893	0.366391	0.366391	0.366391	0.047314	0.047314	0.047314	Natural Environment
736	1	Land	0.995924	0.995924	0.995924	0.087303	0.087303	0.087303	0.554348	0.554348	0.554348	0.075738	0.075738	0.075738	General Surface
1363	1	Land	0.597946	0.597946	0.597946	0.09707	0.09707	0.09707	0.34923	0.34923	0.34923	0.169335	0.169335	0.169335	Natural Environment
8716	1	Land	0.650528	0.650528	0.650528	0.675322	0.675322	0.675322	0.505163	0.505163	0.505163	0.817338	0.817338	0.817338	General Surface

Table 10.5 Number of Clusters With Each Descriptiv Value

Landform	5
Tidal water	8
Natural environment	56
General surface	8
Inland water	3
Total	80

Table 10.6 Comparison of Descriptiv Values for Data Instances and Cluster Instances

Descriptiv	Data Instances		Cluster Instances	
Landform	196		6	
Natural environment	2811		2589	
General surface	5387		9476	
		8394		12,071
Tidal water	1010		197	
Inland water	781		4	
		1791		201
Building	1053			
Structure	73			
Glasshouse	2			
		1128		
Roadside	393			
RoadorTrack	507			
Path	19			
		919		
General surface, structure	2			
General Surface, Tidal Water	2			
Historic Interest, Landform	4			
Tidal Water, General Surface	3			
Natural Environment, Road Or Track	14			
Inland Water, Natural Environment	2			
Landform, road or track	2			
Path, structure	9			
		38		
Unclassified	2			
		2		
Total	12,272	12,272	12,272	12,272

A second issue highlighted by this is that it may be appropriate to merge some of the clusters. For example, eight clusters have Tidal Water as their dominant descriptiv value, and while the members of all of these clusters are long and sinewy in shape, the members of each cluster vary in the length and complexity of the geometry, as shown in Figure 10.6.

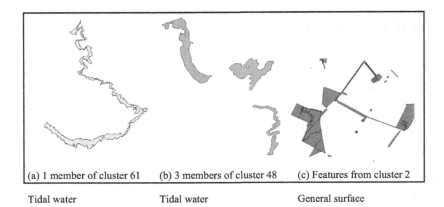

(a) 1 member of cluster 61   (b) 3 members of cluster 48   (c) Features from cluster 2

Tidal water   Tidal water   General surface

FIGURE 10.6
Data examples.

Figure 10.6 also shows some members of cluster 2, with dominant descriptiv General Surface. Both of these examples indicate that the measures used in this phase are not sufficient to effectively identify class membership. Parts (a) and (b) show that potentially similar instances are put into different classes largely as a result of their length and complexity. In some cases, this may be appropriate, if larger and longer water features are classified differently from smaller ones (e.g., river vs. stream). In contrast, (c) appears to group too many similar things together (although this is difficult to confirm as the theme and descriptiv values are not fine-grained), and in this case additional measures to distinguish shape characteristics (e.g., right angles) may be appropriate, as they suggest objects of human origin (e.g. buildings, land parcels, or fields).

Discussion

The issues identified in this analysis highlight the problem of context (referred to as the symbol grounding problem) (Fiorini, Abel, & Scherer, 2013). Manually built ontologies at the domain level incorporate judgements about the way the world is divided up into categories, and these are based on the purpose of the ontology and the worldview of the group building the ontology. That is, ontologies are usually grounded in the minds of users (this is what forms the links between ontology concepts and the real world). Fiorini et al. (2013) propose that we can instead ground ontologies in data, by defining domain concepts in terms of visual primitives. They define concepts in terms of their properties (visual characteristics adopted from an upper ontology), which can then be connected to raw data. They do not attempt to define ontology classes, but use a manually defined mapping from domain concepts to visual characteristics to perform automated classification of instances to ontology concepts.

They test this approach in the domain of petroleum geology, to stratigraphic interpretation of well logs.

We consider that while the definition of ontology concepts is grounded in the minds of users, there are some physical characteristics that can be used to gain an indication of these concepts. This rests on our claim that if we were to randomly select a geographic feature ontology, it would be possible to find or draw pictures of exemplars for each class (indicating that members of each class have physical characteristics with at least some degree of uniqueness) and that those pictures would in most cases look different between classes (indicating that physical characteristics have at least some degree of uniqueness between classes). The main challenges for the problem of ontology learning that we are addressing in this work, are (1) determining which of those physical characteristics are important, and (2) being able to measure them. While in many cases it may be true that classes are differentiated by physical characteristics, these may not all be accessible through a standard two dimensional geospatial dataset. For example, if we want to differentiate between a seasonal river and a permanent river in our ontology, while this is evident from the physical characteristics of the river at different times of the year, it is not likely to be evident from a standard geospatial dataset. It may be detectable from an aerial photograph or satellite image, but this work aims to derive ontologies from standard, openly available geospatial datasets.

Despite this claim about the importance of physical characteristics, we do maintain that the scope of ontologies created without the incorporation of the worldview or an individual or group is limited. For example, one might consider the case of an ontology that classifies water bodies purely on the basis of the water quality, without considering geometric characteristics at all. The work proposed in this chapter only applies to ontologies for which geometry is a relevant factor, and in many cases may require an additional level of human intervention to differentiate between class boundaries that are relevant for the purpose for which the ontology is being created.

This case study has described an approach for geospatial ontology learning that attempts to learn ontology classes from geospatial data instances. In many ways, it has raised more questions than answers, and is a first step toward more detailed research. In particular, the challenge of identifying a wider range of characteristics to use to define clusters, and the question of how to identify which of those are most relevant in a particular context, are important for the further development of the work. It is also possible that the results may be improved by a postprocessing step in which clusters that are sufficiently similar are combined, or that clusters that are significantly different are divided. The clustering algorithms are limited in their ability to deal with special cases and to allow fine tuning according to particular aspects of the input data, and this requires further attention for the future development of this work, as well as depending on the ontological issue of identifying relevant characteristics to ground the created ontology that has already been mentioned. Finally, this work has made use of the attribute values that were included in the data to evaluate the success of the approach, but the use of more comprehensive ontology evaluation tools is appropriate in future work.

CONCLUSIONS

In this chapter, we have provided an overview of the different kinds of geospatial reasoning that may be used with open geospatial data, and briefly discussed the structure of the knowledge representations that support that reasoning. We have also provided two case studies that show the use of geospatial ontologies and reasoning in action, giving an indication of the kinds of issues and challenges that must be considered when working with semantic aspects of geospatial data, when considering the representation of geospatial knowledge, and when reasoning over that knowledge.

References

Aurnague, M., & Vieu, L. (1993). Towards a formal representation of space in language: a commonsense reasoning approach. *IJCAI-93 workshop on spatial and temporal reasoning*, 123–158.

Baglioni, M., Masserotti, M. V., Renso, C., & Spinsanti, L. (2007). Building geospatial ontologies from geographical databases. In *GeoSpatial semantics* (pp. 195–209). Berlin, Heidelberg: Springer.

Belgiu, M., Tomljenovic, I., Lampoltshammer, T. J., Blaschke, T., & Höfle, B. (2014). Ontology-based classification of building types detected from airborne laser scanning data. *Remote Sensing*, 6(2), 1347–1366.

Bennett, B. (2001). What is a forest? On the vagueness of certain geographic concepts. *Topoi, 20*(2), 189–201.

Bitters, B. (2009). Spatial relationship networks: network theory applied to GIS data. *Cartography and Geographic Information Science, 36*(1), 81–93.

Bobillo, F., & Straccia, U. (2011). Fuzzy ontology representation using OWL 2. *International Journal of Approximate Reasoning, 52*(7), 1073–1094.

Borgo, S., Carrara, M., Garbacz, P., & Vermaas, P. E. (2009). A formal ontological perspective on the behaviors and functions of technical artifacts. *Artificial Intelligence for Engineering Design Analysis and Manufacturing (AIEDAM), 23*, 3–21.

Bühmann, L., & Lehmann, J. (2013). Pattern based knowledge base enrichment. In *12th International semantic web conference*, 21–25 October 2013, Sydney, Australia.

Bühmann, L., & Lehmann, J. (2012). Universal OWL axiom enrichment for large knowledge bases. In *Proceedings of EKAW 2012* (pp. 57–71). Berlin: Springer, 2012.

Cai, G. (2007). Contextualization of geospatial database semantics for human–GIS interaction. *Geoinformatica, 11*(2), 217–237.

Carlson, A., Betteridge, J., Kisiel, B., Settles, B., Hruschka Jr., E. R., & Mitchell, T. M. (2010). Toward an architecture for never-ending language learning. In *Proceedings of the 24th conference on artificial intelligence (AAAI)* (pp. 1306–1313), Vol. 2, 2010.

Chen, W. K., Sui, G., & Tang, D. (2011, June). A fuzzy intelligent decision support system for typhoon disaster management. In *2011 IEEE international conference on fuzzy systems (FUZZ)* (pp. 364–367). IEEE.

Clementini, E., Di Felice, P., & Hernández, D. (1997). Qualitative representation of positional information. *Artificial Intelligence, 95*, 317–356.

Clementini, E., Skiadopoulos, S., Billen, R., & Tarquini, F. (2010). A reasoning system of ternary projective relations. *IEEE Transactions on Knowledge and Data Engineering, 22*(2), 161–178.

Cohn, A., & Gotts, N. (1996). The 'egg-yolk' representation of regions with indeterminate boundaries. In P. Burrough & A. Frank (Eds.), *Proceedings GISDATA specialist meeting on spatial objects with undetermined boundaries* (pp. 171–187). Francis Taylor.

Cohn, A., & Hazarika, S. (2001). Qualitative spatial representation and reasoning: an overview. *Fundamenta Informaticae, 43*, 2–32.

Cohn, A., Bennett, B., Gooday, J., & Gotts, N. (1997). Qualitative spatial representation and reasoning with the region connection calculus. *Geoinformatica, 1*, 275–316.

Cohn, A. G., Magee, D., Galata, A., Hogg, D., & Hazarika, S. (2003). Towards an architecture for cognitive vision using qualitative spatio-temporal representations and abduction. In Spatial cognition III, lecture notes in computer science, vol. 2685 (pp. 246–262). Berlin: Springer.

Costa, P., & Laskey, K. B. (2006). PR-OWL: a framework for probabilistic ontologies. In *Proceedings of the conference on formal ontologies and information systems*, November 2006 (pp. 237–249).

Du, H., Alechina, N., Stock, K., & Jackson, M. (2013). The logic of NEAR and FAR. In *COSIT 2013: conference on spatial information theory*, Scarborough, UK, 2–6 September 2013.

Dubois, D., & Prade, H. (1980). *Fuzzy sets and systems: theory and applications*. London, UK: Academic Press.

Effati, M., Rajabi, M. A., Samadzadegan, F., & Blais, J. R. (2012). Developing a novel method for road hazardous segment identification based on fuzzy reasoning and GIS. *Journal of Transportation Technologies, 2*(01), 32.

Egenhofer, M., & Herring, J. (1991) Categorizing binary topological relations between regions, lines, and points in geographic databases. Technical Report, Department of Surveying Engineering, University of Maine.

Fiorini, S. R., Abel, M., & Scherer, C. M. (2013). An approach for grounding ontologies in raw data using foundational ontology. *Information Systems, 38*(5), 784–799.

Fisher, P., Wood, J., & Cheng, T. (2004). Where is Helvellyn? Fuzziness of multi-scale landscape morphometry. *Transactions of the Institute of British Geographers, 29*(1), 106–128.

Frank, U. (2001). Tiers of ontology and consistency constraints in geographical information systems. *International Journal of Geographical Information Science, 15*, 667–678.

Freksa, C. (1992). Using orientation information for qualitative spatial reasoning. In A. U. Frank, I. Campari, & U. Formentini (Eds.), *Theories and methods of spatiotemporal reasoning in geographic space* (pp. 162–178). Berlin: Springer.

Fu, G., Jones, C. B., & Abdelmoty, A. I. (2005). Ontology-based spatial query expansion in information retrieval. *Lecture Notes in Computer Science, 3761*, 1466–1482.

Gahegan, M. (1995). Proximity operators for qualitative spatial reasoning. In *Proceedings of the international conference on spatial information theory: a theoretical basis for GIS (COSIT 1995)* (pp. 31–44), LNCS 988.

Granell, C., Díaz, L., & Gould, M. (2010). Service-oriented applications for environmental models: reusable geospatial services. *Environmental Modelling and Software, 25*, 182–198.

Guesgen, H. W. (2005). Fuzzy reasoning about geographic regions. In *Fuzzy modeling with spatial information for geographic problems* (pp. 1–14). Berlin, Heidelberg: Springer.

Guesgen, H. W., & Histed, J. W. (1996). Towards qualitative spatial reasoning in geographic information systems. In *Proceedings of the AAAI-96 workshop on spatial and temporal reasoning* (pp. 39–46), Portland, OR.

Guesgen, H. W., Hertzberg, J., Lobb, R., & Mantler, A. (2003). Buffering fuzzy maps in GIS. Spatial Cognition and Computation (Special Issue on Vagueness, Uncertainty and Granularity), 3(2&3):207–222.

Hernandez, D., Clementini, E., & Felice, P. D. (1995). Qualitative distances. In *Spatial information theory: a theoretical basis for GIS*, edited by A. Frank & W. Kuhn, Lecture Notes in Computer Science 988 (pp. 45–58). Berlin: Springer-Verlag.

Hobona, G., Fairbairn, D., Hiden, H., & James, P. (2010). Orchestration of grid-enabled geospatial web services in geoscientific workflows. *IEEE Transactions on Automation Science and Engineering, 7*(2), 407–411.

Hois, J., & Kutz, O. (2008). Natural language meets spatial calculi. In *Spatial cognition VI. Learning, reasoning, and talking about space* (pp. 266–282). Berlin, Heidelberg: Springer.

Hois, J., Tenbrink, T., Ross, R., & Bateman, J. GUM-Space: the generalized upper model spatial extension: a linguistically-motivated ontology for the semantics of spatial language. Technical Report. Universität Bremen SFB/TR8 Spatial Cognition, http://www.ontospace.uni-bremen.de/ontology/TechnReport09GUMspace.pdf, 2009.

Hudelot, C., Maillot, N., & Thonnat, M. Symbol grounding for semantic image interpretation: from image data to semantics. In: *Tenth IEEE international conference on computer vision*, Los Alamitos, USA, 2005, p. 1875.

Janowicz, K., Scheider, S., Pehle, T., & Hart, G. (2012). Geospatial semantics and linked spatiotemporal data: past, present, and future. *Semantic Web, 3*(4), 321–332.

Jha, M. K., & Keele, R. A. (2012). *Using dynamic Bayesian networks for investigating the impacts of extreme events.* INTECH Open Access Publisher.

Klien, E., Lutz, M., & Kuhn, W. (2006). Ontology-based discovery of geo-graphic information services: an application in disaster management. *Computers, Environment and Urban Systems, 30*, 102–123.

Klir, G. J., & Folger, T. A. (1988). *Fuzzy sets, uncertainty, and information.* Englewood Cliffs, NJ: Prentice-Hall.

Laskey, K. B., Wright, E. J., & da Costa, P. C. (2010). Envisioning uncertainty in geospatial information. *International Journal of Approximate Reasoning, 51*(2), 209–223.

Lehmann, J., & Hitzler, P. (2010). Concept learning in description logics using refinement operators. xvi. *Machine Learning Journal, 78*(1–2), 203–250.

Lehmann, J., Auer, S., Bühmann, L., & Tramp, S. (2011). Class expression learning forontology engineering. *Journal of Web Semantics, 9*, 71–81.

Lisi, F. A., & Esposito, F. (2010). Nonmonotonic onto-relational learning. In *Inductive logic programming*, Volume 5989 of Lecture notes in computer science (pp. 88–95). Springer, 2009.

Liu, J. (1998). A method for spatial reasoning based on qualitative trigonometry. *Artificial Intelligence, 98*, 137–168.

Lutz, M., & Klien, E. (2006). Ontology-based retrieval of geographic information. *International Journal of Geographical Information Science, 20*(3), 233–260.

Mädche, A. (2002). *Ontology learning for the semantic web. Ontology learning for the semantic web.* Berlin: Springer Science & Business Media.

McGuinness, D. L. (2003). Ontologies come of age. In D. Fensel, J. Hendler, H. Lieberman, & W. Wahlster (Eds.), *Spinning the semantic web: bringing the World Wide Web to its full potential.* MIT Press.

Moratz, R., & Wallgrun, J. (2012). Spatial reasoning with augmented points: extending cardinal directions with local distances. *Journal of Spatial Information Science, 5*, 1–30.

Mukerjee, A., & Joe, G. (1990) A qualitative model for space. In *AAAI-90 proceedings* (pp. 721–727), July 29–Aug 3, Boston, MA.

Neuhaus, H., & Compton, M. (2009). The semantic sensor network ontology. In *AGILE workshop on challenges in geospatial data harmonisation* (pp. 1–33), Hannover, Germany.

Neumann, B., & Moller, R. (2008). On scene interpretation with description logics. *Image and Vision Computing, 26*, 82–101.

Nguyen, H. T., Kreinovich, V., & Tolbert, D. (1993). On robustness of fuzzy logics. In *Proc. 2nd IEEE international conference on fuzzy systems* (pp. 543–547), San Francisco, CA.

Niles, I., & Pease. A. (2001) Towards a standard upper ontology. In C. Welty & B. Smith (Eds.), *Proceedings of the 2nd international conference on formal ontology in information systems (FOIS-2001)*, Ogunquit, Maine, October 17–19, 2001.

Pawlak, Z. (1991). *Rough sets: theoretical aspects of reasoning about data*. Dordrecht: Kluwer Academic Publishing.

Pérez-Miñana, E., Krause, P. J., & Thornton, J. (2012). Bayesian networks for the management of greenhouse gas emissions in the British agricultural sector. *Environmental Modelling & Software, 35*, 132–148.

Petry, F. E., Cobb, M. A., Ali, D., Angryk, R., Paprzycki, M., Rahimi, S., ... & Yang, H. (2002). Fuzzy spatial relationships and mobile agent technology in geospatial information systems. In *Applying soft computing in defining spatial relations* (pp. 123–155). Physica-Verlag HD.

Raskin, R. G., & Pan, M. J. (2005). Knowledge representation in the semantic web for Earth and environmental terminology (SWEET). *Computers & Geosciences, 31*, 1119–1125.

Schockaert, S., De Cock, M., Cornelis, C., & Kerre, E. E. (2008). Fuzzy region connection calculus: an interpretation based on closeness. *International Journal of Approximate Reasoning, 48*(1), 332–347.

Shariff, A. R., Egenhofer, M., & Mark, D. (1998). Natural-language spatial relations between linear and areal objects: the topology and metric of English-language terms. *International Journal of Geographical Information Science, 12*(3), 215–246.

Stock, K., Karasova, V., Robertson, A., Roger, G., Small, M., Bishr, M., Ortmann, J., Stojanovic, T., Reitsma, F., Korczynski, L., Brodaric, B., & Gardner, Z. (2013). Finding science with science: evaluating the use of scientific knowledge and semantics to enhance discovery of scientific resources. *Transactions in GIS, 17*(4), .

Stock, K., Leibovici, D., Delazari, L., & Santos, R. (2015). Discovering order in chaos: using a heuristic ontology to derive spatio-temporal sequences for cadastral data.. *Spatial Cognition & Computation, 15*(2), 115–141.

Stuckenschmidt, H., & Visser, U. (2000). Semantic translation based on approximate re-classification. In *Proceedings of workshop on semantic approximation, granularity, vagueness, workshop of the seventh international conference on principles of knowledge representation, reasoning*, Breckenridge, CO.

Studer, R., Benjamins, R., & Fensel, D. (1998). Knowledge engineering: principles and methods. *Data and Knowledge Engineering, 25*(1–2), 161–198.

Tomlin, D. (1990). *Geographic information systems and cartographic modeling*. Englewood Cliffs, NJ: Prentice-Hall.

Völker, J., & Niepert, M. Statistical schema induction. In G. Antoniou, M. Gro-belnik, E. Paslaru Bontas Simperl, B. Parsia, D. Plexousakis, P. De Leenheer, Jeff, Z., Pan (Eds.), *The semantic web: research and applications – proceedings of the 8th extended semantic web conference (ESWC)*, Heraklion, Crete, Greece, May 29 to June 2, 2011, volume 6643 of Lecture notes in computer science, pp. 124–138. Springer, 2011.

W3C OWL Working Group. (2012). OWL web ontology language overview. W3C Recommendation 11 December 2012. http://www.w3.org/TR/owl2-overview/. Accessed 10.07.15.

Winter, S., & Yin, Z. C. (2011). The elements of probabilistic time geography. *GeoInformatica, 15*(3), 417–434.

Worboys, M. F. (2001). Nearness relations in environmental space. *International Journal of Geographical Information Science, 15*(7), 633–651.

Wu, Z., & Palmer (1994). Verb semantics and lexical selection. In *32nd annual meeting of the association for computational linguistics* (pp. 133–138).

Zadeh, L. A. (1965). Fuzzy sets. *Information and Control, 8*(3), 338–353.

Zimmerman, K., & Freksa, C. (1996). Qualitative spatial reasoning using orientation, distance and path knowledge. *Applied Intelligence, 6*, 49–58.

Zimmermann, K. (1994) Measuring without measures - the Δ-calculus Graduiertenkolleg Kognitions-wissenschaft, Universität Hamburg, Report 39, 1994.

Subject Index

Printed in the United States
By Bookmasters